CRIME IN AMERICA

OBSERVATIONS ON ITS NATURE, CAUSES, PREVENTION AND CONTROL

by Ramsey Clark

WITH AN INTRODUCTION BY
Tom Wicker

SIMON AND SCHUSTER
NEW YORK

Chapter 13 has appeared in a different form in *Playboy* magazine.

Third printing

SBN 671–20407–6
Library of Congress Catalog Card Number: 78–128604
Designed by Irving Perkins
Manufactured in the United States of America

TO RONDA

Contents

Introduction

Washington

The most revolutionary public voice in America today is that of Ramsey Clark. His rhetoric is by no means violent, and in political terms there are plenty who speak more wildly, of overthrowing government and standing people up against the wall. But no one in American life today calls as frequently or as eloquently for a genuine revolution in human conduct—in the way men manage their affairs, deal with one another, and regard themselves.

It is a constant theme of Clark's speeches and of *Crime in America,* for instance, that Americans can master their own destinies and conquer their vast and debilitating problems, even though he believes they face in the last third of this century swifter and greater change than will ever in history have affected any people. It is all, Ramsey Clark keeps trying to tell us, a "matter of will."

In May 1970, speaking to the Congressional Conference on Justice in America, he briefly spellbound a roomful of authorities with an informed and penetrating, nevertheless visionary, talk. Here he is, for instance, saying the kind of thing most of us would never think to say, probably wouldn't say if we did think it, for fear of being ridiculed by "practical" men:

"We have to change human attitudes. How do you do that? We have to condition violence from the people's character. It can be done. It has to be done, because we are all up against it. When there are violent people, others will be affected by it.

"There are efforts going on now to find out how you go about purging violence, purging racism. . . . We just have to learn to be very introspective and learn as individuals how to purge violence and fear and racism and qualities like this from our being. I think the young people see this. . . ."

Now that is truly revolutionary talk and about as far from the general cynicism as it is possible to get. Interestingly enough, when Ramsey Clark says such things, few people scoff—as they tend to do at dreamers. A rangy six-footer, just 42 years old, with wide ears, a furrowed brow but a ready smile, and plenty of his native Texas in his voice, Clark also can and often does rattle off impressive strings of statistics or quickly demolish a faulty legal argument or penetrate to the heart of a matter in a phrase ("A right is not what someone gives you; it's what no one can take from you"). By no means a mere theorist, he is himself "practical" enough to have received an incredible array of tributes from law enforcement types of all varieties, compiled an excellent record as one of our youngest Attorneys General, and achieved dubious fame by becoming Richard Nixon's prime target in the 1968 Presidential campaign.

In a notable act of putting up rather than shutting up, he appeared in Judge Julius J. Hoffman's courtroom in 1969, ready to testify for the defense in the conspiracy trial of the Chicago Seven. It was not his fault that Hoffman ruled out his testimony before it could be given, carefully keeping from the jury even the fact that the former Attorney General was willing to speak for the supposed conspirators.

Just as straightforwardly, as President Johnson's chief law officer, Clark authorized the prosecution of Dr. Spock and the Rev. William Sloane Coffin for conspiring to counsel evasion of the draft. ("The question was not what was right or wrong morally. The question was whether the law was violated. The system must have integrity. . . . It never seemed wrong to me that Thoreau and Gandhi were prosecuted or that they went to jail. That was their point. They so disagreed with their governments that they would sacrifice freedom itself to show their concern.")

Clark is a sober, in some ways even a melancholy, young man; it is hard for an intelligent person encumbered with personal conscience and a social ethic to be otherwise in the wake of the wounding sixties. But he has not lost his sense of humor or his dry wit. He once brought the house down at a Women's National Press Club dinner with a discussion of the relative merits of a bugged martini or a bugged Gibson; and on the subject of the kind of J. Edgar Hooverish crime statistics that he most mistrusts, he can be devastating:

"What do we know when we are told there is a murder every 43 minutes and a rape every 19? If that time clock applied to the Virgin Islands, everyone there would be murdered in five years, after having been raped twice."

This fancy has a serious point—"We torture ourselves with things like that; we lead ourselves to fear rather than to constructive action"—and, in fact, Ramsey Clark is an awesomely knowledgeable professional in the law-and-order field. He has his own kind of statistics, which tell their own story:

"In every major city in the United States you will find that two-thirds of the arrests take place among only about two per cent of the population. Where is that area in every city? Well, it's in the same place where infant mortality is four times higher than in the city as a whole; where the death rate is 25 per cent higher; where life expectancy is ten years shorter; where common communicable diseases with the potential of physical and mental damage are six and eight and ten times more frequent; where alcoholism and drug addiction are prevalent to a degree far transcending that of the rest of the city; where education is poorest—the oldest school buildings, the most crowded and turbulent schoolrooms, the fewest certified teachers, the highest rate of dropouts; where the average formal schooling is four to six years less than for the city as a whole. Sixty per cent of the children in Watts in 1965 lived with only one, or neither, of their parents."

Readers of this book will find, nevertheless, that Clark is generally and genuinely sympathetic to the problems and plight of the police, as shown by his recommendations for professionalizing local forces, paying them more as well as training them better, and according them more status and respect in the community. Richard Nixon never said much about *that* when he was blaming crime in America on the "permissive" Attorney General Clark, nor did the candidate let his Republican rallies in on, say, the fact that it was Ramsey Clark who introduced and organized the first of the federal "strike forces" that have begun to make serious inroads on organized crime, and who reorganized the archaic Bureau of Prisons to provide new kinds of rehabilitation programs.

And it was Clark who coordinated the defense of the Pentagon in October 1967, during a peace march of about 50,000 demonstrators —at least five times as many as went into the streets of Chicago during the 1968 Democratic national convention; but after Chicago, the Pentagon march could be seen to have been handled with the least possible violence and the most leeway possible for the marchers.

Clark is getting to be something of a political figure himself, now that he is not under the confinement of the Justice Department. He is in demand for speeches, books, television. His name is bandied about in Presidential speculation, and there is even a Clark-for-President Club in the unlikely location, among others, of Raleigh, N.C. But the taste of it does not seem much in his mouth; at Senate hearings in the summer of 1970 he characteristically disregarded conventional political wisdom and flatly contradicted President Nixon's contention that there is nothing that can be done about de facto school segregation, most of which Clark believes has official roots. Anyway, he says, "the essential fact is that segregation in schooling is bad, whatever the cause."

It might be splendid to have him debating that and similar issues in the 1972 campaign with Mr. Nixon; but the crass fact is that to win the Presidency, or even a party nomination to run for it, a man usually has to want to win more than he wants anything else—which means that he will do things to win that he would not have done for any other cause. That is not Ramsey Clark's way; and, in any case, a campaign does not seem quite the right cup of tea for a man who says flatly that we need "a billion dollars more for correction," advocates stiff gun control laws, and refused to use wiretaps even after

Congress voted him the authority to do so ("The future potential to invade privacy is total").

This, of course, is a book about crime and its causes, but Clark is distinguished among our public men for his ability to see that crime is not an isolated matter among our other failings, or merely the culpable result of evil men and lax officials. Crime, he tells us at the outset, "reflects the character of a people . . . of the entire society." So there is more—much more—in this wise, compassionate, intelligent book than crime statistics or exhortations to support your local cops. Ramsey Clark knows well, for instance, that all the Supreme Court decisions of the last century mean less to the frequency of crime in America today than the cold, indisputable facts of change and growth and upheaval: "In the 1960's more than two million Negroes, 8 per cent of all in the nation, left the South for the cities of the North, the Midwest and the West. They got off buses and out of old cars in places like Watts, first stop for the newly arrived poor in Los Angeles. In just five years, from 1960 to 1965, massive migrations caused the percentage of black children in public schools in Baltimore to increase from 50 to 61, in Chicago from 42 to 50, in St. Louis from 49 to 60 and in San Francisco from 24 to 32. There was no clearer indication of the immense new segregation coming in central city America. The consequences were clear, too."

But we have done all too little about them—either those among us who may want to set up a sort of concentration-camp America with all the bad guys locked away, or those who, more nearly seeing the real nature of the problem and its magnitude, have either turned aside in despair or insisted on doctrinaire and outmoded solutions. In the teeth of this failure, Ramsey Clark's voice, like that of any true revolutionary, is singularly confident, remarkably clear:

"If we are to deal meaningfully with crime, what must be seen is the dehumanizing effect on the individual of slums, racism, ignorance and violence, of corruption and impotence to fulfill rights, of poverty and unemployment and idleness, of generations of malnutrition, of congenital brain damage and prenatal neglect, of sickness and disease, of pollution, of decrepit, dirty, ugly, unsafe, overcrowded housing, of alcoholism and narcotics addiction, of avarice, anxiety, fear, hatred, hopelessness and injustice. These are the fountainheads of crime." And then he adds, with the kind of calm, unshakable sense of human possibilities one cannot even imagine in most of the alarmists and jingoes of crime: "They can be controlled."

Clark can be that calm and that confident because beyond everything else—beyond the knowledgeable professional, the experienced and skillful official, the analyst of social conditions, the able and prolific speaker and writer—beyond all these, Ramsey Clark is a man who believes in mankind with the passion and tenderness of a lover. He sees us bound together here in our vale of tears, inextricably, mystically, we southern sharecroppers and we ghetto blacks and we corporation executives—all the children of the universe.

"The poor don't know a lawyer," he once said. "They couldn't call one if they wanted to because they don't have a dime to use the phone and they couldn't get the secretary to put the lawyer on the line if they did because they couldn't pay a fee." The profound burden of this book, together with its information and its analyses and its professionalism, is that we don't have to treat each other like that; *we* are the trouble. "Why should people who have the ability to enforce their rights, to hire lawyers, have advantages over people who don't have the ability to enforce their rights, to hire lawyers?"

It is, he insists and insists again, a matter of will. "How much do we care? How much foresight, initiative and energy will we devote to the quality of life and the human condition in the exciting years ahead?" That is the only truly revolutionary question before us, and in *Crime in America* Ramsey Clark asks it with courage and persistence and eloquence—but, above all, with that generosity and understanding for his fellowman that marks him as a public figure and private friend.

TOM WICKER
July 1970

PART ONE

Nature and Causes

Crime reflects the character of a people. This is the painful fact we do not want to face. Other premises are easier to accept, other causes easier to control. There is no simple reform for defective character. It is as stubborn, durable and strong as ourselves. It is ourselves.

All those qualities in life that make us what we are determine our capacity to commit crime. Heredity and environment, the interaction of individual and society, the totality of human nature and human experience—these are the elemental origins of crime. No part by itself will tell us all we need to know to effectively prevent antisocial conduct.

Crime is not just sordid happenings—it is human behavior. People commit crime. Some consider that man is essentially good and that, given the chance, he will develop as a benign being. Others conceive man to be essentially evil and believe that he must be controlled for his own protection and the existence of an ordered society. To the former, liberty is the essential condition for man to develop fully the capabilities for good within him. To the latter, permissiveness will bring out the basic weakness and selfishness of man, who must be carefully disciplined to control his baser instincts.

Perhaps most of us believe that there are inherently good people and inherently bad people. Philosophers have debated the issue since man first reflected. With the enlightenment of science, the answer is more obscure than ever; the question itself of doubtful utility.

What we know when crime occurs is that there are individuals who care so little for others, or have such disregard for the systems and standards of society, or who have so little control over themselves that they will hurt people, take property that is not theirs and violate the rule of law. So long as a society includes such individuals, crime will occur. However effective government may be in its effort to control crime, while its citizens have the will to violate the law, society is in a contest it can never finally win. Nor can there be lasting comfort in safety that is dependent on a policeman, for police can never be omnipresent. What happens when they are not there? And who, finally, protects us from the police? Where crime occurs constantly, we cannot help but view our neighbors with apprehension, however close the precinct station. To look at our fellow citizens through eyes filled with fear is not to live in a happy place.

Nature conspired to make social instability and concomitant crime common in America. A frontier, a totally foreign and largely uncivilized aboriginal people, an early and brutalizing slavery of a different race from a distant continent, pioneers moving beyond the reach of established institutions, the interaction of a wide range of cultural, racial, ethnic and social backgrounds in a new melting pot, an early and devastating civil war, a tradition of guns, immense population growth both native and immigrant, vast industrialization and urbanization, high mobility and rootlessness, and sweeping technological development—all these and more contributed to change and turbulence beyond that experienced by any other people at any time in history.

In a sense our people were subjected to the trauma of exploring several New Worlds simultaneously—not just the geography of North America, but the mixing of many different peoples from different countries and continents with wide racial, cultural and social disparities, and the totally new environment of mass population, high urbanization and accelerating technological development. We fared well, considering all the pressures of change. We must hope other nations destined to experience many of the same forces fare as well.

Crime reflects more than the character of the pitiful few who commit it. It reflects the character of the entire society. How do people capable of stealing a car or mugging a cripple, of embezzling from the bank that trusted them or raping an eighty-year-old woman, come to be that way? All they are and all they have experienced that drove them to commit that crime overcame all that sought in vain to restrain them. What they are and what they experienced came largely from society—from its influence on them and on their forebears.

If we are to deal meaningfully with crime, what must be seen is the dehumanizing effect on the individual of slums, racism, ignorance and violence, of corruption and impotence to fulfill rights, of poverty and unemployment and idleness, of generations of malnutrition, of congenital brain damage and prenatal neglect, of sickness and disease, of pollution, of decrepit, dirty, ugly, unsafe, overcrowded housing, of alcoholism and narcotics addiction, of avarice, anxiety, fear, hatred, hopelessness and injustice. These are the fountainheads of crime. They can be

controlled. As imprecise, distorted and prejudiced as our learning is, these sources of crime and their controllability clearly
emerge to any who would see.

We are cruelly afflicted with crime because we have failed to
care for ourselves and for our character. We are guilty of immense neglect. Neglect, not permissiveness, is the culprit. Do
not blame the precious little true freedom that the individual
can squeeze out of mass society for the sins of generations of
selfish neglect. It was from too little love and help, not too
much liberty, that the child across the street ran with the gang.
We—his family, friends, neighbors, school, church—all watched
him for years, and no one was truly surprised when, just back
from the reformatory again, he was arrested for murdering a
store clerk while committing armed robbery. What can his
mother—an alcoholic, unemployed, husbandless with four children—do for him? What can a fifth-grade ghetto schoolteacher,
barely able to maintain classroom order among forty students,
do to help such a youngster? Can we hope to create a just society
and assure domestic tranquillity by reacting in anger with force?
We will assure violence if government acts only to keep the
poor in their place.

It was another form of neglect—indifference, not helplessness
—that caused the wealthy suburban father to give his teenage
son a new car and let him stay out all night. Such a father has
no cause to speak of ingratitude, after all he has done for his
son, when the boy is arrested for gang-raping a fifteen-year-old
girl. He gave his son nothing of himself.

The crucial test of American character will be our reaction to
the vastness of crime and turbulence in which we live. It will
not be an easy test. The obvious and instinctive reaction is repressiveness. It will not work. You cannot discipline this turbulent, independent, young mass society as if it were a child.

Repression is the one clear course toward irreconcilable division and revolution in America. The essential action is to create a wholesome environment. Healthy people in a just and concerned society will not commit significant crime.

To fail this test is to destroy liberty for the individual in mass society. To pass it is to liberate the powers of the individual for the good of mankind—to provide even for the most miserable among us the chance to fulfill himself, to do all he can, to be whatever he has within him to be.

We are not yet so far from the jungle that self-preservation has ceased to be our basic instinct. Crime threatens self-preservation and stimulates age-old emotions. The most dangerous of these is fear. Reason fades as fear deprives us of any concern or compassion for others. When fear turns our concern entirely to self-protection, those who must have our help if crime is to be controlled lose that chance. Finally, fear can destroy our desire for justice itself. Then there is little hope. We are prepared to deny justice to obtain what unreasoning, overpowering emotion falsely tells us will be security. Arm yourself, suppress dissent, invade privacy, urge police to trick and deceive, force confessions, jail without trial, brutalize in prisons, execute the poor and the weak. Due process can wait—we want safety! Naked power becomes sovereign. Only force can rise to meet it. The end is violence.

Fear was a saving reflex for the cave man. His survival depended on it. There were threats in nature he could not control —savage tribes and saber-toothed tigers with which he had to contend. Alerted by fear, he could flee or, through cunning, destroy and thereby survive. For modern man, who cannot escape his mass society, fear threatens survival. Nature holds few perils we cannot control, and our problems are far too vast and complex to let unreasoning fear direct their resolution. Population growth and technology have made the individual so totally dependent upon others that his very safety and welfare depend upon theirs. Personal preservation can no longer be found in flight or self-defense except in the most temporary way. Safety can come only from service to others, because until the basic human needs of all are fulfilled, there will be a vast unrest at work that cannot be stilled by force or by admonition to respect the law.

To insist on the dignity of the individual, to assure him health and education, meaningful employment, decent living conditions, to protect his privacy and the integrity of his personality, to enforce his rights though he may be the least among us, to give him power to affect his own destiny—only thus can we hope to instill in him a concern for others, for their well-being, their safety and the security of their property. Only thus can we bring to him a regard for our society, our institutions and our purposes as a people that will render him incapable of committing crime.

If we are to prevent crime in the midst of increasing anxiety and fear, of complexity and doubt, our greatest need is reverence for life. A humane and generous concern for each individual, for his safety, his health and his fulfillment, will do more to soothe and humanize our savage hearts than any police power that man can devise. When society seeks vengeance, when it cheapens one life, it demeans all life. Violence will nourish violence so long as we do not revere life. Violence in mass interdependent technologically advanced society threatens everyone. There is no escape. It is no longer tolerable as a problem solver —in private or public hands—in international or interpersonal affairs. There is little evidence that some new wisdom which could not restrain the club will stop the bomb.

Most Americans are incapable of committing a serious crime —but far too many can, and do. Our character as a people determines this capability. There have been and are now whole societies where but a very few, and they only under extraordinary circumstances, can bring themselves to injure another or take what is not theirs. But in America, we have cultivated crime and hence have reaped a bountiful crop. Crime is the ultimate human degradation. A civilized people have no higher duty than to do everything within their power to seek its reduction. We can prevent nearly all of the crime now suffered in America—if we care. Our character is at stake.

1

CHANGE AND CRIME

CHANGE is the dominant fact of our time. It separates us from all history. For two millennia and more after it was written in Ecclesiastes that there was no new thing under the sun, this wisdom sufficed. Then things began to change, slowly at first, but rushing now beyond our comprehension with acceleration the only foreseeable course. The nature and dimension of change must be constantly observed, its impact assessed and direction determined, if man hopes purposefully to affect his fate. No significant or lasting issue can be intelligently considered without reference to change. Today change is the main cause of crime and offers the best opportunity for its prevention.

Change is created principally by two interrelated dynamics. Both are uncontrolled human conduct: population increase and the application of science through technology. To ignore them in present conduct and future planning is to miss the great forces of this epoch—and to err.

The Union was formed in 1787 with fewer than 4 million people. By the time it was determined less than a century later that such a nation could long endure, we had grown to 32 million, 4 million newly emancipated from legal slavery though far from being free. Lincoln had foreseen a population of 200 million by 1900. He missed by a wide margin—we were 76 million at the turn of the century—but he had detected the main truth. We were growing rapidly.

In each of four consecutive decades before World War I the number of immigrants arriving from Europe exceeded the entire population of the United States when the Constitution was ratified. By 1920 there were 100 million Americans. Less than fifty years later we were 200 million. In the 1950's alone our numbers increased by more than seven times the total population of 1787. During the first two-thirds of the twentieth century the population of the United States grew two and one-half fold. The final third promised to add as many people as were added in the first two-thirds.

When the big census clock in the lobby of the Department of Commerce in Washington announced we were 200 million in October 1967, it failed to count perhaps 8 million—twice the population of the nation at its birth. Many of those not found by the census takers did not want to be found. They had wives and children, creditors, police or others looking for them. Many were simply lost in the enormity of our numbers. They were mere individuals in a mass society who didn't count except as trouble. They lived in overcrowded tenements, drifted from shanties and stairwells through all-night theaters and public rest rooms to bars, sidewalks, alleys and jails. Nearly all were poor. Perhaps half were Negroes. All the factors that make Americans hard to count make it harder to count black Americans.

Compared to most of the world, our population growth is slow now. The birth rate in the Philippines is twice that of the United States. As medical science, health services and good nutrition are provided in developing countries during the final thirty years of this century, decades will be added to life expectancy there. Only months will be added to life in advanced nations that have previously benefited from better health afforded by medicine and good food. Indeed, some believe slight declines in the length of life have already resulted from the many environmental pollutants—air, water, artificial foodstuffs, noise, anxiety—of technologically advanced urban nations. Longer lives to a greater degree than more births will explode populations. We think of ourselves as a young nation. Half of our people are under twenty-six years—but half of Brazil is under seventeen.

The earth will have a billion more people living on it in a mere decade. World population will double by the year 2000, adding 3 to 4 billion. Three-fourths of the total will be black, brown or yellow. Hundreds of millions will know hunger and many will starve in the remaining years of the century.

Science and technology affect our lives even more intimately than population increase, if the two can, with any realism, be considered separately. To measure the impact of science and technology we need not go back before our own century. Millions of Americans can remember the first horseless carriage that came to their town. Today there are more automobiles—85 million—on the highways than there were people in 1900 and as many cluttering our environment, sitting on blocks in back yards, resting stripped and smashed upon city streets and alongside freeways and country roads or piled high in junk yards on the outskirts of town. Often during the 1960's the weekly bumper crop of automobiles manufactured in Detroit exceeded the babies born throughout the nation. They make us the most mobile people who ever lived. Only one person in five in the United States today resides within fifty miles of his place of birth, while in most places and at most times perhaps fewer than one in five ever ventured fifty miles from where he was born. It was dangerous out there. Barbarians threatened on land and you could sail off the edge of the sea.

And yet the automobile as we use it will not survive the century. Even sprawling Los Angeles is one-third pavement, and traffic delays increase steadily. The contest between more freeways and mass transit is only slowly coming to a climax. The burdensome delays, expense and inconvenience of essential travel will reach crisis proportions for the poor before adequate facilities can be provided.

The social effects of travel are just beginning to work their way. Supersonic aircraft will carry hundreds of passengers in intercontinental flight less than seventy years after the Wright brothers abandoned bicycles to launch a heavier-than-air craft aloft for sixty-eight seconds at Kitty Hawk, North Carolina. They will bring Kuala Lumpur closer to Liverpool in time and familiarity than Canterbury was to London in Victoria's day.

In December 1901 Marconi startled the world by transmitting a feeble signal between Cornwall and Newfoundland over air waves. The present older generation, still remembering the crystal set, are the first people in history to hear by radio of important events in distant places—the Armistice in Europe, the stock market crash, the invasion of Poland, the atomic bomb dropped on Hiroshima—almost instantaneous with the occurrence, and thereby sense the meaning in their lives of things once comfortably remote and our growing interdependence.

While it informed whole populations of the new, mass communication also created a new commonness. Throughout the country people who before could have only vaguely known of one another's existence laughed simultaneously to the jokes of Fibber McGee and Molly and danced to the tunes on the Hit Parade. Television demonstrated at the New York World's Fair in 1939 was a curiosity. By 1955 television networks covered the United States, and by 1967 Telstar provided the possibility of instantaneous audio-visual communication between any two places in the world. In 1969 we could send radio waves back from a spaceship passing Mars. Today millions of preschool and school-age children see more and learn more from television than from parent or teacher. Yet no one can estimate the effect of television on the nature of man and society. Few even wonder and only the most inquisitive imagine ways of measuring. But that its impact is immense is undeniable.

Man has built more structures in the past thirty years than in the preceding six thousand. He will duplicate the feat in the next twenty years with better, cheaper structures. Still, millions will be ill housed, and huge urban slums will contain most human misery.

From the time nomadic man, hunting and grazing, first broke ground with a stick or a bone to cultivate the soil, ten thousand years elapsed before McCormick's reaper harvested the bounty of the prairies. Within a few decades millions had moved from the broken soil of the countryside to the asphalt pavement of the city. The revolution in agriculture liberated man from the soil. While 90 per cent of mankind throughout history had toiled to feed and clothe all, now less than 10 per cent of the labor force provides surpluses of food and fiber in bountiful America. And our government pays farmers not to produce more, though malnutrition is widespread at home and millions starve abroad.

Atomic energy, undreamed of when our senior scientists were schoolboys but now harnessed by man's ingenuity, offers more power and peril than all of the mules, fossil fuels, steam, wind and waterfalls of the world combined. When today's schoolboys are senior scientists, they will smile sentimentally at present primitive understanding of nuclear science just as we smile at the image of James Watt contemplating a whistling tea kettle and wondering how he might capture its force.

Science is only beginning to penetrate the mysteries of nature, while technology constantly narrows the time lapse from discovery to market surplus. We double our knowledge of the physical world each decade. With no acceleration in scientific development, a physicist or chemist conferred his Ph.D. today must expect, before the end of his career, to work in a field sixteen times broader in basic knowledge than the entire learning of all his professors and the most advanced researchers and visionary theoreticians of this time.

In 1900 there were roughly 10,000 scientific journals regularly published. By 1950 there were 100,000, and merely to cover published indexes to the journals a scientist would have to read one each working day

Perhaps one-fifteenth of all the people who ever lived live

today, but probably three-fourths of all the scientists who have labored labor today. They labor with a learning, a sense of direction and an institutionalized support that make them productive far beyond the potential of their predecessors.

Isaac Newton is ancient history to the physical scientists, while his contemporary John Locke remains a principal source for political scientists. But the human and governmental needs of our society were no more dreamed of in the philosophy of Locke than was our world of science by Newton.

Population growth and technology together have caused urbanization. In 1787 New York City, then, as now, our largest metropolis, had 33,000 people, and Philadelphia, second largest and host to the Constitutional Convention, had 20,000. Barely two dozen settlements had more than 2,500 people, and fewer than one in twenty of the total population lived in them. The rest were sprinkled very lightly over the Eastern seaboard on the edges of fields cleared of the forests but strewn with stones and tree stumps.

By 1900, 20 per cent of our people lived in towns of 25,000 or larger, but only sixty-five years later 80 per cent lived in and around cities of more than 50,000. Demonstrating the trend, the population of Texas increased 27 per cent between 1950 and 1960 while more than 200 of its 254 counties declined in population. Life in or near a city became a necessity—for nearly all.

In the 1960's more than 2 million Negroes, 8 per cent of all in the nation, left the South for the cities of the North, the Midwest and the West. They got off buses and out of old cars in places like Watts, first stop for the newly arrived poor in Los Angeles. In just five years, from 1960 to 1965, massive migrations caused the percentage of black children in public schools in Baltimore to increase from 50 to 61, in Chicago from 42 to 50, in St. Louis from 49 to 60 and in San Francisco from 24 to 32. There was no clearer indication of the immense new segregation coming in central city America. The consequences were clear, too.

We have witnessed more fundamental change in the way people live and in the nature of their society during this century than in all previous history. We shall witness more change in the remainder of this century than throughout history to date.

It is change that causes revolution; not revolution, change. There has never been revolution in a static society. No people ever arose violently from stagnation. Often it is change for the better that first brings the realization that something better, or even something different, is possible. Ferment, the turbulence of motion, the awareness of present misery, the vision of greater fulfillment and the recognition of avoidable injustice give rise to the impulse to revolt.

The volume and velocity of change we are experiencing are unknown to history. What has changed is not understood and what will change is not foreseeable. But the impact of change—of population increase, of science and technology and of urbanization—is profound. It shapes and conditions human conduct.

Irresistible forces have made us the most urbanized, anonymous, interdependent, transient, technologically advanced people who ever lived, and still greater change will come. In so complex a mass society it becomes increasingly difficult for the individual to find human dignity, a sense of purpose and meaning in his life. His impotence to affect in the slightest way things of utmost importance overwhelms him.

The crowding of millions of poor people with their cumulative disadvantage into the urban ghettos of our affluent and technologically advanced society not only offers the easy chance for criminal acts—it causes crime. The utter wretchedness of central city slums, crammed with most of the sickness, poverty, ignorance, idleness, ugliness, vice and crime of the whole metropolis, its residents impotent, incapable, incommunicado and physically isolated by surrounding freeways without exits, slowly drains compassion from the human spirit and breeds crime. From there the poor view another country—powerful and affluent—on television and know as the poor have never known before the full dimension of their degradation. Rootless, detached from the land by agricultural revolution, mobile and anonymous, the poor and powerless have become dependent on society not only for their well-being but for survival itself. No longer can man fare alone. There is no place to garden, no cornfield, no fish and game or wild fruits and berries in the slums, there is only your fellow man. The nomadic subsistence possible to the ghetto poor without money, jobs or welfare is derived from crime.

Nor is there a place to escape. Even in Alaska the native peoples—Eskimo, Aleutian Islander and North American Indian—can no longer flourish in the most isolated and unaffected natural habitat remaining. The salmon that once assured him food now feed people over six continents; the three best species are extinct, and the native must venture farther and fish longer, often among great refrigerated ships, to fill his needs. The seals, once so plentiful, now fur ladies in Moscow, Paris and New York, and trophy hunters seeking a head to hang on the wall or a skin to cover the floor steadily diminish game. Twenty per cent of the people in our largest state, enduring the most hostile climate in America, are left without adequate food, clothing or shelter; they are poor, uneducated, jobless—and dying young. Their life expectancy of only 34.3 years, per capita income of less than one-fourth that of white Alaskans and their inability to get half the calories needed daily only show the consequences of our times to those who are left out. So it is to a lesser degree in pockets of rural poverty throughout the nation. The growing wealth of the nation does not touch Appalachia, rural Mississippi and the Imperial and Central Valleys of California. Often it drains a little more from the remaining poor.

Such distortions in the distribution of increasing affluence are vast. Millions may cross the poverty line, but other millions are plunged more deeply into different forms of poverty. Proportionately they may be a steadily smaller part of the whole, but in absolute numbers they are millions. Americans living today in life-crushing poverty exceed the population of the entire nation on the day Grant and Lee met at Appomattox. Growing fortunes for already advantaged suburban dwellers are matched by the deadly decline to less and less in Harlem, Hough and Watts. The affluence provided by technology—so readily visible to all —creates a new and intolerable poverty for those it passes by. The automobile, the high rise, television and chemistry have an immense influence not only as forces of change but as causes of crime. The anxieties arising from technology cause most of our instability and heighten the desire to manifest contempt for our existing values and to escape to something different. Addicts, alcoholics and the mentally ill are products of that anxiety and contribute most of the crime in America.

Young people, frustrated, neglected, skeptical and unable to escape the truth that surrounds them, wonder at our purpose. Powerless as are the poor to affect in the slightest way the things that matter most to them, youth can only protest a war that calls on them to kill and die, demonstrate against electronic, chemical and nuclear instruments of mass destruction, endeavor to change the schools that fail to provide fulfillment, seek to stop the bulldozers that destroy the remaining places of recreation and beauty, and try to prevent further pollution of air and water and of foodstuffs by synthetic chemicals.

Old ideals founder. Family breakdown, anonymity of the individual, the inundation of ceaseless communications, the sounds of civilization—passing trucks, trains and airplanes, TV, radio, neighbors—and the total inability of people to provide their own necessities create an environment in which values are difficult to identify and older virtues depreciate rapidly. The quick change in the human condition creates uncertainty, unfamiliarity and fear. From new teachers who do not know us we learn lessons they do not intend. The horror of war in Vietnam, the inhumanity of hunger in Biafra, the injustice of apartheid in South Africa, the cruelty of malnutrition in Mississippi have dawned slowly on us these past years. The impact of similar situations that will emerge in the next several decades will profoundly shape our destiny. We cannot expect domestic tranquillity or a tidy order in the midst of such turbulence.

In the light of our ability to completely annihilate one another, some people doubt that man has a future. Others, viewing population increase, technological explosion and the mindlessly swift current of events, question whether man is in control of his destiny. Beyond these is the enigma of the meaning and worth of the individual in mass society. Combined, the forces that cause the loss of direction and sense of purpose and that question even our continued existence have demeaned human dignity, cheapened life and eroded resistance to antisocial conduct.

It has all happened in a remarkably short period of time. Two lives can span the entire epoch of America. Thousands of people born before 1787 were alive in the 1870's and 1880's. Tens of thousands born in the 1870's and 1880's live today. Any two, linked death to birth, can span the American story, as Jefferson Davis and Harry S. Truman nearly do.

To live in ordered liberty we must develop social disciplines and institutional actions relevant to present conditions and future directions. The time has long since passed when we can afford the leisurely adaptations of yesteryear. They are hopelessly inadequate.

Vast effort in making government and social organization meaningful and effective is clearly essential. We must give our highest priority to mastering the art of effecting change in institutional conduct. Law, science, education, social service, industry, labor and religion must all be enlisted as effective instruments of social change. Our neglect of government and the quality of life, our inability to disenthrall ourselves from the old to see the new and our hypocrisy have brought us perilously close to a condition in which youth sees nihilism as the answer to present ills and anarchy as the most desirable alternative.

Vast numbers of a thing—anything—depreciate its value. The magnitude of today's numbers compels computerization. Only computers can store, coordinate, retrieve and deliver data necessary to judgment in many current endeavors. Only computers can calculate with the speed required by the quantum of facts in mass society. Like most products of technology, computers are not without risk. They cannot make moral judgments. Man must do this. As with nuclear energy, which will be essential to the preservation of man in mass society, computers can destroy. They can become the master rather than the servant of man.

To master the profusion of data, to weed out the obsolete, to force relevance in our actions, to develop priorities and to implement decisions, we must simplify. Simplification is an essential process in a society which manufactures proliferation. Social stability cannot be attained until we so simplify the complexities of our lives that the individual can see some sense of order and proportion in society. Change and the countless numbers it has produced compel simplification.

Far from being only a stimulant of crime, change offers man's best chance, if a perilous one, to reduce substantially his antisocial conduct. Through technology this generation first liberated mankind from bondage to nature. The question now is whether technology will in turn master man. If human reason and purpose can control technology, they can vastly enrich the human condition. The underlying causes of crime will crumble before the forces of change when they are directed to create conditions elevating human dignity and creating reverence for life. Population control, health, knowledge, human usefulness, wholesome environment and beauty can be achieved through change. For all the problems change creates, its opportunities exceed them many times over.

There have never been people at any time in history who so clearly and abundantly possessed the potential to meet all of their problems and provide for all of their needs as do Americans today. We do not release half the energies of our people. Through technology we can build new cities—clean, ample and beautiful. We can educate, employ and fulfill all of our people. Tragically neglected processes of criminal justice can enlarge both security for society and liberty for the individual. We can find justice. The question is one of will.

2

THE MANY FACES OF CRIME

CRIME has many faces.

White-collar crime converts billions of dollars annually in tax evasion, price fixing, embezzlement, swindling and consumer fraud.

Organized crime reaps hundreds of millions in gambling, loansharking, drug traffic, extortion and prostitution, corrupting officials and resorting to force, including murder when necessary, to accomplish its purposes.

Crime in the streets, as we have come to call it, encompassing a wide variety of crimes against people and against property—robbery, mugging, burglary, larceny, theft and looting—produces millions of hard-earned dollars for its perpetrators.

Crimes of passion, emotion overwhelming reason, include most murders, rapes and assaults. Conduct once deemed immoral and made criminal—gambling, prostitution, alcohol and drug abuse, profanity, abortion, homosexuality, fornication and obscenity—is a pervasive face of crime accounting for hundreds of thousands of arrests annually.

Violations of regulations designed to protect the public health, safety and convenience—traffic control, building codes, fire ordinances, minimum standards of quality, mandatory safety precautions, misrepresentation—involve highly antisocial conduct in mass society causing hundreds of thousands of deaths each year.

Revolutionary crime and illegal conduct intended to alter institutions impose rioting, mob violence, unlawful confrontation, arson and trespass on a weary society. Terrorist actions—sniping, bombing and ambushing—common in parts of the world, are an ever increasing risk in America.

Corruption in public office—bribes, payoffs, fixes, conflicts of interest—occurs in every branch of government, legislative, executive, judicial, administrative, and at every level, federal, state and local.

Police crime—wrongful arrest, brutality and blackmail—is not unknown.

Types and methods of crime are as varied as human behavior in our complex and changing society. Persons capable of crime act within the range of their opportunity, their conduct shaped by their situation. Bankers rarely rob banks. There are easier, safer, more successful ways of obtaining money. The poor do not fix prices. They do not even have the price. But among those capable of crime each finds his own way.

It is the crimes of poor and powerless people that most enrage and frighten the affluent, comfortable and advantaged majority. Riots, muggings, robbery and rape are loathsome not only because they are inherently irrational and inhumane but because they and their causes are so foreign to the experience of people with power that they are incomprehensible. If opportunities open to the poor offered more rational and humane avenues to the ends sought by crime, these means would be utilized. It is the inhumane and irrational condition of the poor that finally causes some among them to commit such crimes.

Few people think analytically when they consider the problem of crime. It is an emotional subject. First to mind come crimes we have experienced. Then we think of crimes we sense with greatest horror—those we fear most. As a result we ignore many types of crime. We are aware of the crimes decried in the headlines but remain unaware of most crimes. Comparatively rare occurrences in the world of crime become so notorious that they form our basic impression, even knowledge, of crime. But to conceive of crime as only an inhuman murder or rape or a filling station robbery is like viewing measles as a mere skin blemish. The real danger is beneath the surface. It is fever and damage to body tissue. It is mutation of basic human qualities that may be transmitted to the next generation. The simplistic diagnosis of crime leads to the wrong prescription: all that is necessary is to control a few individuals. But crimes are inter-related. Society cannot hope to control violent and irrational antisocial conduct while cunning predatory crime by people in power continues unabated.

Any nation that wishes to prevent crime must be conscious of the whole range of criminal activity.

Each type of crime exists because we are what we are. Our national character and condition create capabilities for crime, cause us to suffer them and inhibit commitment to their control. Different crimes are related in their causes and in the motivations of those who commit them. For these reasons prevention and control of nearly all categories of crimes will be achieved by the same social reforms and law enforcement practices.

To think of controlling street crime while organized crime flourishes is to ignore their clear connections. Narcotics supplied by the professionals nourish thefts, burglaries and sometimes robberies and muggings by the addicted driven to buy more drugs. To believe crimes of violence can be controlled while property crimes are widespread is to assume a discipline in a mind capable of crime which experience does not reflect. The values that permit theft from an empty car are unlikely to prevent armed robbery of a bus driver. Where white-collar crime is accepted, burglary, larceny and theft must be expected. If a poor man capable of crime had custody of the company books, he would rarely burglarize when he could embezzle. Embezzlement is easier and safer and if the perpetrator is caught, the penalties are relatively insignificant. Nothing so vindicates the unlawful conduct of a poor man, by his light, as the belief that the rich are stealing from him through overpricing and sales of defective goods or that middle class employees abscond with cash receipts.

The crimes to which we pay least attention are those committed by people of advantage who have an easier, less offensive, less visible way of doing wrong. White-collar crime is usually the act of respected and successful people. Illicit gains from white-collar crime far exceed those of all other crime combined. Crime as practiced among the poor is more dangerous and less profitable. One corporate price-fixing conspiracy criminally converted more money each year it continued than all of the hundreds of thousands of burglaries, larcenies or thefts in the entire nation during those same years. Reported bank embezzlements, deposits diverted by bank employees, cost ten times more than bank robberies each year. Bank robberies are always known because by definition bank employees are present and money is taken by force. Bank robbery is nearly always reported because insurance cannot be claimed unless it is. Embezzlement, on the other hand, is frequently not reported when restitution is possible or if the amount involved is small. Sometimes embezzlement is not discovered.

White-collar crime is the most corrosive of all crimes. The trusted prove untrustworthy; the advantaged, dishonest. It shows the capability of people with better opportunities for creating a decent life for themselves to take property belonging to others. As no other crime, it questions our moral fiber.

To the victims the consequences of white-collar crime are often more dire than those that follow theft, burglary or robbery. White-collar crime can dig deeper than the wallet in the pocket to wipe out the savings of a lifetime. The thief takes only what is in the purse or the dresser drawer at the moment of his crime. The embezzler may reach beyond to destroy the equity of a family, ruin a whole firm, or render corporate stock valueless.

Naturally we dread violent crime most—murder, rape, assault and robbery. To many these are the world of crime, and all else is insignificant. But they are only the most extreme manifestations of our capability to injure others. They tell us that people can be conditioned to the ultimate insensitivity—the capacity to take or damage life.

Violent crime springs from a violent environment. Mental illness, addiction, alcoholism, widespread property crime, the prevalence of guns, police brutality and criminal syndicates, all contribute to its dimension. Rioting is followed by weeks of arson and violent skirmishing. Children are deeply disappointed that they missed the excitement of participation and seek another chance, as earlier generations regretted being too young to fight in World Wars I and II. Disturbances on the city streets cause resonant vibrations among inmates in jails and penitentiaries who riot and damage prison property. Campus unrest both reflects and adds to general unrest. The youngest see it all and learn.

The motives of most crimes are economic. Seven of eight known serious crimes involve property. Many crimes against persons, such as robbery, mugging, kidnaping and sometimes assault and murder, are incidental to a property crime. Their main purpose is to obtain money or property.

Property crimes cost billions annually. From kids stealing candy bars to multimillion-dollar frauds, they manifest a lack of concern for other people. This insensitivity largely reflects attitudes developed through social experience. While the contributory factors are many and varied, the capability for crime develops in early childhood when character is forming. Children living in places where people have no rights that they are capable of enforcing will rarely have a regard for rights of others. Since legal rights tend to reflect important values of society, such individuals have little regard for things society considers important. To know that police take bribes, the church treasurer ran off with the building fund, the construction contractor swindled your father out of the cost of new roofing, and three of your friends make more in a night stripping cars than you make in a week washing them is not conducive to respect for law. Some finally rationalize that they would be fools to play it straight when everyone they know is on the make. The next step may be rolling a drunk. For suburban youth living in materialistic abundance the motivations for rapidly increasing property crime are different, diverse and more difficult to identify. Neglect, anxiety, family breakup, emptiness, the loneliness of the individual in huge high schools and lack of identity contribute. Faceless youngsters of affluent families steal cars, burglarize suburban homes and commit acts of malicious destruction most often because nothing else in their lives seems important.

When police crime occurs, it too brutalizes. Where police protection is purchased, it corrupts. Anyone who experiences such things or believes that they happen will have little confidence in law or its enforcement. Where can he turn? If he lives in a world of brutality, he will be brutal. If he lives in a world of corruption, he will be corrupt. The black rage of the ghetto results from an accumulation of inhuman experiences. It evolves from frustration to despair to rage. This is the ultimate product of our inhumanity. Decades ago in the South people we now say suffer black rage were called "bad niggers." Their lives often ended with lynching. We have come to see the same rage among all of our disadvantaged people of every race. We succeed in driving the last drop of pity from some.

Many crimes reflect merely the gap between our preachment and our practice. They expose the dimension of national hypocrisy. We professed to prohibit the production, transportation and sale of alcoholic beverages when we knew their widespread use would continue. The harm that comes from such self-deception is difficult to underestimate. How much respect can there be for the integrity of the law? How is equal justice possible? Only a handful of the known offenders ever felt the sanction of the Prohibition laws. Criminal empires were created because the profits were high and legitimate businesses would not compete. Relationships between police and the communities they served were seriously impaired—the respect and confidence essential to effective law enforcement destroyed. Police, however professional, can never hold the respect of the people when they must endeavor to enforce laws that the public will not obey.

In our turbulent times, when youth seriously questions the purpose, the integrity and the effectiveness of our laws, we must have the courage to face honestly and answer truthfully such difficult issues as the continued prohibition of marijuana and other mild stimulants and depressants, gambling, prostitution, abortion, and sexual relations between consenting adults. Nothing is worth while for the individual, or for his society, unless his own actions are honest. The failure to face and answer such issues is as dishonest as the false answer. The consequence in the lives of millions is immense.

There are still many, nurtured on the Puritan ethic, who believe drink and debauchery are so much more alluring to the multitudes than justice and rectitude that they conceive of goodness as merely self-denial. They insist that the law prohibit those who would not deny themselves. But prohibition is impossible. Forces more powerful than the fear of police are at work. If society really intends to control gambling, drugs and prostitution, it must work to educate, to humanize, and to civilize.

Laws that cannot be enforced corrupt. Partial enforcement of laws against known violators is inherently unequal except in the most sensitive and skillful hands, and usually even then. We become a government of men rather than of laws, where men choose who will be arrested and who will remain free for the same infraction. Those arrested are bitter, while those permitted to continue unlawful activity corrupt others and themselves. The watching public is cynical.

Political campaign financing is a classic illustration of the hypocrisy we will tolerate. At the federal level, and generally at the state, a major portion of the funds for political campaigns is raised in violation of law. Federal law says that not more than

$3 million shall be spent by a presidential nominee in pursuit of that office. National parties have spent many times that amount in recent elections. Estimates of the total cost of the presidential campaigns of 1964 and 1968 exceed $100 million each. The Federal Corrupt Practices Act limits candidates for the United States House of Representatives to $10,000 and for the Senate to $25,000. Candidates have spent more than $1 million seeking a Senate seat. It is impossible for a major candidate with opposition to comply with such unrealistic limits. Evasion is forced, because the practicalities and prior practice leave no choice. The losers are the law and the people.

Criminal codes must be simplified. Unenforceable laws, antiquated laws, laws that are inconsistent with the moral standards of the public or the economic facts of life must be repealed. New laws and new techniques of control relevant to the needs of the day must take their place. Only then can society look at crime with a straight face. Only then can the law be an effective instrument of public policy.

Of the many faces of crime, the most tragic is never recognized by many. The rubble it leaves in wasted human lives exceeds many times over all the injury of violent crime. Assaults, rapes, even murders are counted in the thousands and tens of thousands. But millions fall victim to the cruelest of all crimes, which takes its toll in miserable, empty and wasted lives. It is the crime of power over impotence—the crime of a society that does not insure equal protection of the laws. It is crime against people who have no rights—the crime of a society which seeks to maintain order without law. From it grows most crime of violence and much property crime.

It is the crime of failing to provide fire escapes, condoning faulty wiring and other fire hazards, permitting overcrowding in unsanitary tenements infested with rats, all in violation of ordinances with criminal penalties. It is the illegal sale of rotten meat and impure bread at excessive prices—and racial discrimination in employment in violation of federal statutes and state fair employment practices acts.

It is the willful violation of basic constitutional rights. The United States Supreme Court in 1954 declared racially segregated schools inherently unequal. That most fundamental of rights has been denied to more than 95 per cent of a whole generation of black students in the public schools of the eleven states that were the Confederacy—a majority of the black school children of the nation. Does government have a greater duty to prevent a physical assault than the theft of an education? Would you rather have your child brutally beaten or deprived of his chance for a good education? Poor young blacks wind up suffering both. The cost to America of this one huge crime of deprivation is immeasurable.

Our society permits conditions to exist in which laws cannot be enforced. Gambling, narcotics, prostitution, extortion and loansharking are open and notorious. Police see it and know it. Areas of our cities are so dangerous that neither life nor what little property people who live there have is safe. The basic solution for most crime is economic—homes, health, education, employment, beauty. If the law is to be enforced—and rights fulfilled for the poor—we must end poverty. Until we do, there will be no equal protection of the laws. To permit conditions that breed antisocial conduct to continue is our greatest crime. We pay dearly for it.

3

THE CRIME COUNT:
IGNORANCE, MYTH AND FACT

IGNORANCE is perhaps the greatest barrier to effective crime control. We know little; we misconceive much. Leadership unwilling to concede how little it knows—but often willing to exploit the escalation of anxiety—tortures us with our own lack of understanding.

The crime clock used by the Federal Bureau of Investigation is a notable example. It measures only the frequency of crime reported to police throughout the nation, not the rate of crime based on the whole population. It does not attempt to tell us why we have crime, what causes it, who commits it, or whom it finds for its victim. What does it mean to tell the nation that seven serious crimes are committed each minute of the day, that a murder occurs every thirty-nine minutes, a forcible rape every seventeen minutes, a robbery every two minutes? It means that you take the public for a fool. For how many people are born, how many die, how many homes burn, how many suffer heart attacks, how many are injured in automobile accidents in the same period? If the same frequency for crimes were applied to China with its fourfold greater population, the clock would toll one-fourth the crime per capita it indicates here. If the crimes measured occurred in the Virgin Islands the whole population would be dead of murder in three years, having been previously raped twice and robbed eighteen times. If all these crimes occurred in places known to you or me, we would all be annihilated in a matter of weeks or months.

The clock alarms but it does not tell the time. You look at the sweep second hand and hold your breath for the next auto theft forty-one seconds away—even though it may be thirty minutes and will occur in a distant city you have never visited, among people you have never known. The clock presents a two-dimensional world that is unreal—minutes measuring occurrences—but there are many dimensions to this world and we must measure more than two if we are to know anything about crime.

Most crime is never reported to police. And much crime is inaccurately reported. Erroneous crime statistics are often used to create the impression that the new chief is doing a good job, or to support a movement to add more police. Frequently an apparent increase in crime really reflects an improved effectiveness in law enforcement, or in the reporting of crime itself.

The better the police, the more they learn of crimes that are actually committed. Today some cities suffering far more crime than others take false comfort from lower rates of reported crime because of weaker police departments. Most lives in America are unmarred by serious crime. The only meaningful impression such people can have about the incidence of crime is from the press, other communications media and the police. As crime becomes more topical, the tendency of distorted impressions to mislead increases.

Wherever crime is not reported we know the police are not effective, trusted or respected. Too many people there would rather suffer crime in silence than report it. It is a bother, useless, gets you involved—or, worse, in trouble yourself. The lives of some are so saturated with crime that they take it for granted, like the weather. Who reports the weather? The last time you reported a burglary, the police ignored the call, or perhaps caused more inconvenience than the crime itself: two hours of questioning, an argument with your son, a trip to the precinct station, twice viewing line-ups—and no results. Report crime, and you cause trouble for a friend or relative or with a neighbor you fear. It should not be surprising that those who suffer most crime report it least. Crime among the well-to-do is usually reported. For one thing, you cannot collect insurance for losses resulting from crime that is not reported. For another, crime is relatively rare among the well-to-do. They are shocked when it occurs, and in their contacts the police have nearly always been polite. The poor have had a different experience.

We cannot assume, however, that because a crime is reported, it actually occurred. How many reported thefts are really efforts to defraud insurance companies? How many alleged assaults are motivated by anger or vengeance? Rape presents an extreme illustration: 18 per cent of all rapes reported to the police in 1968 were determined by investigation to be unfounded. Efforts must be made not only to secure full reporting of crime but to be sure reports are truthful and accurate.

Over the years the FBI has developed an increasingly uniform and complete report of crime from an ever greater number of jurisdictions. By 1968 reporting covered 97 per cent of the people living in major cities and 75 per cent of the people living in rural areas, accounting for 92 per cent of the nation's total population. Still, we have only the beginning of an accurate, comprehensive crime report.

The more serious the crime the more likely it is to be reported. Murder will out. There must be some explanation for the corpse or the absence of the deceased. Of all crimes murder is probably the most accurately reported. Some murders are not detected—a disappearance, a fire thought to be accidental, a mistaken medical judgment as to the cause of death—and some, we assume, just died, and no one cares enough to question. There are a few murders we still ignore: a Negro killed while being questioned in a rural county jail, a person shot fleeing an officer in a slum, a convict stabbed to death in a prison fight, or an alcoholic vagrant found in an alley.

While most murder in America has always become known to the police, police have not always kept a careful count or fully and accurately reported murders to the FBI, which assembles the national uniform crime reports. We hear of the Southern counties that experienced a murder a week in the 1920's. But how many sheriffs kept careful reports or accurately transmitted information for national statistical purposes?

To the extent that it has been accurately reported, murder occurred less frequently per capita in the United States in the 1960's than during the 1920's and 1930's—and probably, though we do not know, well below the rate during the nineteenth century. In 1967, for instance, the murder rate was 14 per cent lower than in 1933. If we knew of all the murders committed in that earlier period, the contrast might be considerably sharper. Certainly our crime statistics generally became substantially more all-inclusive between 1933 and 1967. But because they are so questionable, reliance on even the murder statistics for the last thirty years is risky.

The comparison with earlier years, if accurate, is important. It can help measure our heritage of violence. It is relevant in considering the causes of murder. Is there some correlation between murder and the anxieties created by an economic depression such as we experienced in the 1930's or the greater affluence of the 1960's? The comparison is also critical in forming public opinion. How can we know whether we are becoming more violent except by an accurate comparative statistical count?

Consideration of crime trends for lesser crimes is even more speculative. Perhaps 90 per cent of all murders are reported to the police, but at the far end of the crime spectrum probably as few as 10 per cent of minor property crimes are reported. This fact reflects a sad lack of concern and a callousness about ourselves and, more importantly, our youth who commit most minor property crimes. By accepting the unacceptable—minor crimes—we invite worse. Young people sense this and they are not motivated toward decency. To succeed with one crime may well encourage another. Indifference to crime causes its repetition.

Crimes in America are so many and varied that we endeavor to count only those defined as serious for national reporting purposes. Millions of serious crimes are unreported each year. Tens of millions of lesser crimes such as minor thefts and larcenies are not counted, though they differ little—often only in the value of the property wrongfully taken—from serious crimes of the same nature. All the other risks to society may have been the same—the same window pried open, the same gun or knife in hand, the same addict who if caught might assault or murder, the same wallet or purse or cash register—but in one case only fifteen dollars was there, while in the other it was fifty-five dollars.

Of the types of serious crime, seven are chosen for the most comprehensive statistical reporting. They include most serious crimes and tend to indicate general crime trends. Called "index crimes," they are murder, rape, assault, robbery, burglary, larceny and car theft. Of 3.8 million index crimes reported to the police in 1967, and 4.5 million in 1968, approximately 12 per cent are classified crimes of violence—494,000 in 1967 and 589,000 in 1968. Four categories of the seven are included under crimes of violence—murder, rape, aggravated assault and robbery. Robbery, with over 200,000 reported incidents in 1967 and 261,000 in 1968—40 per cent of all violent crime reported—is a crime of violent potential rather than of violence as an end in itself. Its purpose is to take property; violence, threatened or used, is only the technique.

Violent crimes are constantly emphasized in national coverage of reported crime, while many other crimes—particularly white-collar crimes—are virtually ignored. This pattern both reflects and shapes our interest and concern. Ironically, news coverage of violent crime tends to increase rather than deter violence, while reporting of white-collar crime is a strong deterrent to its commission. Reputation is important to the businessman.

A tax fraud indictment is ruinous. The indictment and conviction of a prominent businessman has a deep effect on the business community. When a prison sentence is imposed there is often profound shock, but prison sentences are rare for white-collar crime. There are federal judicial districts in which there has never been a conviction for tax fraud and many where conviction has never resulted in imprisonment.

Constant reporting of violent crime, on the other hand, seems to add to the climate of violence. There is a psychotic response, almost a resonant vibration, to reports of arson, bombing, riot, murder and rape. People otherwise docile for the time respond to reports of violence as if it were a contagious disease and the reports were a carrier. And for the kid from the slums the only time he is likely to see his picture in the paper may be when he is in police custody following arrest for a violent crime. Far from destroying a reputation, this is the best chance for fame— or at least notoriety—that fate offers him.

To the extent that statistics on violent crime are accurate, the individual's chance of being the victim of a crime of violence in the United States in 1967 was one in 400 during the year, or once in 400 years. The odds are one in 146,000 per day. If you assume only half of all violent crime comes to the attention of the police—a reasonable assumption—the individual's chances are then twice as great, or once in 200 years.

The odds, however, vary immensely with location and condition. Crime is not spread evenly over the nation. The chance of being a victim of violent crime is much greater for the city dweller. Robbery is the most urbanized of all violent crimes. Robberies per capita in cities of more than 250,000 people occur ten times more frequently than in surrounding suburban jurisdictions and thirty-five times more frequently than in outlying rural areas. The murder rate in big cities is four and a half times higher than in the suburbs and two and a half times above the rural rate. The big-city rates for aggravated assault, rape, burglary, larceny, and theft exceed both suburban and rural rates by two to four times. The rate of auto theft is fourteen times greater in urban than in rural areas.

The murder rate in the Southern states is twice that of the nation, and assault is 50 per cent higher there. Robbery is more common in the Northeast, while rape is reported most frequently in the Western states.

The general averages indicate only a small part of the geographic concentration of crime, because there are further concentrations within the city or the region that compound its presence there. Crime is heavily concentrated in small geographic areas of the inner city and pockets of rural poverty. Here, where fewer than one-fourth of the people live, more than three-fourths of all arrests occur. Here the cost of police per capita and per square mile is many times the police cost elsewhere in the city or countryside.

While on the average a citizen may be the victim of violent crime only once in 400 years, there are indications that the poor black urban slum dweller faces odds five times greater—one in eighty. Since violent crimes are more frequently unreported in the slums, the chance of being a victim there may be substantially higher. If only one-fourth of the violent crime of the ghetto is reported, which is quite possible, the odds for those living there of being a crime victim within a year are one in twenty.

The white middle class city dweller by contrast is likely to be the victim of violent crime at the rate of once every 2,000 years, while upper middle income and rich suburbanites have one chance in 10,000 years.

The brutalization of poverty, racism and discrimination in the United States is graphically demonstrated by the dimension of violent crime reported among Negroes. Violent crime in the black ghetto is probably reported less frequently than anywhere else in America. Even so, Negroes, composing at most 14 per cent of the total population, were involved in 59 per cent of the arrests for murder in 1967. This does not mean that Negroes in fact committed 59 per cent of all murders. Negroes are arrested more frequently and on less evidence than whites and are more often victims of mass or sweep arrests. But 54 per cent of all known murder victims were black in both 1967 and 1968—this is a body count, mathematically precise excepting human error. Blacks are nearly always the victims of black violence and suffer some white violence as well.

Nearly one-half of all persons arrested for aggravated assault during 1968 were black—and, again, blacks were the primary victims of the assaults. Sixty-one per cent of all persons arrested for robbery were black, with black victims bearing most of the burden. Forty-seven per cent of those arrested for rape were black, while approximately one-third of all arrested for serious property crimes were black. Blacks were their principal victims. The most tragic and dangerous risk of racism in America today is that it may cause us to misconstrue the meaning of crime among poor blacks. That crime flows clearly and directly from the brutalization and dehumanization of racism, poverty and injustice. Black America has shown itself to be far gentler and more humane than white America. There is nothing inherent in black character that causes black crime. On the contrary, the slow destruction of human dignity caused by white racism is responsible. This is the most pitiable result of this huge wrong of the American people.

More than one-fourth of all murders reported in 1968 were within a family, a majority involving husband and wife. An additional half of the murders resulted from arguments in which the participants usually knew each other. One murder in fourteen resulted from lovers' quarrels. One-fourth of all murders occurred in connection with the commission of another felony —a burglary, rape or robbery—or where such a felony crime was suspected. The victim often knew his assailant before the crime in these situations.

Studies indicate that up to 85 per cent of all murders occur within families or among acquaintances. Murder, usually a

crime of passion, naturally occurs where emotions are strongest
—husband and wife, father and son, a psychotic, a drunk, the
angry neighbor, the lovers' quarrel, beer-drinking buddies. The
crime we fear most—murder by a stranger, the mad killer, the
shadow in the night—accounts for fewer than one murder in
five. If you are afraid of being murdered, there is more safety in
deserting your family and having no friends than in additional
police, who rarely have the opportunity to prevent friends and
relatives from murdering one another. Any substantial reduction in the number of murders will come slowly with the stabilizing of our national character. Humane and gentle people do not
injure one another.

Probably two-thirds of all aggravated assaults occur within a
family or among neighbors or friends. They happen in areas
where social dynamics put most pressure on people—where
families are disintegrating. Even rape is committed more often
than not by a person known to the victim. Only robbery, of the
crimes defined as violent by the FBI, is committed most frequently by a stranger. As reported, about 20 per cent of the
victims know the robber. Usually, people who commit robberies
do not know people of property.

Three categories of offenses against property—burglary, larceny and car theft—are included among the seven index crimes.
These account for nearly 90 per cent of all serious crime reported to police. Since violent crimes are more likely to be reported, property crime probably comprises closer to 95 per cent
of all serious crime that actually occurs.

Crime is selective both as to seasons and times of day, but all
crimes do not prefer the same seasons, or criminals the same
working hours. Violent crimes tend to be more frequent in the
summer. Murder, rape and assault occur most often in July,
when they range up to 20 per cent above the annual average,
while in January they are more than 10 per cent below average.
Negligent homicide, aided by icy streets and the closeness of
indoor living, is highest in December—more than 30 per cent

above the annual average, while in June it is 20 per cent below.

Robbery, burglary and auto theft occur most frequently in the fall. Robbery and burglary reach their peak in December, while auto thefts recede with winter weather. Robberies nation-wide tend to be 30 per cent higher than the annual average in December and 15 per cent lower in April and May. Burglaries, larcenies and auto thefts will run 10 per cent above normal in peak months and 10 per cent below in slow months.

Auto theft and burglary occur at residences half the time. Two-thirds of all auto thefts occur under cover of darkness. Only slightly more than half of all residential burglaries are at night, because people are more likely to be at home then, while 95 per cent of all nonresidential burglaries are at night, after people have left the office, store or plant. Since burglary is a crime of stealth involving forceful or other unlawful entry, it is naturally most often committed when people are least likely to be present.

Larceny for purposes of the Uniform Crime Reports is the unlawful taking of property valued at more than fifty dollars without the use of force, violence or fraud and without an unlawful entry into a building. Inflation is clearly a factor in the increase of reported larceny. Many items worth far less than fifty dollars ten years ago cost a good deal more than fifty dollars now. Theft of such an item in 1960 was not reported as a serious crime, but today it is.

The most common larcenies are stripping autos, theft of valuables left inside unlocked cars and from open buildings, theft of bicycles, shoplifting, purse snatching, pocket picking, and taking money from coin-operated machines. Some 1,047,100 larcenies were reported in 1967, and police know of over 2 million additional thefts of property valued at less than fifty dollars. Both figures represent a small fraction of all larcenies. An urban crime, it occurs five times more often per capita in cities of over 100,000 than in rural areas.

For 654,000 automobiles reported stolen in 1967, 130,000

arrests were made. In comparison 86 per cent of the stolen cars were recovered, 55 per cent within forty-eight hours. The high recovery results from the fact that three-fourths were stolen for transportation only—chiefly by juvenile joy riders—and cars are hard to hide. Two-thirds of all persons charged with auto theft in 1967 were under eighteen years of age.

Law enforcement is not a major deterrent in property crimes. Arrests are made for less than one reported burglary, larceny or car theft of every five reported. Convictions are obtained in something less than one in twenty cases of even the serious crimes against property that are reported to police.

Nearly the entire increase in arrests for the commission of serious crimes during the 1960's is accounted for by minors. Youngsters between eleven and seventeen, composing 13 per cent of the population, are convicted in over 50 per cent of all prosecutions for burglary, larceny and car theft. Half of all property crime is committed by people under twenty-one.

Arrests for all criminal acts excepting traffic offenses increased 18 per cent between 1960 and 1969. Arrests of persons under eighteen increased 100 per cent in this same period, while the total population between ten and eighteen years of age grew 25 per cent. But because of changing enforcement standards reflected in new arrest patterns, few conclusions can be drawn. For instance, of 3.5 million arrests in 1960, 1.25 million were for drunkenness, while of 4,146,000 arrests in 1968, only 1 million were for drunkenness. Drunkenness is not an offense of the young. The one clear fact is that more young people are being arrested, whatever the charge.

Suburban youth are involved in a substantially greater proportion of all suburban arrests, nearly 40 per cent, than are urban and rural youth in their communities. Arrests of females under eighteen increased 149 per cent between 1960 and 1967, while arrests of males in this age group rose 92 per cent. But male arrests were still seven times higher than female arrests in 1968. Crime generally, and violent crime particularly, is the act of the nation's largest minority—the male. Of all ages from cradle to grave, sixteen-year-olds are arrested most frequently. The rate drops every year thereafter.

Violent crime is predominantly adult crime. It takes longer to harden the young to violence. Fifty-four per cent of all persons arrested for robbery are under twenty-one, but only thirty per cent arrested for aggravated assault are minors. In 1967, 9 per cent of all persons arrested for murder were under eighteen, compared to 64 per cent of those arrested for car theft. Only 37 per cent of all persons arrested for murder were under twenty-five.

Youth is the time in life with the rarest exception when those who live lives of crime take that road. The most important statistic of all in the field of criminal justice is the one which tells us that probably four out of five of all felonies are committed by repeaters—that 80 per cent of all serious crime is committed by people convicted of crime before. The first crime was committed nearly always as a teenager. Approximately half of all the persons released from prisons return to prison, many again and again. In federal youth centers nearly all prisoners were convicted of crimes that occurred after the offender dropped out of high school. Three-fourths came from broken homes. The ignorance that afflicts so much of our thinking and data about crime provides no excuse for our failure to act here. We know the facts about recidivism. The individuals who repeatedly commit crimes are identified and the high probability that they will commit yet more crimes is tragically clear. We also know that for most of them rehabilitation is possible. This crime is controllable—if we care.

4

THE MOTHER OF CRIME

WITH the vast increase in population and urbanization, the poor—an ever smaller proportion of the whole but numbering millions—have been concentrated in older parts of the inner city and more remote pockets of rural poverty. Here among a fraction of all of our people is most cultural and economic deprivation with all its consequences. Gradually separated from the whole by mushrooming suburbs and bypassing freeways, entire sections of sprawling cities exist in lonely despair while in Appalachia and rural Mississippi the poorest are left behind as the young, the strong and the educated move toward urban America. Segregated, their ability to assist one another limited, few are reached by helping hands from outside. Public assistance is essential to survival in interdependent mass society, but the present system of welfare only increases their inability to free themselves from poverty and often destroys the initiative necessary to do so.

As if through a one-way mirror, the urban poor watch the outside world speed by in expensive automobiles. They see steel and glass skyscrapers of affluent America rise from the slums where they used to live. Television reminds them all day long that most opportunity is barred to them. They see out from the slums, but few see in. The first generation to suffer poverty in the midst of plenty, they are the first to be stigmatized by poverty. In the past nearly all were poor. Now in America the poor are a small minority. The frustrations arising from this fact, not experienced by the poor heretofore, compound the anguish of the interdependence of urban life.

Most crime in America is born in environments saturated in poverty and its consequences: illness, ignorance, idleness, ugly surroundings, hopelessness. Crime incubates in places where thousands have no jobs, and those who do have the poorest jobs; where houses are old, dirty and dangerous; where people have no rights. A fraction of our people live there—less than one in five —but they number 40 million, more than our total population of a century ago. More people are jammed in several city blocks today than populated our biggest city in 1787. Probably four in five of all serious crimes flow from places of extreme poverty and most are inflicted on the people who live there. Yet most who live in poverty never commit a serious crime.

It is well to be concerned about crime among affluent suburban teenagers, drugs in high schools and protests by college students. These are matters with which we must deal sensitively and effectively. To the segregated country club set, they encompass much of the direct experience with crime. But beyond this narrow life is the real world of crime and violence that is the overwhelming part of the whole. It is the poor, the slum dweller, the disadvantaged who suffer most, and most tragically, the crime of America. It is here that the clear connection between crime and the harvest of poverty—ignorance, disease, slums, discrimination, segregation, despair and injustice—is manifest.

Every major city in America demonstrates the relationship between crime and poor education, unemployment, bad health, and inadequate housing. When we understand this, we take much of the mystery out of crime. We may prefer the mystery. If so, we are condemned to live with crime we could prevent.

Take the map of any city—your city—and mark the parts of town where health is poorest. Health is essential to joy in life. Without good health there is little chance for happiness. The mentally ill are not themselves. The physically ill can be only a part of themselves—that part painful. Poor health, as your map will show, is not spread evenly through your city.

Find the places where life expectancy is lowest—seven years less than for the city as a whole—where the death rate is highest —25 per cent above the rate for the entire city. Some census tracts will reveal an incidence of measles and mumps 50 per cent higher than in the remainder of the same city; rheumatic fever and whooping cough, 60 per cent higher; hepatitis infections, meningitis and encephalitis, 25 per cent higher; food poisoning and venereal disease, 100 per cent higher. Fetal and infant deaths are more than twice as high there. Most narcotics addiction will be found in parts of the city where 10 per cent of the people live. Alcoholics will constitute a substantial part of the adult population there.

Mental retardation occurs in some parts of your city at a rate five times higher than in the remainder. Twenty-five per cent of some prison populations are mentally retarded. And mental retardation does not just happen; it is caused. The causes are many and most are preventable. Disease, brain injury, lack of pregnancy care, malnutrition for generations or in the mother or during infancy and early childhood, all contribute. A German measles epidemic among the ghetto poor will leave hundreds of infants with profound brain damage in the following months. Deficiencies in diet, irregular meals and unwholesome food play a major part in creating the climate of crime in a nation that pays farmers not to produce more food.

Of 4 million births in the United States annually, 250,000— one in sixteen—or more are infants with significant defects. Of these, fewer than one in five can be attributed to inherited genetic defects and even these often involve the effects of past environmental influence. Infants with birth defects are heavily concentrated among the poor, who often do not recognize them and cannot adequately provide for their special needs. Those born to wealthy parents will be cared for. The causes for most of these tragic defects are remediable. Those who live where most occur know this, too.

Mental and emotional illness afflicts substantial proportions of the population in some parts of town, while in others it is comparatively rare and carefully treated. Mental illness among children on welfare has been estimated at twice the rate of other children of poor families living in the inner city—affecting nearly one in four. Dangerous psychotics devoid of any human pity may be your neighbors in the slums. Most people who commit serious crimes have mental health problems. Those who have lived or worked among serious offenders in prison know that nearly all need psychiatric help and emotionally stabilizing influences.

We are ignorant of many of the facts about health in the central city slums, because illness there is so frequently unreported, untreated, and even unrecognized. Besides, so many there feel little can be done about illness anyway. Hospitals are distant, clinics unknown, doctors few and often unprofessional.

Accidental injuries, broken legs, burned hands, fractured skulls are not spread evenly among the population of your city. A small minority of the people suffer the great majority of all accidents. Some arise from the greater danger of the surrounding physical environment, others from a mental attitude or propensity for accident. Where the accident rates are much higher than elsewhere, broken limbs have mended crooked for the want of a doctor to set a bone. This is where the poor people live. Mark it on the map.

Now mark the parts of town where education is poorest. Education is the basis today for most individual opportunity. Without a good education only the very exceptional or fortunate will have a chance for fulfillment. Formal education in the past largely reflected advantages of family. Only the children of the rich and the highly educated went to college. They were a small fraction of their age group. College education for them added little to opportunities already provided by the very advantages that sent a person to college in the first place. Not so now. Today half of our college-age population is in college. Fact explosion, science and technology, and the complexity of our society make an intensive education imperative for all who will realize their full potential.

Find those parts of the city where the oldest schools stand, where there are no national honor society students, where classrooms are most crowded and there are no playgrounds, where the teachers' qualifications are lowest, class days shortest and dropout rates greatest, where the ratio of students to teachers is highest and books and supplies are scant. Mark the areas where illiteracy is above 15 per cent, where three-fourths of the people do not finish high school, where the average period of formal education is four years less than for the city as a whole. These are objective criteria that can be measured.

Now locate the schools where there is the most classroom disruption, where violence and drugs have been common for years, where students who do not understand their courses are passed or forced out of school, and where most students wait the day and the year through without interest or involvement in education.

Next mark the parts of town where unemployment is highest. Unless wealth is inherited, married, or stolen, employment is the individual's chance for independence. Only when he can support himself and his family, choose his job and make a living wage can an individual and his family exercise real freedom. Otherwise he is a servant to survival without the means to do what he wants to do. Employment is man's major chance to make a contribution, to develop his own talents, to live to the fullest, to be somebody and do something.

We are unjustifiably proud of a national unemployment rate that has been below 4 per cent for most of the past few years. But 4 per cent of the labor force in our mass society approaches our total population of 1787. With gross insensitivity we speak of a 2 per cent increase in unemployment and fail to see that we speak of the means of living for millions. Nor is this the 1930's. We cannot go back to the farm. Unemployment today is intolerably cruel at any rate. Since man is no longer able to exist on the land, we must provide employment or support for everyone. Otherwise, crime will be the way of subsistence for the urban poor.

The overall unemployment figure is one of those facts that is the enemy of truth because it does not tell enough. In parts of cities everyone is employed or living comfortably on accumulated wealth. In some blocks of the slums most people are unemployed—and all live in poverty.

Locate those parts of your city where one-fourth of the employables are unemployed. Unemployment nationwide for Negro teenagers averages 25 per cent for boys and 33 per cent for girls. In parts of the black ghetto it will be twice the average and more. Among those employed, most will have menial jobs with little chance for promotion—janitor, garbage collector, car wash, domestic servant. They are the last hired and the first fired. A generation which has lived with comparatively high employment often believes blacks can get jobs if they want to. They did not experience the rage of their parents in the depression who desperately sought work and could not find it.

Many seeking jobs will be turned down because of arrest records. Such records do not demonstrate guilt of any crime. They sometimes reflect a practice of repression by police. Rarely is there any relationship between his arrests and the fitness of an individual for the job he seeks. In some ghetto areas, most boys have arrest records. Intense bitterness arises when those records are used as a basis for denying employment.

Discrimination in employment on account of race bars many from any decent job. Some major corporations listed on the New York Stock Exchange, among the largest employers in their cities, do not hire Negroes, or hire them in segregated, unskilled jobs with no chance for advancement. Nationwide patterns of racial discrimination in employment, sometimes sanctioned or insisted on chiefly by labor unions which have done so much for the poor, bar a major segment of Negro America from participating in the mainstream. Even the well-educated and skilled Negro in America is usually underemployed.

Crowding poor young blacks in urban slums—school dropouts unable to find jobs and somehow sensing society itself stands in their way—is not conducive to social stability. Their chances of being somebody, of doing something important or getting rich—not a rare American aspiration—are slim indeed. And they know it.

In the most comprehensive investigation of job discrimination ever made, the United States Equal Employment Opportunity Commission reported, in a 1969 survey covering minority job patterns in 123 cities, 50 states and 60 major industries involving 26 million workers, that two-thirds of the Negroes, Mexican-Americans and Indians were held back from jobs by outright racial discrimination, not by lack of skills or education. In the slums of those cities nearly every person of a minority race was affected.

Find now the parts of town where the average per capita income is 60 per cent of the average for the city as a whole, where —as in the Hough area of Cleveland and Watts in Los Angeles —average individual income actually declined between 1960 and 1965, while, nationally, individual income rose 13 per cent.

The dynamics of urban growth are such that even in the most prosperous times some poor get poorer. Through economic and social pressures they tend to wind up together, thereby compounding their plight. People with no capital, no savings, little property—and that dilapidated and mortgaged for more than it is worth at usurious rates of interest—have small stake in the general welfare. There are millions in such circumstances.

The north wind made the Vikings. Both social and physical environment shape character. Wordsworth believed children must grow up in an atmosphere of beauty and simple human affection if they are to become honest, open, trusting and generous people concerned for others. To live where air is fresh, where you can be alone, find quiet, see beauty, where some things are new and clean, is stabilizing for a person. In parts of your town this is impossible—and people live there.

Then mark on your map the areas where the oldest buildings and houses stand—those that average twice the age of all the structures in the city. Half of the buildings in Harlem were built before 1900, while half the buildings in the world have been built in the last three decades. There will be whole blocks and neighborhoods where most buildings violate safety and health ordinances. They are overcrowded with four times the city's average occupancy per room, parts of three families share two rooms, and someone sleeps on the landing. They have no fire escapes, there are broken steps on the one staircase. The stove and wiring are a fire hazard. Fire alarms occur ten times more frequently in proportion to population there. The plumbing doesn't work. The rooms are unbearably hot in summer, unbearably cold in winter. The air is always stale. Rats and roaches thrive. Old lead-base paint flakes off, finds its way to children's mouths and damages their brains, or kills them— hundreds each year.

The population per city block in this part of town may be twice or even ten times the city's average. A square mile may contain three or thirty times more people than the average square mile, depending on whether you are in Oakland or Harlem. Home ownership will be one-half or one-tenth the rate for the city as a whole, but in some parts of town no one owns the place where he lives. Everyone is too poor. The streets are dirty and full of chuckholes. It is the last place the city gets around to picking up the garbage, removing the snow, repairing the gas leak.

Most of the people who work there do not live there. Businessmen, clerks, landlords, teachers, politicians, even preachers, live elsewhere. Police, firemen and schools will be present, but the welfare office, state employment commission, union hiring halls, county hospitals, medical clinics and the social security office are nearly always outside the area. Sometimes these critically needed services are located in areas the poor cannot find or where they fear to go—downtown, near the police station or jail, by city hall—two transfers and thirty-five minutes away on public transportation.

Merchants learned decades ago they must sell their wares where the people who will buy them live. Government is only slowly learning it must provide its services most effectively where they are needed most urgently. Among the elderly poor perhaps one person in five who has earned social security benefits fails to receive them, however desperate the need, because of ignorance or difficulty of access, while the rich widow with investment income secures legal counsel to be sure she is receiving her entire social security payment.

Public transportation in poverty areas is usually poor. It is nearly always less adequate than in more well-to-do areas. New routes tend to be located where people with political and economic power want them, where customers can pay and where drivers and passengers are safe. The isolation of the slum dweller increases as public transportation bypasses the ghetto.

Life in the urban slums destroys families. In the south-central section of Los Angeles called Watts, where 14 per cent of the citizens of the city resided in 1964, over half the children under eighteen years of age lived in broken homes—with only one parent or with neither. One-quarter of all families received public assistance. The divorce rate was one and a half times that for Los Angeles as a whole, difficult as it is for the poor to finance a divorce. The number of households headed by a female was far higher than elsewhere in the city. Other areas in other cities were worse off.

When we read that the percentage of black children raised in families headed by women rose from 23 per cent in 1960 to 30 per cent in 1968, we must remember that is the national average. The average for the 40 per cent of the Negroes living in poverty is much higher. Middle and upper class blacks tend to have strong families with few children. They know the risk of being poor and black. In contrast to the 30 per cent for black families, only 12 per cent of all white families were headed by women in 1968.

Where the poor live, there are few enforceable rights. City building, safety and health ordinances and pure food laws are ignored. Consumers are defrauded with impunity.

Laws prohibiting discrimination on account of race are only slowly implemented. Most black students continue to be denied constitutional rights to an equal education, and essential rights in employment and housing are unenforced throughout the country.

Most rights are denied by poverty itself. The poor lack the power to enforce their rights. They cannot afford a lawyer to sue in a civil case or secure appointment of competent counsel when charged with crime. Legal aid and neighborhood legal services programs supported by the bar, charities or the government itself do not supply a significant portion of the representation needed by the poor. Rights are only words to people who are powerless to enforce them.

The most fundamental of all rights—security of person and property—is woefully absent in the slums. There is an uneasy order, but there is no law. The people of the ghetto suffer most of the crime in the city.

Finally, mark the highest crime areas on the map of your city. The places where most murders, rapes, muggings, robberies, burglaries and assaults occur. The police know them well. Mark the places where two-thirds of the arrests for serious crime are made and only 10 per cent of the people live—the places where it is really not safe to walk the streets at night. Note the areas where the cost of police per square mile is five or ten times more than the cost for the city as a whole, and even the cost per capita in such densely populated areas is twice or more the cost elsewhere.

Consider how much greater the concentration of police is in these areas and how much less effective their performance. Order is usually maintained, but crime is rarely prevented. Narcotics addiction is concentrated in the slums. Perhaps one-half of all the heroin addicts of the nation live in the ghettos and barrios of New York City. Nearly one-third of all arrests in the nation that do not relate to traffic control involve persons under the influence of alcohol. Most of these occur where fewer than 10 per cent of the people live. Prostitutes walk the streets of the ghetto and their houses are known to their neighbors, who wish they were not there, and to the police, who do nothing about them. Numbers, bolito and other illegal gambling are wide open because chance is the best opportunity to escape for most who are imprisoned by urban poverty. Mark the part of your city where crime flourishes.

Now look at the map of your city. You have marked the areas where there are slums, poor schools, high unemployment, widespread poverty; where sickness and mental illness are common, housing is decrepit and nearly every sight is ugly— and you have marked the areas where crime flourishes. Behold your city—you have marked the same places every time. Poverty, illness, injustice, idleness, ignorance, human misery and crime go together. That is the truth. We have known it all along. We cultivate crime, breed it, nourish it. Little wonder we have so much. What is to be said of the character of a people who, having the power to end all this, permit it to continue?

Perhaps the greatest reflection on our character is that we were relatively unconcerned for decades while crime festered in the slums. Thousands of heroin addicts died annually there and we barely noted it. Our concern arose when new social dynamics and population movements brought crime and addiction out of the slums and inflicted it on or threatened the powerful and well-to-do.

You will not eliminate crime by eliminating poverty, ignorance, poor health and ugly environments. But it is clear that such conditions are demonstrably responsible for most crime— for nearly all crime that is foreseeable and can be prevented.

People do not commit crime because they are black or poor or sick or ignorant or unemployed or live in ugly homes. They started much as you and I, fully capable of every human emotion. Many of our most benevolent and gentle people have suffered extreme poverty and severe illness. Indeed, history offers no better evidence of the indestructibility of the human spirit than the great man emerging from the modern urban slum. But the cumulative effect of all these disadvantages, their concentration among so small a part of the population, the total inability of most to escape their constant presence and the enormity of injustice take a heavy toll. Many who fall are the strongest and most sensitive. They cannot endure the inhumanity of their lives. They live in an environment that is so full of violence, frustration, despair and hopelessness; that witnesses so much misery and inequality and crime; that is so powerless to help itself, that they are slowly conditioned to see no wrong in hurting others or taking their property. They have known little else. Cruel experience has crushed the last drop of compassion from some. Many seeing the plight of the urban poor doubt the essential fairness of our people, assume hypocrisy in all our conduct and, lacking respect for our society, do as they want and take what they can. Much of the unrest among our affluent youth reflects an awareness of these conditions and an unwillingness to accept their continuation.

The most ironic and profound tragedy threatened by the prevailing fear of violent crime is that because of it those who suffer least, the powerful, may deprive those who suffer most, the powerless, of the very programs that attack the major underlying causes of crime. Without a massive effort to eliminate these underlying causes, crime can only increase and thereby cause still more fear. Thus, fear, turning us away from concern for others, destroys hope and opportunity.

The solutions for our slums, for racism and crime itself in mass society, are basically economic. We must make an economic commitment to end them. If we are to control crime, we must undertake a massive effort to rebuild our cities and ourselves, to improve the human condition, to educate, employ, house and make healthy. And with the vastness of our growth and the immensity of change we must move urgently.

5

ORGANIZED CRIME:
THE LIMITED EMPIRE

SOME Americans believe there is no such thing as organized crime. Others see organized crime as the scourge of the nation, the heart of the crime problem. One view is as far from the fact as the other. There is organized crime. And it is a serious problem. But it is a minor part of our total crime. It is a part that can and should be eliminated, for it corrupts government, preys on the weak and contributes to our climate of lawlessness.

Whole civilizations and societies have existed without organized crime. Whole nations today are free of it as are entire states and regions of this country. Nowhere is it the principal part of crime, but in some of our major cities its tentacles wield power over many people and reach into high places.

Organized crime supplies goods or services wanted by a large number of people—desperately needed cash, narcotics, prostitutes, the chance to gamble. These are its principal sources of income. They are consensual crimes for the most part, desired by the consuming public. This fact distinguishes the main activities of organized crime from most other crime. Few want to be mugged, have their assets embezzled or their cars stolen, but it is public demand that creates the basis for the activities of organized crime. Where this demand is great, law enforcement is working against the strong desires of a significant sector of the populace and will not therefore prevail in a free society—or for long under any circumstances.

There are several aspects of life in America that make it a natural culture for organized crime. First, we try to prohibit things that people want—gambling, drugs, money at excessive rates of interest, prostitution, liquor—knowing we lack the means and the will to fully enforce our own prohibition. An organization is necessary to provide significant or dependable supplies of any commodity or service in a mass market. People who organize to supply illegal goods and services necessarily operate outside the law. The risks may be high, but so are the rewards. Nor do the perpetrators make nice distinctions among the laws they choose to violate. When customers do not pay their debts or fail to perform their part of agreements, when there is a threat to report illegal activity to the police or to compete in illicit conduct, force is employed to compel compliance, to prevent interference or to destroy competition.

A second aspect of our culture conducive to organized crime is our tolerance of conditions where millions of people, as a practical matter, have no significant rights they can enforce. The poor are so often the helpless victims of crime that for them crime has become acceptable, even natural. They do not bother to report it. They protect themselves and the little property they may have by their wits. Helpless and hopeless, the poor urban slum dweller is the natural prey of organized crime which thrives in his environment.

Here are thousands who want to gamble. So limited is economic opportunity for them that the daily number is a major hope in their lives. They have no credit. When they need, or badly want, money, only Shylock will deal with them—and he is a stern creditor.

Who in our society is more likely to seek the escape offered by narcotics than the poor who live in the devastating misery of urban slums? Drugs will temporarily liberate a person from the wretchedness there without his ever leaving. Both desirous of drugs and powerless to protect himself against his suppliers, he is the ideal customer for organized crime. Isolated and afraid of the police, he can be coerced with impunity.

Finally, we have made it easy for organized crime to operate by our tragic neglect of law enforcement, which could effect control and impose limitations on organized criminal activities. But ghetto crime too often concerns society at large only when it threatens general disorder or spills over into middle class neighborhoods. Consequently, police departments have not been staffed, trained or professionalized to cope with organized crime.

In 1967 President Johnson's Crime Commission reported that only a few jurisdictions in the United States had well-developed organized-crime investigative units. The Commission's nationwide survey showed that but twelve of the nineteen cities acknowledging the presence of organized crime within their jurisdictions had special police units investigating its activities. Less than one-third—six—had special prosecutive units. Of the forty-three police departments that reported no organized crime activities in their jurisdiction, only three had units in their departments that gathered information to determine whether organized crime was present.

The police are widely exposed to temptations of bribery by their inadequate salaries and lack of professional competence and pride. Why should an underpaid officer moonlight four hours a day when he can make as much by ignoring a bookmaking operation that seems impossible to stop anyway? What's the harm? Slowly the rackets buy protection, corrupting a sergeant or a lieutenant, several patrolmen, a court clerk or magistrate, an assistant district attorney, a deputy warden or probation officer. The major restraints on organized crime ultimately become the self-discipline of the bosses, who do not want to risk a public outcry, and the limited purchasing power of the poor.

As long as we satisfy some vague moral need by outlawing conduct we cannot control, and while we care so little that we crowd poor and powerless people in violent slums, and while through neglect we rely on underpaid and undertrained police for law enforcement, we will have organized crime in many forms and a steady supply of illegal goods and services to the poor. This should surprise no one.

The marvel is that we do not have more organized crime. President Johnson's Crime Commission surveyed seventy-one cities and found evidence of organized crime in only twenty-five. Of the cities surveyed, four of the five with more than 1 million citizens acknowledged the presence of some organized crime, but only one in five with populations between 250,000 and 1 million appeared to have any organized crime. Still, more than half of the smaller cities surveyed with populations between 100,000 and 250,000 thought they had organized crime, and federal intelligence indicated some presence of organized crime in a few cities where local reports denied it.

The activities of organized crime are wide-ranging, but gambling has been its greatest source of income since the repeal of the Prohibition Amendment. Gambling lends itself to criminal conduct. Chance rather than effort determines whether or not you succeed. It is an easy-come, easy-go, cash business.

Loan sharking, sometimes called "juice," is believed to be the second most significant source of income for criminal syndicates. Here, as with gambling, organized crime deals with large numbers of people. Its rates of interest are exorbitant, and loans are often repaid several times over in a period of months. Threats and violence are quickly used to collect money where necessary.

Importation and wholesaling of narcotics engage some groups in organized crime, and prostitution and the production and sale of illegal liquor are still frequent endeavors. Extortion, protection, bribery, blackmail and shakedowns are also frequent practices in the world of organized crime, but they are incidental to the real moneymaking activities of a successful mob.

Organized crime tends to vertical integration. It manufactures, processes, distributes and retails many of its criminal products. It controls, to the extent it can, all essential activities both to minimize risks and to maximize profits, but its ultimate market is at the retail level because it is dealing in consumer trade. Insulated as it may try to remain from the street action—from the numbers runner, the dope mules, the hotel bellboy, the collector—it still must depend on these as its agents. Even when the street operators are independent contractors, they require careful supervision; the business they are in does not attract the most reliable sorts, and it is a dangerous, highly visible activity. One informer or weak link can jeopardize a territory, suppliers and, potentially, the leaders themselves.

Diversification is important to organized crime. When the heat is on gambling, the syndicates look elsewhere. They have abandoned most retail narcotics and marijuana traffic largely to small-time pushers, frequently addicted themselves, and to free-lance operators. The risks of the narcotics trade are too high for the overlords as the new markets shift from the safely isolated and usually ignored slum to the diffuse and turbulent student population. Organized crime presents a stationary target for law enforcement because of its ongoing activity and the large number of customers depending on its supply. These factors, together with the difficulty of re-establishing contacts abandoned during a cleanup effort, have caused La Cosa Nostra and others to seek new fields of endeavor.

Increased sophistication and affluence have led those in organized crime into many legitimate businesses. Such varied activities as banking, securities, brokerage firms, hotels, transportation, labor organizations with their trust funds, government services and contracts, and licensing and zoning bodies have felt their influence. When it moves into legitimate businesses, organized crime brings its old ways—strong-arm tactics, violence and fear. Firms have been bilked of assets, fraudulent stocks issued, planned bankruptcies executed, trust funds and loan accounts manipulated, and competitors driven out by unfair trade practices and direct criminal acts. Mobsters make dangerous partners.

It is easy, however, to exaggerate this movement into major business. The occasions when control of large enterprises is sought are rare. The vested—and usable—wealth and power of organized crime are not that great. Most of the top leaders of organized crime maintain some legitimate business activities, but they do not touch one-tenth of 1 per cent of American business.

Legal activities tend to make organized crime conservative. The bosses no longer need to run the high risks of constant criminal activity. They have vested interests and a stake in the status quo. The occasions on which violence or other unlawful activity is a sound risk diminish. The strict discipline essential to daily criminal conduct is not necessary. They go soft in comparison to their earlier days.

The wealth and income of organized crime are exaggerated beyond reason. Twenty-six billion dollars is a figure suggested by some as its annual gross income, and by others as its net profit. Even the President's Crime Commission in 1967 estimated $6 or $7 billion as the probable net income for organized crime on which it does not pay taxes. If true, this would make the profits for organized crime comparable to those of the ten largest industrial corporations combined. General Motors, Standard Oil, Ford, General Electric, Chrysler, IBM, Mobile Oil, Texaco, Gulf and U.S. Steel together netted $7.2 billion in 1968 after taxes, and they employed more than 2.5 million people. The high estimates of syndicate income would average $1 million a year for 26,000 individuals and the low a million each for 6- to 7,000 persons. Even the lower estimate of the Crime Commission is wildly improbable. The FBI sets the total membership of La Cosa Nostra at less than 6,000. Where can so much money go? How could it remain so well hidden? There is big money in organized crime for a few, but for most it is dangerous, hard, dirty work for uncertain middle class incomes.

Because it is an ongoing business, with payrolls to meet, dealing constantly with tens of thousands of customers, organized crime cannot flourish without law enforcement protection. At the very least, local law enforcement must be neutralized, because major organized crime activities are impossible to conceal. You cannot conduct a retail business and seek customers without public awareness. Significant continuous gambling, loansharking, narcotics traffic, prostitution, extortion and other widespread organized criminal acts cannot long escape the notice of police.

Perhaps the greatest harm to come from organized crime is the corruption of officials. This damage affects a community in ways well beyond the reach of its criminal conduct. Where some police are corrupt, law enforcement generally is likely to be bad. Where government officials are bribed, the moral climate of the whole community is affected. Public confidence is undermined. Cynicism inhibits corrective action and stimulates others to cut corners and perhaps commit crime. A moral looseness sets in because the system itself seems to have no integrity.

As with all crime, we oversimplify our definition of organized crime. There is far more to it than La Cosa Nostra. Our society is much too complex to expect only a single syndicate or type of illegal activity. There is no one massive organization that manages all or even most planned and continuous criminal conduct throughout the country. There are hundreds of small operations that engage in organized criminal activity—car theft rings, groups of burglars, safecrackers working together, gangs of armed robbers, combinations that occasionally smuggle and distribute marijuana and dangerous drugs—scattered throughout the nation. These people deliberately engage in crime for profit, but it tends to be ordinary crime, not widespread consensual crime that offers high profits for satisfying the wants of a segment of the public. They act sporadically and do not monopolize territories. They are essentially joint ventures in crime.

Areas that are free of major organized crime are not necessarily free of substantial criminal activity of the types conducted by organized crime. Market demand in such places is supplied by small operators, a pimp and three girls, a floating crap game, the landlord who loans money at 20 per cent a month. There are many small groups of organized criminal activities in limited geographic areas that are wholly independent of and unknown to outside criminal elements.

Major organized crime in America is committed by large cohesive groups exhibiting similar patterns of activity in cities separated by hundreds or even thousands of miles—New York, Las Vegas, Chicago, Miami. They are essentially a loose confederation. Together their membership numbers in the low thousands. They are remnants of the old Mafia—by chance and FBI public relations now called La Cosa Nostra.

The Mafia exists in the United States. It was first identified on our soil in the nineteenth century and came here with immigrants, principally from Sicily. In terms of the power it wields, the extent of its operations, the numbers of its membership and their capability for violence, it is probably less significant today than in the 1920's, the 30's or the 40's. Gang wars of the 1920's and 30's exceeded anything we have witnessed since World War II. Bosses with hundreds of gunmen held mass meetings in the days of Prohibition. On September 11, 1930, the day the self-proclaimed Boss of Bosses, Salvatore Maranzano, was assassinated, forty members of La Cosa Nostra died by gunfire.

Millions of Italians have migrated to America. Many came to escape the Mafia, but among the immigrants were also some of its members. Once here, the Mafiosi helped bring more from the old country. In the late 1920's Benito Mussolini put such pressure on the Mafia in southern Italy and Sicily that many left for America. With reinforcements, the Mafia consolidated domination of the more lucrative criminal operations in cities where they worked. Al Capone, Lucky Luciano, Frank Costello and Vito Genovese became household names throughout the country.

Mafia members are of course an infinitesimal part of the Italian migration to America—a few thousand out of many millions. Italo-Americans have contributed immeasurably to the quality of life in America in every area of endeavor. Organized crime is as abhorrent to the Italians in America as it is to our society as a whole.

The earlier markets for criminal operations of the Mafia, the ethnic ghettos of recent immigrants, have disappeared. The new markets, Negro, Puerto Rican, Mexican-American, have proven more difficult. As the Jewish merchant in the black ghetto yields to small businesses owned by blacks, the monopoly of the Mafia in organized crime gives way to the black or Spanish-speaking entrepreneur.

Historically the Mafia was a family affair. Genealogists are still important sources of intelligence units investigating organized crime, because blood relationships remain a major element. Whom can you trust if not your own family? But few cultures from foreign countries—even the nature of family life—have survived the melting pot of America without substantial dilution. Most disappear except as unconscious qualities merged with other cultures in the American mainstream.

The family tradition has weakened within the Mafia. The strict discipline and tight organization compelled by constant danger have moderated. The younger generation have gone off to college and displayed much of the independence of their generation generally. Some sons have become professionals—lawyers and doctors. Outsiders have been let into the hierarchy of the families. Still, there is a Cosa Nostra and its influence hurts this country.

The federal government has a major role to play in the control of organized crime. The incidence of interstate activity is high among the syndicates. Rarely are the activities of a significant family of La Cosa Nostra confined to a single state. By the division of powers in the Constitution and by the inherent difficulty of coping with an organization only partly within their jurisdiction, state and local governments are limited in their potential effectiveness.

The overriding need for federal action stems not from jurisdictional niceties, however, but from a far more debilitating fact. The presence of any significant organized crime necessarily means local criminal justice has been corrupted to some degree. The Wickersham Commission surveying crime in America for President Hoover observed this in 1931, as did President Johnson's Crime Commission in 1967. The major role of federal enforcement against organized crime is as a liberator of local law enforcement. Federal agents can strike at organized crime that has paralyzed local police. Federal action can place local law enforcement in control again.

Federal police, as conceived and staffed today, cannot control the retail activity in which organized crime engages. This is too vast a task for its comparatively few agents. The criminal conduct involved is as essentially local as the business of the corner grocer.

Federal enforcement can seek to break up major interstate networks and control importation and interstate shipments of narcotics, but when the action gets to the street, where the demand is, and where supplies will be found to meet demand, regular policing would require a vast national force if the federal government were to assume responsibility. But there is no more reason to think such a national police would be effective than would a single poverty agency or education office endeavoring to serve the entire nation. All the dynamics of mass society compel local control and performance. The local police are the only law enforcement body present in sufficient numbers to control the retail activity of organized crime. They know the areas, the streets and the people, if any law enforcement agency does. Local police outnumber the FBI fifty to one.

Local police should be involved in federal enforcement action against organized crime whenever possible. If arrests are made, or raids conducted by federal agents without advising local authorities, there is the very real danger that local officials may mistake what is happening and interfere, or be unprepared to provide support, should federal manpower be inadequate. Local participation is desirable at the time of federal action not only to prevent direct confrontations between United States agents and local law enforcement but because urban police must ultimately come to grips with organized crime if it is to be controlled. Too often, however, where organized crime flourishes, federal agents cannot safely advise local police of the place and purpose of an imminent raid on a gambling or drug operation until it is under way. There have been occasions when local police have been advised in advance and federal raids have failed because illegal operators have been warned and suspended their activities.

Organized crime presents a variety of difficult enforcement problems because its activities cross so many interdepartmental and police jurisdictional lines. Police departments and federal agencies are divided into groups that operate independently of each other. Organized crime, however, does not respect fine jurisdictional lines. The narcotics squad, the vice squad, the detectives, the precinct patrolmen, the sheriff's office and state police each with separate units, the FBI, the IRS Intelligence Division, the Alcohol and Tobacco Tax Division, the Secret Service, Customs, postal inspectors, the Federal Bureau of Narcotics and Dangerous Drugs—all have jurisdiction over some part of organized crime activity. Each has developed information within its area of responsibility about organized criminal activities. To confront organized crime effectively all law enforcement agencies must pool their knowledge and coordinate their actions. Unlike individual crimes, which usually concern only a single agency, or at most several agencies, organized crime with its network of wide-ranging daily operations concerns nearly all agencies of law enforcement.

The demands of the marketplace and the desire for success in its ventures and security from police have compelled crime to organize. We might ask, then, If crime can organize, why can't law enforcement? Too often law enforcement agencies fear their independence will be lost if they coordinate with other agencies. And they are often right. But consolidation and reorganization are frequently a real need, because there can be no justification for thousands of existing local police departments. They are too small to be effective, but like most institutions they cling to what they have. As a result they impede effective enforcement. To be effective against organized crime, law enforcement must organize itself.

The concept of the federal strike force was developed in 1967 to attack organized crime in city after city on a highly coordinated basis.

To begin, a strike force gathers and analyzes all available police intelligence about organized crime—its leaders, subordinates and activities—in a target city. By collecting relevant data possessed by all law enforcement agencies operating in an area, an immediate and substantial reservoir of information is available for designing a plan of attack.

After collecting and analyzing all available intelligence, a strike force staffed with professional investigators from the major agencies involved begins to function. Teams vary greatly in size, depending on the nature of the city involved and the dimension of organized crime activity there, but typically a score or more of investigators from at least several federal agencies—the Federal Bureau of Narcotics and Dangerous Drugs, Internal Revenue Service Intelligence Division, Customs, Secret Service, the Labor Department, Alcohol and Tobacco Tax Division of Treasury, postal inspectors and others—are assigned full time with half a dozen or more lawyers. The FBI, state and local police and on occasion the Canadian Royal Mounted Police provide substantial support. Allegations of criminal conduct are thoroughly investigated. Potential leads to evidence of criminal acts are carefully followed. A special grand jury is convened to hear matters presented by the strike force prosecutors.

Beginning in Buffalo, strike forces have been sent to Detroit, Chicago, New York, Miami, Philadelphia, New Jersey, Massachusetts, Connecticut, Rhode Island and other centers of organized crime. Their success has exceeded the expectations of their strongest advocates. More federal indictments have been returned against organized crime figures in months than in preceding decades. Each strike force has obtained more indictments in its target city than all federal indictments in the nation against organized crime in as recent a year as 1960.

Closer working relations established among law enforcement units working with a strike force have improved coordination after a strike force leaves. No longer does one agency sit on information unrelated to its responsibility that would provide vital leads or a missing link to those working in another field or save the life of an informer. Local police are given the chance to perform duties long abandoned—to make arrests where protection existed. They are again in control.

Strike forces have been successful against the leaders of La Cosa Nostra. More known members of La Cosa Nostra were indicted in 1967 and 1968 than in the preceding twelve years combined. With a dozen strike forces operating constantly, moving from city to city, returning from time to time, major units of organized crime can be broken up and their activity substantially curtailed.

While the FBI used electronic surveillance in organized crime investigations from the late 1950's until June 30, 1965, such surveillance was never used by strike forces from their inception through January 20, 1969. Scores of agent years were devoted to electronic surveillance in the early 1960's, but the FBI itself denies that a single conviction was obtained on the basis of information from its bugs. To admit that a conviction was thus obtained could void the conviction, since it might then be based on evidence secured unlawfully, but the review of scores of trials in which it was discovered that defendants were overheard on bugs has yet to reveal one in which it can be determined the evidence used at the trial came from, or was discovered through leads from, a bug.

Perhaps a great deal was learned from electronic surveillance. Certainly a lot of time was wasted. But clearly the control of organized crime can be effected without its use. A professional local police is the essential element in its control. Without that, organized crime will never be long or effectively controlled. Without that, police use of bugs is itself a risk. They would bug the wrong people.

The FBI came slowly to the organized crime field. For such a natural adversary, this is surprising. It was still making pursuit of the Communist Party its claim to fame long after there was any risk to national security from that source. The CPUSA, as the Bureau calls it, has been reactionary and irrelevant to new radical movements for years while the FBI continues dramatizing its peril.

La Cosa Nostra operated extensively in the United States for decades before the FBI would admit its existence. It was the late 1950's when the Bureau changed. It was now ready for a new crusade, this time against the scourge of organized crime. Today La Cosa Nostra is the FBI's new thing.

When Robert F. Kennedy became Attorney General, he brought to that office from his rackets investigation experience the first real understanding of and commitment to the control of organized crime. In the spring of 1961 he began a massive coordinated drive. He sought and secured legislation that provided new tools to enlarge federal power to combat organized crime. He increased and vitalized the organized-crime section of the Department of Justice and visited major centers of organized crime throughout the country to get the drive moving. As he took center stage, the FBI stepped aside, and remained on the periphery until 1965. The conflict between Attorney General Kennedy and the FBI arose from the unwillingness of the Bureau to participate on an equal basis with other crime control agencies. The FBI has so coveted personal credit that it will sacrifice even effective crime control before it will share the glory of its exploits. This has been a petty and costly characteristic caused by the excessive domination of a single person, J. Edgar Hoover, and his self-centered concern for his reputation and that of the FBI.

Despite halfhearted gestures by the FBI, the federal effort mounted. From 19 indictments of organized crime figures in 1960, a negligible record, it climbed steadily to 687 in fiscal 1964. Then it leveled off and even declined temporarily before ascending sharply to 1,107 in fiscal 1967 and 1,166 in fiscal 1968.

Constant and increasing enforcement effort can erode the influence of major interstate criminal organizations. While this does not mean gambling, illicit drug sales, loansharking or prostitution will stop, it means the concentration of power from such activities will be scattered and the risks to society diminished.

There is no reason why La Cosa Nostra should not be relegated to history within a few years. It is on the ropes now. The main question is why we have endured it so long. The answer says far more about the commitment of the American people than about the criminal power of La Cosa Nostra.

Do not expect, however, that organized crime will disappear with La Cosa Nostra. Without vast efforts to eliminate underlying conditions that cause crime and without a substantial professionalization of police we could come to wish La Cosa Nostra was still around. It is disciplined. It protects its territory. It deals in goods and services of comparatively good quality. Vacuums will be filled. Competition could be great. Impure and dangerous drugs that La Cosa Nostra would not deal in because it knows the public would not stand for deaths and deformities would be traded by amateurs looking for a quick dollar. The old professional knew that dealing in inferior products wasn't good for business.

Ultimately the control of organized crime rests with the citizens and local law enforcement. It is the people who support organized crime. While its goods and services are in great demand, law enforcement cannot be successful in controlling their supply. There will be a great demand as long as millions of poor, hopeless and powerless people are crowded in urban slums.

Organized crime is something everyone can hate. It arouses no pity, no compassion. It is fashionable to glamorize organized crime, to vastly overstate its power and create for it an image as the consummate evil. It fascinates the public. It is cheap to handle, too. Arrest a bunch of Sicilians and the latest "crime wave" is over—and America lives happily ever after. For many, organized crime is the alien conspiracy that absolves us of responsibility for crime in America. This self-deception only causes a serious diversion from the real problems and urgent needs of crime prevention.

We may well question how much law enforcement manpower has been wasted persecuting minor hoods so that some district attorney or chief of police or federal agency could make a reputation for itself. We should stop playing games with something so important and end this corrupting business in the only way it can be done.

But we must not deceive ourselves—organized crime is a very small part of America's crime. What does it have to do with the juvenile offender who accounts for most of the increase in crime? True, it supplies some narcotics, and thereby contributes to drug-related crime. But the narcotics it supplies are a minor part of the total illegally consumed in America, and they will be found in one form or another, one way or another, while conditions causing the demand for them continue. What does organized crime have to do with street crime—murder, rape, assault, mugging, robbery? Practically nothing. Is it possible that one violent crime out of a thousand is committed by criminal syndicates, or results from their activities? Since America had more addicts of opiate derivatives in 1900 than in 1969, can addiction fostered by organized crime then be a major cause of the increase in violent crime? White-collar crime, protest, riot, school disturbances, the general violence of our environment are barely touched by organized crime. It only preys on them. We will no more make our streets safe or our society tranquil by eliminating organized crime than we would make the seas safe from sharks by eliminating the remora.

The greatest harm we could suffer from organized crime would be to permit it to distract us from the major problems we face if we are to control crime in America.

6

DRUGS: WHEN CHEMISTRY AND ANXIETY MEET

In 1900 OFFICIALS estimate there were between 250,000 and 1 million addicts of opium and its derivatives in the United States—the equivalent of at least 1 person out of 400 in the total population of 76 million. The opiates taken in 1900 were raw and straight. The normal dosage then would be lethal for the average heroin addict of our times.

With the population now exceeding 200 million, the Federal Bureau of Narcotics and Dangerous Drugs can identify fewer than 65,000 addicts of opium derivatives, and estimates that there may be an additional 10,000. There are more, but only several hundred thousand at most. Opium addiction today is a minor problem compared with 1900.

To think of dangerous drugs in terms of poppy fields in China, Iran or Turkey, camel caravans bringing opium across deserts to bustling trade centers, and clandestine laboratories around port cities such as Marseilles refining raw ingredients into heroin is to miss the major perils of the present and the future. Change causes the past to mislead. History offers little that is relevant to the control of dangerous drugs today.

Chemistry places us on the threshhold of immense and unrecognized dangers from the use of drugs. American youth has already learned that "speed"—methedrine—kills. It has discovered this fact the hard way—in morgues. Pep pills, amphetamines, barbiturates, LSD and other new chemical synthetics are presently in widespread use with unknown consequences.

Over the next ten years, chemists will invent or discover scores of dangerous new drugs—synthetic chemical compounds unknown today. They will have vast power to stimulate quickly or depress bodily processes or take us out of ourselves. Such drugs can excite the emotions, cause euphoria or "blow the mind." Some will cause brain damage, blindness, injury to vital body tissue and mutations of genes and chromosomes that deform infants born of users. Those who doubt there will be such drugs fail to see the sweep of scientific exploration. Thalidomide, a mild sedative itself, barely indicates the potential for harm.

It is not only the type of drug taken—the shift from the narcotic found in nature to newly discovered synthetic chemicals— that is changing. New portions of the population are affected. Historically, addiction in America has chiefly afflicted the poor, primarily racial or ethnic minorities, in port cities or border towns. Nearly half of the heroin addicts in the United States today live in the New York City area. Most are Negroes and Puerto Ricans.

Young Americans, from junior high schools through university graduate departments, are the growth market for drugs— primarily the new synthetic chemicals. We live in a time of great anxiety and profound doubt. Youth seeks escape from frustration, boredom, lack of purpose, anonymity, anger and despair. Drugs offer escape. Millions of our young in every part of the nation seek drugs—some to show off or for the excitement of a new thing, others from a psychic need or physical dependency. America is confronted with a whole new set of prevention and control problems in the field of narcotics and dangerous drugs.

The evolving and critically difficult challenges of dangerous drug control must be approached on four closely coordinated fronts—research, education, enforcement and health care and cure.

Research is the beginning of any effort to control drugs. Research can tell us the truth about drugs. Which are harmful? Which are beneficial? Above all, we must know the truth before a dangerous drug fills mental institutions with people who cannot reason and causes babies to be born without arms. Only research can do this.

Today's youth is the best-educated, best-motivated generation we have yet produced. Highly idealistic, it is also tough-minded. Young America does its own thinking. It will not accept old wives' tales. We can no longer command our youth to eat spinach because it is good, or not to smoke marijuana because it is bad, with any expectation that we will be obeyed. Times have changed; and for the better, if we have the courage to face it. From now on young people will be persuaded by cold, hard facts and not by myths. Facts linked together can lead to truth. In this scientific epoch, research will provide the facts. Until we make a clear and convincing case that a drug that offers desirable effects is dangerous, we will run the risk of its full potential for injury.

Research must seek, discover and test new drugs before unforeseeable injury results. If government does nothing about a new drug until police see people reacting in strange ways to its use, we will unnecessarily suffer thousands of tragic deaths and injuries. Recognizing the widespread desire for stimulation, sedation and hallucination, we must realize that drugs capable of causing these effects will be used widely by people who do not know the consequences. Through research we can foresee the consequences before dangerous drugs reap their grim harvest in human suffering.

Adequate research will require a very substantial expenditure. Large fully equipped laboratories, our best scientific capability and a close and thorough knowledge of the leading edge of worldwide biological and chemical research must be provided. An initiative and foresight rarely exerised in areas where profit motives cannot operate will be essential to success. We know of the great damage possible from chemistry misapplied to the human body, and we know of the wonders it can work. Scientists—and the universities and corporations that support their research—have an obligation to see the world as it is. They cannot create harmful drugs for potential public use with impunity. Before unleashing their discoveries on a helpless public, scientists must measure the risks of human consumption and know that social agencies are capable of their control. We cannot permit the general public to use drugs until we know their effect. We must stand for people. Drugs are guilty until proven innocent. We may except experimentation in cases of medical emergency and limited but carefully controlled efforts to cure serious diseases where time is of the essence or laboratory work cannot provide needed assurances without human use. But a rational and concerned society must not wait until fifteen years after the discovery of a cyclamate and its subsequent worldwide use in a variety of foods before testing it as a cause of cancer. In the future, with the rapid development that will come, we must make every effort to know of such perils in advance.

In technologically advanced mass urban America, government is the major protector against potentially dangerous drugs. Agencies responsible for research, education, enforcement, care and cure must recognize the ingenuity and the anxiety of our youth. They must carefully regulate the development and marketing of new drugs until we know what they are. Once the formula for a new depressant or stimulant is on the market, it can be produced by tens of thousands of amateur and professional chemists. For many the high school laboratory will do—for others the kitchen sink or a bunch of jars in the garage. The capability of the smart teenager, the petty trafficker and the small-time experimenter to reproduce dangerous drugs under conditions that law enforcement cannot control is clear. The kicks of the future can come from homemade drugs, impure and dangerous beyond present experience and imagination.

Once a drug is proven to be dangerous, the chief task becomes education. The facts must be clearly and forcefully presented if a dangerous drug that also produces a desirable effect is to be resisted. If the educational effort begins in ambiguity, ignorance, misapprehension, suspicion or fear, it will fail to persuade our bright, well-educated and skeptical youth.

Education is no small assignment. Our population is so vast, thousands must work at it. Formal education is the nation's major occupation, involving nearly one-third of our people as students, teachers and administrators. Courses in the danger of drugs should be integrated into school curricula with supporting evidence as solid as geometry. In a society saturated with pharmacies and drugstores, where millions regularly take medication and the use of dangerous drugs is increasing, can anyone say it is more important for people to study the Franco-Prussian War than to know something about the body and its chemistry? H. G. Wells observed in 1920 that civilization is in a race between education and catastrophe. The disaster can result from the failure to educate on drug abuse. In our mass society, with its turbulence, its teeming youth, its anxiety and despair, the danger will not be heard unless it is communicated loud and clear.

The chief target for education is our young people. Comprehensive effort to reach those in greatest danger through every channel available is the best prevention and the most effective drug control investment we can make. Schools, churches, parents, clubs, scouts and other youth groups must be presented with clear and convincing evidence. The medical profession itself must be educated to recognize and treat victims of dangerous drugs.

Many drugs have both beneficial and harmful uses. The opium poppy gives us morphine, which, medically administered, has spared mankind excruciating pain and suffering. Its use with a doctor's prescription is lawful. It also gives diacetylmorphine, $C_{21}H_{23}NO_5$, the white powder we call heroin, which is the chemical agent responsible for most of the addiction in the United States. There is no legal use of heroin. Legal traffic for medical purposes in morphine, and particularly in the amphetamines, barbiturates and other chemical synthetics, presents difficult enforcement problems. Drugs that are addictive or otherwise harmful when used excessively or by people with unusual physical conditions, must be effectively regulated. Illegal sales and thefts of these drugs are a major source of supply for addicts. They will become more so. Pharmacists, the drug industry, distributors and retailers must be fully informed of and accountable for any avoidable diversion of drugs from legal channels to illicit traffic.

Law enforcement agencies, too, must be enlightened about dangerous drugs. Their professional qualifications in chemistry, medicine, forensic science, laboratory analysis and drug detection will determine their effectiveness in law enforcement. Without such skills, their ability to contribute constructively will be limited.

When all else fails, police will be the public's protector. As with all crime, it is late in the day when law enforcement must step in to protect society. But however effective our research and convincing our education, drugs will be sought by millions in this age of anxiety.

No area of police activity calls for greater skill or discipline than drug control. Of all consensual crimes, the victim here is least reliable and least likely to cooperate. His dependence on his supplier is great. Most traffickers are users themselves and therefore doubly dangerous—dangerous as persons dealing in serious crime and dangerous as unstable individuals under the influence of narcotics.

Evidence is difficult to obtain in drug abuse cases. Ferocity of the addict toward enforcement approaches that of the lioness protecting her cubs. Historically, narcotics agents have worked under cover and through informers. Informers, rarely wholly reliable, are even more rarely so in narcotics work. It takes months of undercover effort to gain confidence, to get past small retail purveyors and obtain evidence of sources. Narcotics control is the most dangerous and difficult area of criminal law enforcement.

To keep pace with the discovery of dangerous new drugs and to anticipate new methods of manufacture, new techniques of diverting lawful commerce, new patterns of distribution and new markets among the young around colleges, high schools and junior high schools, will be as difficult as any assignment confronting law enforcement.

Organized crime will continue to operate with the older narcotics, the opiate derivatives. It may move into the synthetics to a greater degree than presently but this is a difficult field for it. The mobs are used to the safe market of the powerless people in the slums and have long profited from the remoteness of the sources of opium and other natural narcotics. But the professional criminal will be active. Forty per cent of all persons arrested by the Federal Bureau of Drug Abuse Control between 1965 and 1968 for the sale or possession of unlawful chemical synthetics had criminal records. Sixteen per cent were armed when arrested. The effort to curb them will remain dangerous.

Still more difficult to control will be the amateurs, the cultists, the free-lance artists aware of a huge market and high profits who want to increase their volume or who are merely attracted by the excitement. In a mass society, mobile, affluent and seeking escape, many will try their hand at trafficking. If arguments unfounded in fact continue as to whether certain drugs are harmful, an aura of respectability—even integrity—will protect their use around universities and secondary schools. A society that uses tobacco and alcohol so extensively will have to make sound distinctions between them and drugs, or well-educated young people will feel challenged to assert their independence by defying what seem to them groundless prohibitions.

Drug traffic among the poor will continue. Its emphasis will change slowly from heroin to chemical synthetics. More effective control in the difficult environment of poverty will depend on the success of federal enforcement in international and interstate transportation and greatly improved local enforcement effort. Because heroin addiction in the slums generates so much crime, control there must have priority.

Drug seizures can be prevention. Recent increases in seizures must continue and accelerate if we are to reverse the trend toward greater use. Opium and opiate derivatives seized by federal agents increased from 128,953 grams in federal fiscal year 1967 to 327,750 grams in 1968. Both were all-time highs. The average injection or capsule taken by addicts contains about four milligrams of heroin. Seizures in 1968 therefore exceeded 80 million doses. Individuals will take anywhere from four to sixty doses a day. Marijuana seizures by federal agents increased from 12,148,126 grams to 31,824,628 grams during the same period, again an all-time high. An average smoke will contain roughly sixty-five milligrams of marijuana, although some will be five times or more that strength, so that federal seizures in 1968 accounted for nearly 500 million smokes.

Seizures of stimulants and depressants increased even more dramatically. Seizures of stimulant capsules incidental to arrest rose from 3,292,583 in fiscal year 1967 to 19,563,607 in fiscal year 1968, while depressants increased from 4,737,440 in 1967 to 11,326,540 in 1968. Seizures by judicial proceedings against illegal inventories of stimulants and depressants rose from 90,-799,518 in 1967 to 558,270,076 in 1968.

Law enforcement must recognize the interrelation between the use of different drugs. If seizures dry up sources for relatively harmless substances like marijuana, while heroin remains available, the result is quite probably new young addicts who otherwise would not have used addictive opiate derivatives. Priorities in enforcement, with the great emphasis on the most deadly drugs, are imperative.

To some extent increases in seizures reflect increased traffic. We must search for the meaning of the great increases in arrests for drug offenses during the last several years. A heavy reliance on drugs has important social implications, especially where the users are young people from well-to-do families. Among the poor, the meaning of addiction remains clear.

Poor mental health, alcoholism and drug addiction are present in most crime. These conditions are interrelated. Most alcoholics and individuals physically addicted to narcotics, as well as those psychologically unable to stop their use, started from a state of personal instability. This vulnerability caused many to seek the relief of drugs or alcohol and increased their risk of addiction. The cure for both alcoholism and drug addiction depends on the restoration of mental and physical health to the individual.

It has finally become clear to the public that alcoholism is a health problem. Law enforcement can provide some marginal control, but it can never cure. Not yet so clear is the fact that drug addiction can never be effectively dealt with as a law enforcement problem. It is much more. It is a social problem of profound implication calling on our greatest medical and sociological skills.

Drug addiction is an illness. Medical science can discover cures and provide care. A medical cure for heroin addiction offers a major opportunity to reduce crime. Thousands of poor people pay as much as twenty-five dollars a day for narcotics—money they can raise only by criminal acts. Though usually nonviolent, addicts seeking ways to support twenty-five- and fifty-dollar-a-day habits account for a substantial part of all serious property crime in cities like New York.

Drug users should be placed in correctional programs that cure and provide the opportunity to stay cured. The user's crime, until it causes him to commit other crimes, is against himself. When an individual is first found to be a user, criminal sanctions are neither necessary nor desirable. Where commitment is necessary, civil commitment of a contractual nature offers the opportunity for physical control over the addict without the stigma of a conviction for crime—and therefore the best chance for rehabilitation. Voluntary participation, which is the basis for civil commitment, creates an attitude helpful in achieving a cure. We move slowly toward such reforms as civil commitment. It was not authorized in federal law until 1965 and remains unknown to the laws of all but a few states.

With cruel slowness, almost as if we did not care, we are seeking ways to break or reduce opium addiction. Medical science could soon find a method of restoring balance in body chemicals to eliminate addiction if adequate effort were made. Methadone now offers escape from some of the tortures of physical addiction. Yet it is only beginning to be available to addicts and is itself only a beginning as a medical remedy. It is even more clearly within our potential to release the terrible hold of psychological addiction. Group therapy has made valuable breakthroughs for the psychically addicted. But society remains unwilling to make a major effort to help addicts. As we were once so deeply embarrassed by mental retardation and alcoholism, we are still frightened by addiction. Society thinks of the addict as a dangerous criminal. By failing to act we commit the addict to a foreshortened life of a greater personal wretchedness than that suffered by the retarded or the alcoholic.

Within the competence of medical science and community care, addicts can be rehabilitated. The savings for society just from the reduction of crime will be great. The enrichment from contributions made by former addicts will add to the national wealth. For the individual it will mean life itself.

It is our failure to understand change that misdirects our efforts to control marijuana. We are dealing with a justifiably skeptical generation of youngsters. The effect on them of mishandling so mild a hallucinogen as marijuana can be disastrous.

To engage in a massive effort to control marijuana—virtually closing borders as we did with Operation Intercept in the summer of 1969—is senseless. It may have caused hundreds of new heroin addicts. In an open society, where millions want marijuana, the effort cannot succeed. It is reminiscent of the frantic enforcement activity in the dying days of Prohibition, when raids indiscriminately and unjustly rounded up thousands of persons who had done nothing different from hundreds of thousands of others. The only thing worse than failure in such a massive enforcement effort would be success. The potential for substitutes for marijuana is beyond any enforcement capability. Heroin is still readily available. LSD and other chemical compounds can be made in the school chemical laboratory or in the kitchen sink. We can drive young people to truly dangerous drugs.

We can also destroy their faith in American justice. The penalties fixed for the sale and possession of marijuana by federal law and the laws of most states are unrealistic and unjust. They can only cause disrespect for law and add to the widespread view among our young people that our laws are hypocritical and do not intend justice. A judge—Solomon himself—confronted with youthful offenders charged with marijuana violations cannot follow the law and do justice, for the sentence required by law often means the end of a promising young career —sometimes the beginning of a life of crime.

Youth sees a society with 7 million alcoholics, police bribed by organized crime pushing heroin, and an eighteen-year-old boy sentenced to five years for possession of marijuana when hundreds of the students in his college have smoked it without consequence. It is easy to understand how they lose the little hope they have for our society.

Conflicting opinions about marijuana based on inadequate research damage society and our system of criminal justice in many ways. Cynicism, division, defiance, and sometimes total loss of respect for the integrity of the system result. We must decide—and soon. Is marijuana harmful? Should it be prohibited, controlled, or permitted? To decide correctly, we need facts. The evidence to date does not support criminal sanctions against the use of marijuana.

Legislators without understanding, who want to show how opposed they are to sin and how greatly they favor economy, vote long penitentiary sentences for marijuana offenses—five years as a minimum—but deny one cent for research needed to determine whether it is harmful. Perhaps this is good politics. If so, our system is in grave trouble. Long sentences embitter thousands—including many opposed to marijuana—who see them for what they are, punishment without reason or compassion.

This combination—irrational punishment and a refusal to seek the truth through adequate provisions for research—makes a rational solution of the marijuana issue impossible, however effective government policing may be. Try to explain the sense or the justice of the law's approach to marijuana to a group of teenagers. It cannot be done. It makes no sense. It is unjust.

After years of argument, evidence that marijuana is more harmful than cigarettes or whisky or that it naturally leads to the use of dangerous drugs is inconsequential. In the continued absence of such evidence, marijuana should be legalized. Legislation accomplishing legalization will have to be carefully drawn. The dangerous drugs commonly associated with marijuana will follow it into safer channels of distribution if care is not taken. When legalized, marijuana must be taken from the crime merchants who stock speed, LSD and heroin.

Delay and indecision over the future handling of marijuana are harmful. Constructive leadership will move rapidly to obtain necessary facts about its effects on humans and make a final judgment. The desire to avoid any increase in the use of stimulants, meritorious as it is, cannot be adequate reason for continued prohibition of marijuana. It would be nice if our people were so stable, our times so anxiety free and our five senses so fully appreciated that the effect of drugs would be noxious to all. But it is not so. There are immense pressures within our society pushing people toward drugs. Regulation must be realistic, practical and effective or we will suffer immense damage.

At the federal level, the Federal Bureau of Narcotics has had the major responsibility for enforcing the laws controlling opium, its derivatives, cocaine and marijuana. Customs agents, the Border Patrol and others are active in drug control, but only incidentally to other primary duties.

Until 1968 the Bureau of Narcotics never had more than three hundred agents. Over twenty were assigned outside the United States. Nearly one-third of the domestic agent power was concentrated in New York City. Until 1965 the California-Mexico border was manned by two agents.

With such limited manpower provided for the purpose, it cannot be assumed we really intended to control narcotics. Enforcement has been impossible—less than a gesture. The few agents involved had the most difficult and dangerous investigative responsibilities in federal law enforcement, working under cover for months, handling strings of informers, sinking deeply into cultures of poverty, crime and addiction. Narcotics agents usually started at federal pay level GS-5, while FBI agents started at GS-10. For their comparatively white-collar duty, FBI agents received 50 per cent higher pay than narcotics agents.

In 1965 Congress created the Bureau of Drug Abuse Control in the Department of Health, Education and Welfare. This small new federal investigative agency was assigned the role of controlling the emerging chemical synthetics. Planned for expansion, BDAC never had more than 270 agents. Staffed largely with personnel recruited from other federal bureaus, primarily Narcotics and the FBI, it was still struggling to identify itself and find its mission when it was reorganized with the Bureau of Narcotics into the Federal Bureau of Narcotics and Dangerous Drugs and located in the Department of Justice in April 1968.

Because of low salary bases, the old agencies were unable to attract men with good educational backgrounds and professional qualifications. The combination of poor pay, difficult work, close contact with criminal elements and low professional standards made the bureaus vulnerable. The result was a record of corruption. Within months after the merger of the Bureau of

Narcotics and the Bureau of Drug Abuse Control into the Department of Justice in 1968, more than fifty agents were dis-
charged and over a dozen indicted for selling narcotics or
accepting bribes. The good agents were among the best in law
enforcement. They had to be to survive. But the old agencies
were ineffective and worse.

The need for the merger was clear. Each agency was understaffed. Resources were wasted in the duplication and the inefficiency of small parallel regional offices covering virtually the
same geographic areas. While much of the narcotic and drug
traffic followed different patterns, the overlap was substantial.
The natural narcotics were primarily in the slums. Nearly one-
half of all narcotics addicts lived in the ghettos and barrios of
New York City. Five states—New York, California, Illinois,
Michigan and Texas—accounted for 80 per cent of all addiction. The synthetics—LSD, amphetamines and barbiturates—
were found largely in the suburbs, around college campuses, in
high schools and junior highs, wherever young people gathered.

History placed marijuana, which is not a narcotic, in the Bureau of Narcotics because when it was first declared illegal there
was no Bureau of Drug Abuse Control. Later BDAC agents
making arrests for the sale of LSD found marijuana present 90
per cent of the time. Before the merger, it was possible for
agents from the FBN and BDAC, having worked separately for
weeks on an investigation, to arrive at a suspect's door at the
same time, armed with search warrants, but unknown to each
other.

The merger offered the first real opportunity the federal government has had to fulfill its responsibilities. The additional
manpower meant it could make a balanced effort to control
heroin. In 1968, 80 per cent of the heroin used in the United
States came from Turkey and was refined in southern France.
Control of this supply is a fairly easy enforcement target. If the
flow were drastically curtailed, the demand would continue, and
the brown impure heroin from Mexico and opium from Laos

and China would soon fill any void. In the meantime, robberies of pharmacies, doctors' offices and hospitals by people seeking morphine and other narcotics would be widespread.

Great effort must be made to prevent human consumption of heroin, which has no legal use or medical purpose, to keep it from the young and to avoid new addiction. But effort must include medical care and cure, or control will never be achieved and thousands of lives will be wasted. The medical disciplines known to BDAC and its close relationship to the National Institutes of Health and of Mental Health offered a broadened outlook for enforcement.

Still, the long-range risks are not "H," or the international traffic in narcotics, via poppy fields in Iran, Turkey and China. However widespread the use of heroin may become, the greatest risks are the new synthetics.

Before the summer of 1968, the federal government had never designated a drug as dangerous until it had been observed in extensive street use. The divisions of responsibility before the merger made it unlikely that designations would be made on the basis of research. Only when police saw people acting peculiarly and found strange pills did they seek chemical analyses to determine the cause. Government research must discover the dangers of drugs in the laboratory—not the morgue, the maternity ward, the hospital or the insane asylum.

In June 1968 synthetic marijuana was designated as dangerous. It has yet to be developed at a cost that is commercially feasible. It will be. Then, a teaspoonful of liquid will impregnate a carton of regular cigarettes with a stronger, purer effect than natural marijuana at its best. No longer will helicopters search the highlands of central Mexico looking for fields of marijuana. No longer will thousands of smugglers risk discovery in border crossings. Cheaper, better and easier to obtain, marijuana can then be manufactured in the kitchen as gin was once distilled in the bathtub.

The designation of synthetic marijuana as dangerous was a

beginning. It meant government no longer felt it adequate to wait until extensive usage creates an enforcement necessity. The new Bureau had begun.

The designation of synthetic marijuana as a dangerous drug also caused a more reasonable penalty to attach to its possession. Because it was designated as a dangerous drug, synthetic marijuana comes under statutory provisions setting a maximum penalty of one year, rather than the five-year mandatory minimum penitentiary sentence which attaches to natural marijuana. The designation could not have occurred without the merger, because the Treasury Department opposed action that would deprive it of enforcement jurisdiction.

Consolidation of offices and cases will more than double the effective power of the former agencies. Substantial increases in manpower should soon make BNDD one of the most important and powerful federal investigative agencies—and none too soon. Aware of the pace of change, it can give comprehensive protection as drug use shifts slowly from old natural narcotics to new chemical compounds. It can stimulate, contract for and even conduct research that must be undertaken. It can contribute to the educational task that must be the major effort if prevention and control are to succeed. Federal agents can provide leadership, professionalism and training for local law enforcement personnel, who will have the principal responsibility for controlling the new patterns of distribution of the far more dangerous drugs to come.

7

GUNS: THE VIOLENT KILLERS

Since 1900 guns have killed over 800,000 persons in America. More than 20,000 people are shot to death and upwards of 200,000 are injured or maimed by firearms each year.

Total casualties from civilian gunfire in this century exceed our military casualties in all the wars from the Revolution through Vietnam. Guns are dangerous even in the best-trained and most responsible hands. In America guns are readily in the grasp of psychotics, incompetents, criminals, addicts, alcoholics, children—nearly anyone who wants them, however dangerous he may be.

Estimates of the number of firearms in private ownership range from 50 million to 200 million. We can only guess. Surveys indicate more than 40 million people own guns. Some have arsenals. They live in slums, high rise apartments, on farms—everywhere. Guns are in attics, garages, bureau drawers, glove compartments, closets, desks, under beds, standing in the corner, hanging on the wall—anywhere you might imagine and many places you might not.

Throughout our history ownership of firearms has been widespread. From earliest times Americans have identified their safety and too often their personal power with guns. Young boys were given guns and owned them with pride. For many, a gun was a thing of beauty. Nothing they possessed manifested such craftsmanship. With their cool blue steel, clean and smooth, the mechanical precision of their parts, the well-oiled natural-grained wood stock, their perfect balance and fine workmanship, guns captured the hearts and minds of male America. Nothing was treated with greater respect. Guns were works of art, things of beauty, sources of power and symbols of manliness.

But we are no longer pioneers venturing into the wilderness, dependent on our rifles for food and protection. We are more than 200 million highly urbanized and interdependent citizens of the most technologically advanced and affluent nation in history. We must control guns or continue to suffer the violence they generate, the crime they cause and the injury they inflict.

We have failed to control firearms because history and habit are more powerful influences on human conduct than reason and recent experience. Customs adapt gradually to meet new conditions. Society is slow to see how change makes senseless, and often dangerous, ancient activities long deemed essential to survival. Guns were once thought to be provider, protector and defender of liberty. Today they murder.

If government is incapable of keeping guns from the potential criminal while permitting them to the law-abiding citizen, then government is inadequate to the times. The only alternative is to remove guns from the American scene. In question is our ability to meet a crisis. It is not hysteria that demands gun control; it is 8,900 murders, 12,000 suicides, 65,000 assaults, 99,000 robberies—all committed with guns in the single year of 1968. The toll will rise until we act.

Between 1964 and 1969 robberies with guns increased 113 per cent and assaults with guns 117 per cent. More than 25 per cent of all violent crimes, which now exceed half a million annually, involve the use of firearms.

The peril has existed for decades. It has been disregarded at an awesome cost, which, when totaled, amounts to a national catastrophe.

Guns are designed to kill. That is their purpose. In mass urban society they are not the beautiful provider and protector. They are the ugly killer. They are death. They add immeasurably to the climate of violence in America. When viewed as a source of power by otherwise powerless people, guns can only mean violent crime. This is the lesson to be learned from the man ironically chosen as the typical prisoner in the District of Columbia Department of Corrections in 1969. Interviewed by the press after his selection and asked what he would do when released again, he replied, "Do what I always did—get a pistol and stick up anything that moves."

The more violence we experience in America, the more guns we stock. Following every riot, firearm sales have soared. With the repeated and compounded reporting of increases in crime known to the police, gun sales steadily rise. Rifle sales in the United States from 1963 through 1967 increased 115 per cent to 1,882,000 annually. In the same period shotgun sales increased 151 per cent to 1,515,000. Pistol sales were up 139 per cent to 1,188,000. Total firearms sales increased during these four years by 132 per cent to an annual total of 4,585,000 in 1967.

Two million firearms are manufactured in the United States annually for private ownership—70 per cent are rifles and shotguns. Of 1,200,000 guns imported annually, 60 per cent are handguns. America is the chief world market for pistols, which have little utility except to shoot people. Most of the pistols imported are inexpensive and so poorly constructed that they are dangerous to the user as well as anyone in the general direction they may be pointed.

The murder and suicide rates by gunfire in our country are incredibly higher than the rates in other advanced nations. Japan, with one-half our population, had 16 murders and 68 suicides by gunfire in 1966 compared to 6,855 murders and 10,407 suicides in the United States. Australia, still a pioneer country herself, had 57 gun murders among its 11 million people in 1965. Here in America the rate is seven times higher. Canada had 98 murders among 19,604,000 people in 1966, one-seventh the rate of its neighbor to the south. England and Wales had 27 murders committed with guns in 1966 among 54½ million people, while Houston, Texas, alone had 150 gun murders among its 1½ million citizens. That same year Sweden, with a suicide rate nearly twice ours, experienced 14 murders and 192 suicides by gunfire. Its murder rate by guns was one-seventeenth as high as ours; its suicide rate by gunfire was one-half as high.

Murders and other crimes committed with firearms occur more frequently where guns are most plentiful and gun control laws least stringent. Surveys indicate 34 per cent of the households in the Eastern part of the United States contain guns, compared to 53 per cent in the West, 55 per cent in the Midwest and 64 per cent in the South. Not only is the percentage of murders committed by firearms higher in areas where there are more guns and weaker laws—the overall murder rate is higher, too. Rhode Island, New York and Massachusetts have strong gun control laws. Arizona, Texas and Mississippi have more guns per capita and very weak gun control laws.

A comparison of these states is informative:

	Percentage of Murders by Gun	Total Murders per 100,000
Rhode Island	24	1.4
New York	31.8	4.8
Massachusetts	35.5	2.4
Arizona	66.4	6.1
Texas	68.7	9.1
Mississippi	70.9	9.7

The inescapable lesson is that easy access to guns causes thousands of preventable murders, suicides and accidental deaths.

While our information is far from complete and comparisons fail to account for such differences as urbanization, industrialization, economic status, climate, ethnic composition and regional history that affect murder rates, it is perfectly clear that lots of guns and little control mean murder.

Every civilized nation but one has acted to control guns. Nearly all have succeeded. The exception is the United States. In Britain, France, Belgium, the Soviet Union, Italy and West Germany the ownership of firearms is a strictly regulated privilege. Britain's Firearms Act of 1937 requires every gun buyer to obtain a police certificate. In issuing the certificate the police must be satisfied the applicant is not prohibited from ownership because of a criminal record and that he is not likely in any other way to endanger the public peace or safety. Hunters, sportsmen, qualified people who live in hazardous places or work at dangerous occupations may have guns, but every transaction involving guns or ammunition must be registered. Jail penalties are prescribed for failure to provide police the required data, and firearms cannot be pawned.

French laws are clear and strict. Mail-order sales are prohibited. A buyer must be over twenty-one. Every sale must be registered. To obtain a permit to buy a gun an individual must undergo a thorough background investigation. Only the police and licensed guards are permitted to carry loaded guns. Private citizens cannot carry concealed pistols on their persons under any circumstances even if properly registered.

Gun control laws in Italy are similar to those of France. In Spain procedures make it even more difficult to buy a gun. Throughout most of Russia private ownership of rifles and revolvers is punishable by up to two years in prison. In most parts of the Soviet Union hunters can own shotguns, but it is only in remote areas of the north and in Siberia that rifles can be bought. All must be registered.

In West Germany citizens of good reputation can buy handguns if they can demonstrate a need, such as a dangerous profession or isolated or dangerous living or working area. Special permits are necessary to carry pistols outside the home. The laws are strictly enforced.

In the United States, by contrast, until 1968 there was no

federal law with effective sanctions to control interstate mail-order purchases of high-powered rifles or concealable pistols by persons the shipper could not identify. Anyone with the price could obtain the most deadly weapon anonymously. Lee Harvey Oswald, living in Dallas, Texas, purchased the rifle with which he assassinated President Kennedy from Klein's Sporting Goods Co., a Chicago mail-order house. On a coupon clipped from an advertisement in the February 1963 issue of the *American Rifleman* magazine, with a money order for $21.45 attached, Oswald wrote in his own hand the post office address and fictitious name to which the Manchester-Carcano 6.5-millimeter rifle was mailed—A. Hidell, P.O. Box 2915, Dallas, Texas. That was all it took to arm Lee Harvey Oswald and to change the course of history. No federal registration or licensing was required. Most states and cities had no effective gun controls; Illinois and Chicago were among them.

Despite the clear connection between the uncontrolled private ownership of guns and the enormity of the violence they cause, millions of Americans are ardently opposed to any restraints on their possession of firearms. The reasons given are several.

First is the right to bear arms. Those who say the Constitution prohibits the registration or licensing of firearms ignore law and history. The Second Amendment provides, "A well-regulated militia being necessary to the security of a free State, the right of the people to keep and bear arms, shall not be infringed." The purpose, as its language clearly shows, was to insure to the states the right to maintain an armed militia. The Second Amendment has nothing to do with the individual ownership and possession of guns, as the courts have repeatedly held. It only prohibits the federal government from interfering with the state militia. The power of governments, federal, state and local, to strictly regulate the possession of guns is legally unquestionable.

A second argument against the control of firearms is that political freedom and personal safety depend on the ability of a people to defend themselves from the tyrant and the attacker. This they want to believe was the real purpose of the Second Amendment.

Whatever protection the private possession of guns may have once afforded, it now offers only violence. In a technologically advanced mass urban society citizens are virtually helpless against a hostile army. Shotguns are no match for tanks or the massive firepower of modern military weapons. Armies are well trained and regimented, while urban dwellers have no chance to organize. Surely Hungary and Czechoslovakia demonstrated this. It is no longer realistic to think of an armed citizenry as a meaningful protection against the tyranny of an oppressive professional military force.

Nor can firearms in the possession of private citizens protect them from crime. A state in which a citizen needs a gun to defend himself from crime has failed to perform its first purpose. There is anarchy, not order under law—a jungle where each relies on himself for survival. The wrong people survive, because the calculating killer or the uninhibited psychotic more often wields the faster gun. The average citizen with a gun acting in self-defense—housewife, bus driver, liquor store clerk—is a greater danger to himself and innocent people in the vicinity than is the crime he would prevent. There are bodies of good people in cemeteries all over the nation which evidence this fact.

What kind of society depends on private action to defend life and property? This is a task for professionally trained police, who have a public duty and are taught to use force safely and only when necessary. Yet even the police will perform more effectively when they do not carry guns. Of over 400,000 persons arrested for serious crime in England and Wales in the early 1960's, only 159 possessed guns. Such a gunless society would be paradise to our police, who run some risk with every arrest. Among 400,000 arrested for serious crime in America, tens of thousands are armed at the moment of apprehension.

Armed vigilante action by private citizens is another potential use of weaponry inconsistent with every principle of justice and order. Through history such action has caused more injustice and created more disorder than it has alleviated—and in a mass society the capacity of vigilantes to trigger a bloody revolution is far greater than at any previous time. Who in good conscience can weigh the vague and improbable risks of a feared impotence arising from gun control against the brutal fact of thousands of murders, robberies and assaults now committed by firearms?

Perhaps the major argument of those who oppose control is that people, not guns, are responsible for the murders, assaults, suicides, robberies and accidental deaths—and that guns are only the instrument. If guns were not available, it is argued, other methods of committing the same crime would be found. This position ignores human nature and the deadliness of guns.

Of course it is people—and not guns—that commit crime. But what enables people to commit crime? If you wanted to rob a bank and had only a knife, you might hesitate. A gun emboldens you. Suppose your victim is bigger than you. Guns more than equalize. With a gun you are eight feet tall. Many armed robberies are inspired by the sheer sense of power arising from the possession of a pistol. No other weapon has such an effect. A pistol can be concealed, directed accurately and used with sudden, terrifying and deadly effect. Surveys indicate one person in five who is assaulted with a gun dies, compared to one in twenty where a knife is the weapon.

Murder is a crime of passion. Few murders are premeditated. The tragedy is that the rifle was standing there in the closet when the son was seized by fury and shot his father, or the pistol was by the bed during a drunken argument and the husband shot his wife.

Suicide, too, occurs more frequently when firearms are readily available. Many kill themselves with guns who could not find the courage to use another way. Guns are easy, quick, sure—a split second and it is all over.

Several thousand die from the accidental discharge of guns each year. The accidental death rate in the United States is forty times the rate in the Netherlands, fourteen times Japan's, four times Italy's. The mere presence of so many guns insures a continuation of a high death rate caused by their accidental discharge.

In England, where police still function without carrying firearms, few officers die in the line of duty by assault. In America, between 1960 and 1968, 475 law enforcement officers were slain in the performance of their duty. Four hundred and fifty-five, or 96 per cent, died from gunfire. Handguns were the murder weapon in 350 cases. Shotguns were used fifty-eight times, and rifles forty-seven. By comparison, four officers were murdered with knives over the eight-year period. Only in desperation or madness will a person attack a policeman with a knife.

Two defensive arguments are found supporting the unfettered ownership of firearms. The first says that perhaps it would be best if there were no guns, but there are guns, criminals have them and there is no way of keeping them from their murderous hands. We should fight crime, not guns—indeed, we should fight crime with guns. We cannot disarm the good people and leave them at the mercy of the criminal.

It doesn't work that way. Crime is not a rational, calculated activity. A decrease in the availability of guns decreases the commission of crime with guns. The uniform experience in nations and states that have controlled guns has been a lower rate of crime committed with guns. The most rational criminal prefers to play the game of crime without guns because his risk is much higher when guns are used. For every law enforcement officer murdered in the line of duty, police kill fifty persons under color of law. But the criminal mind is rarely so logical. When guns are available, they are used. If guns are not at hand, the criminal will not find them. If he does, his possession of a gun should be treated as a crime for which he can be arrested before he commits a more serious one.

Finally, some protest the bother of gun control. They are angry that, as wholesome hunters, sportsmen, public defenders in the old tradition, they—the good folk—should be subjected to the inconvenience and indignity of registration or licensing. All that is at stake is a few thousand murders, a few more suicides and perhaps several hundred thousand robberies, assaults and accidental deaths and injuries. Is it too much trouble for a people who register wives, automobiles, dogs and many other conveniences and necessities that they should have to register their guns?

In mass society it is difficult to learn the lesson of murder by firearms. We can understand that guns are the weapon in 65 per cent of all murders, but the victims are strangers, people we do not know, and there are only 8,900 a year. Eight times that number are killed in automobile accidents. More die slipping in bathtubs than by gunfire.

Some who have died by guns in recent years have not been strangers to any of us. An inspiring young President; the black apostle of change through nonviolence; the Senator of vision who alone seemed capable of uniting young and old, rich and poor, black and white; two blacks seeking equal justice for their race, one from Mississippi, one moved to Harlem—John Kennedy, Martin Luther King, Robert Kennedy, Medgar Evers and Malcolm X. Their deaths were so stunning and capricious that the role of the gun was obscured. But if these assassinations do not show us that guns kill, destroy, ruin, what will?

After the two tragic assassinations in April and June of 1968 —Dr. King and Senator Kennedy—it seemed that then if ever was the chance for America to come to grips with its gun problem. The nation was shocked as it had been only once before in the century—on November 22, 1963—but by 1968 violence in America seemed all-pervasive.

In April of 1968 the Harris Poll found that by a margin of 71 to 23 per cent the American people favored the passage of federal laws that would place tight controls on the sale of guns.

Organizations of citizens under the leadership of John Glenn, James V. Bennett, Senator Joseph D. Tydings of Maryland and others pressed vigorously for effective gun control action. Groups including church, professional, business, labor, education and civil rights associations joined the fight. By June of 1968 the same survey found 81 per cent of the American people favoring registration of all firearms.

In the great emotional wave following the second assassination it seemed briefly that our lingering love for guns could be shattered. The nation wanted strict gun control laws. Yet they did not come. We must question the capabilities of the democratic system to deal with urgent needs when we fail to act under such circumstances.

Gun control laws in the United States the day Martin Luther King was assassinated were hopelessly inadequate. Interstate control was, for practical purposes, nonexistent. No state can hope to control guns effectively within its borders while interstate mail orders and shipments are uncontrolled. But most state legislatures have not indicated a serious desire to control firearms anyway. For one thing, it is difficult to enforce state and local gun control laws when guns can be bought in neighboring states by felons convicted of violent crimes, by the mentally unstable, by addicts, alcoholics, and juveniles. For another, the gun lobbies organized better and fought harder than the diffused interests that wanted control.

Nationally, in the spring of 1968, the law was at best a patchwork of no controls, ineffective controls, unenforced and unenforceable controls, with only occasionally a jurisdiction where a comparatively effective effort was made.

After a major legislative battle, and the ardent urging of President Johnson, Congress—as a part of the Omnibus Crime Control Act of 1968—finally gave the federal executive departments some opportunity to control the mail-order purchase of handguns. Under the new Act, only federally licensed dealers could buy, sell or ship handguns in interstate commerce. Licenses were to be carefully regulated with strict qualifications imposed, careful record keeping on every gun required and regular inspections made.

The limitation of controls to handguns resulted from several factors. Handguns have little other purpose than for use as a weapon against people. They are more dangerous because they can be so easily concealed. Statistics indicated that handguns are used in over 70 per cent of all homicides committed by firearms, while rifles are used in only 10 and shotguns in 19 per cent. Hunters, an effective political force, were concerned primarily with rifles and shotguns, though they clearly feared that regulation of handguns would be only a beginning.

Testimony on the danger of mail-order sales of guns had been convincing. Mail-order weapons were regularly delivered into dangerous hands. A survey of mail-order gun recipients in New Jersey, a state with strong gun control laws, showed 40 per cent did not hold permits required by law and 44 per cent of those without permits had prior criminal records. In the District of Columbia 25 per cent of the persons receiving guns by mail order had criminal records.

The new law provided a small beginning. Some progress toward effective control of handguns was possible, but it was far from the protection so desperately needed.

Even following passage of the Omnibus Crime Control Act with the first new federal firearms control provisions in thirty years, more comprehensive controls were sought. Proposals were advanced to extend the mail-order ban to rifles, shotguns and ammunition. In addition, some sought what must come if there is ever to be effective control: federal registration and licensing. In August, Congress extended the earlier prohibition of unlicensed shipment of handguns to include the interstate mail-order sale of long guns—rifles and shotguns—and, importantly, of ammunition. It failed to require federal registration or licensing of all firearms. The National Rifle Association, the major factor in the nation's failure to control firearms, had prevailed.

There must be federal registration of all firearms and licensing of all who possess them. State and local laws cannot provide an adequate base for registration and licensing. Ninety per cent of the guns confiscated following the Detroit riots of July 1967 were not registered as required by Michigan law. A majority of the unregistered guns were obtained from a nearby city in a neighboring state that had no gun controls. We are far too mobile and interdependent to rely on a network of state and local laws to protect us from guns.

Every gun in the United States should be registered so that its owner and its full identification are known. This data should be in computers available to all law enforcement agencies. Sirhan Sirhan was identified from leads supplied in seconds by a state computer in Sacramento which recorded the name of the prior owner and the identification of the pistol used to murder Robert Kennedy. The FBI National Crime Information Center, placed in operation in January 1967, now has computer data on hundreds of thousands of stolen and missing firearms. This data bank can be extended to include all firearms.

The power to prevent crimes with guns where permits are required is very real. Police know this and favor strong licensing laws. A person found carrying a gun can be charged with illegal possession if he has no permit. Police characters and crime repeaters known to the police cannot qualify for a permit where the law is adequate, and they can be arrested if found with a gun in their possession. This is a practical and effective deterrent.

No one should be permitted to have a gun in his possession unless he is licensed to possess it. Only then can we begin to control the use of firearms to commit crime. If this mass gathering of data proves expensive, we can afford it; what we can no longer afford is the violence caused by guns.

If we are really serious about controlling crime, we must control firearms. With violent crime increasing and crime with guns increasing even more rapidly, with the continuous risks of snipers and guerrilla warfare and further assassination, responsible leadership must cut through political consideration and insist on gun control. Far from hitting America in its manhood, gun control will show we have men who will stand up for the clear and urgent public interest.

America pays a terrible price for its heritage of guns. We are virtually unique among nations that know guns in our failure to control them. Guns have scarred our national character, marking many of the most terrible moments of our history. Destroyers of life, causers of crime, guns bloody the present and imperil the future. They make lions of lambs. We must create a reverence for life and seek gentleness, tolerance and a concern for others. Guns glorify the power of violence while ignoring its pity.

How long will it take a people deeply concerned about crime in their midst to move to control the principal weapon of the criminals? How long will it take us to realize that times have changed, that indiscriminate traffic in guns needlessly subjects thousands annually to death, injury, fear and property loss? How long will we neglect our duty to do what we can to prevent the majority of our murders, and the tens of thousands of robberies and assaults committed annually with firearms?

How long will we permit guns in the hands of the assassin to threaten our political system? How many summers will we risk sniper fire which can terrorize whole sections of great cities? When will we act?

PART TWO

Criminal Justice

Society deals directly with antisocial conduct through a system of criminal justice, the basic elements of which are police, prosecution, courts and corrections. Too often, though, we think of crime control exclusively in terms of the criminal justice system. This is a dangerously narrow view. Vital as they are to safety and liberty in America, the processes of criminal justice can deal with little more than the immediate peril of crime as it occurs. America must reduce the causes of crime if it hopes to significantly reduce its occurrence. Merely to contain the effects of conditions that breed crime is to engage in an endless and losing battle.

Crime can never be controlled through the criminal justice system alone. Even the most powerful and arbitrary police state in a simple rural environment will be unable to frustrate the deep desires and secret acts of people. The capacity of the system of criminal justice to prevent and control crime in our mass society is extremely limited, however great the effort, however effective its techniques. While the role of the system of criminal justice is critically important, it can never be but a minor fraction of the total effort necessary to prevent crime. To believe police can control the conduct of millions of poor and powerless people, the teeming ghettos that breed crime, the bristling energies of swarming college campuses and the pent-up anxieties of interdependent anonymous urban populations in a technologically advanced society is to dream. The dream will become a nightmare.

Misused, the system of criminal justice can destroy liberty and cause crime. A national police, false arrest, invasions of privacy, the intimidation of dissent, wrongful prosecution, denials of due process, corrupt officials, excessive use of force, failure to fairly enforce the law, police brutality, denial of rights, injustice—all threaten freedom and all cause crime. The American people must understand the limitations of law enforcement and criminal justice and the great danger of exceeding those limits.

For the system of criminal justice to succeed, it must understand its role and adhere to that role with absolute fidelity. Police, prosecutors, judges and correctional workers must respect the limits of their proper function, avoiding conduct in excess of their authority while fully performing their duty. To succeed, the people working within the system must be highly professional and sensitive. The criminal justice system was never more important, because of the prevalence of crime and the increasing complexities of its successful control and because of the restless doubts of young Americans that government in general can be effective and that American government in particular intends to do justice.

The paradox of overreliance on criminal justice to control antisocial conduct and the incredible neglect that characterizes the system itself raises the question whether we really want to prevent crime. Neglect and a demand that it do the impossible are the principal reasons our system of criminal justice is failing.

8

THE FAILING SYSTEM

I n its most direct contacts with crime—prevention, detection, apprehension, conviction and correction—the system of criminal justice fails miserably. Since most crime is never reported to the police, agencies of criminal justice are ignorant, at the very threshold of their opportunity, of most of the conduct they are designed to control.

Of the several million serious crimes reported annually to police, ranging from murder to car theft, barely one in nine results in a conviction. The rate of solution varies with different crimes. Murder is usually reported, and 86 per cent of all reported murders lead to arrests. Among those arrested, however, only 64 per cent are prosecuted and but 43 per cent of the cases prosecuted result in convictions. Of persons prosecuted for murder, 19 per cent are convicted of a lesser crime, such as assault, arising from the same incident, and 38 per cent are acquitted or dismissed. Even as to murder, then, fewer than one in four of those known to the police results in a conviction.

In contrast, only 19 per cent of all the burglaries reported to the police lead to an arrest. Four out of five arrested are prosecuted and 56 per cent are found guilty. Thus for every twelve burglaries reported there is one conviction. The FBI reports that among 2,530 cities with an estimated population of 63 million, there were 616,000 known burglaries in 1968, while there were convictions for 19,950, or 3.2 per cent, of those burglaries.

If one-half of all burglaries in those cities are reported, there is less than one chance in fifty that a burglar will be convicted. But burglary, involving the unlawful entry into a home or business and taking of property without the owner's knowledge, usually is never brought to the attention of police. It is doubtful that one burglary in five is reported. If so, the odds of conviction for burglary may be on the order of a hundred and fifty to one.

Robbery—taking property from a person by force or threat of force—is a crime of violent potential, dangerous to life and increasing rapidly. But chances of a robber being convicted from the commission of his crime are slight. Only 27 per cent of all robberies lead to an arrest. Of those arrested, 63 per cent are prosecuted, of whom one-half are convicted. Fewer than one reported robbery in twelve results in a conviction.

For the most common index crimes—burglary, larceny and car theft, which include 3.8 million of the 4.5 million index crimes reported in 1968—fewer than one in five led to an arrest and fewer than one in twelve resulted in a conviction. If you commit a serious crime and it happens to be reported to police, the chances are better than one in five that you will never even be arrested. But this is not the real measure of risk, because chances are that your crime will never be reported, and if reported the chances of acquittal or dismissal are high. Preventive efforts by police cannot be very effective when risks of detection, apprehension and conviction are so slim.

Less than two-thirds of the cases in which charges are filed against individuals for murder and robbery are prosecutable. Often the reasons are inadequacies in the evidence. The person charged may well be innocent. Because the crimes are so serious, arrests are sometimes made on insufficient evidence. Frequently cases cannot be prosecuted because of failures in the offices of district attorneys and delays in the courts. Legal advice to the police may have been erroneous or incomplete, available evidence may not have been developed, or young and undertrained lawyers may have performed ineffectively. Long backlogs in the criminal docket force many dismissals because witnesses die or disappear, evidence is stale or lost, and the very importance of proceeding is diminished by antiquity.

Long delays in trials dissipate any deterrent effect that might possibly result from convictions in such a small fraction of crime. Deterrence through prosecution arises from the belief that a wrongful act will result in conviction. As we have seen, it rarely does. But even if conviction is certain, deterrence is slight unless it is also swift. A speedy trial is essential if a relationship between wrongful conduct and correctional effort is to be felt.

When the record of rehabilitation by correctional agencies is considered, the failure of the criminal justice system is compounded. While there may be only one conviction for every fifty or more serious crimes, only one in four convicted will go to prison, and most who are imprisoned will commit subsequent crimes. Thus from among the very small portion of all the people who commit serious crimes and are ultimately imprisoned, the system fails to rehabilitate the majority. Rehabilitation is the major chance the criminal justice system has to reduce crime, yet even here it fails.

It is difficult to conceive of a criminal justice system operating in our environment, however sanguine we may wish to be, which could achieve four times the convictions presently secured from among the same number of crimes as are now committed. However vast the resources available and however brilliant the skills applied, there is a limit to what is possible. With a fourfold increase in effectiveness, conviction would still not be obtained in a majority of the reported index crimes. When convictions are compared to the vast number of unreported crimes as well, the fraction of crimes leading to conviction would be less than one out of ten. Without improved correctional capability the increase in convictions might more probably increase than decrease crime. Society cannot look to convictions as its best protection from crime.

The criminal justice system is a process in which each stage must contribute to the same goals—the prevention and control of crime and the rehabilitation of offenders. Performance must flow efficiently from one discipline to the next—from police to prosecutor to judge to jailer. The success of each function depends on the effectiveness of all, and their interdependence exists not only among different disciplines in the same jurisdiction but among the disciplines in different geographic jurisdictions as well.

If police are not effective in preventing crime, prosecution, courts and prisons are flooded. If police fail to solve crimes, prosecutions cannot proceed and courts cannot do justice—the rest of the system never has its chance. When a district attorney's office inadequately or dishonestly presents cases developed by police, the deterrent effect of the process is lost. Guilty persons are not convicted and the public is not protected.

If courts have huge backlogs and are unable to reach criminal cases for many months, burdens are placed on police, who may be confronted with a series of crimes committed by people released on bail pending trial. Prosecution offices face the difficult task of keeping up with witnesses, constantly reviewing old matters and endeavoring to present stale evidence when trial is reached. Jails will be overcrowded with defendants who are not released pending trial. Additional burdens on manpower and facilities are costly, but more costly still is the loss of deterrent effect through delay.

For the accused, delay often means an increased capability to commit crimes or a diminished chance for rehabilitation because of continued exposure to forces tending him toward crime —the old gang, the broken home, the narcotics habit—because crimes may be committed while he is waiting trial, or because of associations and experiences in jail before trial. For the innocent person accused of crime, delay means prolonged anxiety. If held in jail pending trial, the accused faces reduced ability to obtain evidence or witnesses to establish innocence and, innocent or not, possibly the loss of a job, the breakup of an unsupported family, exposure to homosexuality and the development of antisocial attitudes.

Finally, if corrections fail to rehabilitate, then all the efforts of police, prosecutors and judges can only speed the cycle of crime. Longer sentences usually only harden people who spend years waiting to be released. The long sentence does not deter others on the outside and impedes rehabilitation of the persons sentenced. On the average, the same number of prisoners will be released every day as are incarcerated, whether their sentences are for one year or ten. The question is not how long they were in jail, but what they will do when they are released. Public safety depends not on the length of the sentence but on rehabilitation.

No single effort can perfect the criminal justice process within a given jurisdiction. Just to add more police or merely increase the district attorney's staff or simply provide additional judges or only build a new jail will not be enough, unless that happens to be the one deficiency in the system within that jurisdiction. There is no such jurisdiction.

Nor can protection be adequate even where the agencies within one jurisdiction are excellent if those in other jurisdictions are poor. A good police department in one city is confronted with crime it cannot effectively control when adjoining jurisdictions protect gambling and prostitution or tolerate narcotics traffic. Cooperation among police departments in different cities is necessary to combat gambling syndicates, safecrackers, robbery gangs and burglary and stolen car rings that work from city to city. The apprehension and return of wanted persons and the detection and transmission of evidence and witnesses may require the assistance of several jurisdictions.

We will hear more and more about crime spilling over from central city into the suburbs. Suburban fears activating the economic and political power in control of their greater-metropolitan areas will often incite police repressiveness in the inner city slums. Suburban bank robberies, burglaries and assaults committed by people conditioned to crime in the ghetto are a concern of law enforcement in adjacent affluent suburban areas now. Coordination with the major metropolitan police force is the best chance to prevent such crime. Friction between such departments, which frequently exists because of the often higher pay and always easier work of suburban police, can be terribly costly to the public.

Weak prosecution and long delays in criminal trials affect people outside the jurisdiction involved because we are such a transient people. Every day persons with indictments pending in several distant states are arrested on new charges in states they have only recently entered.

When wardens confine first-offender juveniles in jail with hardened criminals, as happens to more than 100,000 youngsters a year, and prisons release inmates bent on further crime, distant places and people are affected. Inmates released from brutalizing Cummins and Tucker prison farms in Arkansas have later committed crimes in Missouri and Texas and California. Because we are mobile and interdependent, agencies of criminal justice must be strengthened throughout the country to be fully effective anywhere. There is no way in our open society that one city or county or state can protect its citizens adequately when crime is rampant in the remainder of the nation.

Effective coordination among agencies of criminal justice is imperative. Beginning in 1966, the federal government sponsored the creation of State Coordinating Councils to review the experience and needs of all police, prosecutors, courts and corrections within each state. After the passage of the Crime Control Act of 1968 these links were formalized and financed to provide promising opportunities for coordination, establishing priorities, more effective distribution of funds and education.

Even more important has been the creation of Urban Criminal Justice Coordinating Councils. To have an overview of a metropolitan area, to plan meaningfully, to establish necessary relationships within a system, all elements of the criminal justice system must work together. The greatest needs of criminal justice within a metropolitan area can be determined only when a professional staff with access to necessary information and experience can survey all activities. Leadership can then be educated, public support organized, priorities established, relentlessly pursued, and hopefully met. Mayor John V. Lindsay with the support of the Vera Foundation has provided a model for the nation and invaluable leadership for criminal justice through establishment and support of such a council in New York City.

The criminal justice system has been tragically neglected in America for generations. It is a system in theory only. At a time when our major domestic concern is crime and violence, the nation spends more on household pets than on police. For all police, prosecutors, courts and corrections—the entire criminal justice process, federal, state and local—our annual expenditure by 1970 was barely $5 billion. This compares with $9 billion spent for tobacco and $12.5 billion for alcoholic beverages. Until the last several years our annual expenditure for the criminal justice process increased by about 5 per cent, barely enough to keep up with population, inflation and the higher cost of newly developed and badly needed equipment.

An added danger of the years of neglect is that they make the addition to the criminal justice system of more of the same a potentially harmful investment. More untrained police in communities where relations with the public are hostile, where crime isn't reported, where riots are a constant risk, is not in the public interest. More judges where there is no effort at court administration, where techniques of efficient docket control are not developed, will only diminish the role of the individual judge and the chance for equal justice. More juvenile detention homes that brutalize the young, more jails where homosexuality is rampant, more prisons hardening criminals will not enhance the public safety.

The need is to establish priorities based on successful experience, on clear needs, on newly developed technology, on a comprehensive evaluation of the entire system. In a society so complex, with governments so fragmented, with existing isolations and conflicts and an overriding ignorance of the nature, causes and cures for crime, this is no easy task. A high level of public commitment and an organized approach are essential.

In a climate of fear it is ever more difficult to adhere to basic principles of government. It would be easy to reshape law enforcement or to place too much power in federal and state government. From all the pressures, we could easily lose liberties that are not only essential to human dignity but that are basic to crime control itself. It will take a stern, even fierce, self-discipline to maintain clear, firm principles. Pragmatism nourished by anxiety can blur the lines of the framework of government and important principles within the processes of criminal justice until they disappear.

In a simpler day we started with local government as the source of law enforcement: the sheriff, the constable, the policeman. As the nation grew, new jurisdictions were established to serve new needs. With the automobile and highway traffic, most states for the first time entered law enforcement with substantial manpower. Slowly as urbanization, mobility, mass population and interdependence increased, the federal government took on more investigative and enforcement functions.

Of more than 400,000 full-time law enforcement officers throughout the nation in the late 1960's, fewer than 26,000 were in federal agencies. The states, though varying widely in relative size and jurisdiction, had fewer than 45,000 officers. Local jurisdictions employed the remainder, more than 80 per cent of all civilian law enforcement. The New York City Police Department alone has over 30,000 officers.

Local law enforcement serves in more than 40,000 different jurisdictions. This figure standing alone manifests the irrelevance of so much of our government structure to present and future needs. The fragmentation necessarily impairs effectiveness and reflects absurd and debilitating stresses and distortions in the model of government.

Many believe that a national police force is desirable. With it they see professionalization, integrity, efficiency, and effectiveness, England the model. They miss the major currents of need in mass society and the practicalities of American law enforcement. Perhaps the FBI with 6,500 agents can be efficient. Could it be efficient with 300,000 agents?

History, habit, geography, climate, population density, ethnic and racial composition, economic levels, mobility, age and dozens of other factors make our cities different. Such diversity is part of our strength. Resulting wide differences in patterns of criminal conduct are found between cities. Law enforcement must be sensitive to such differences and responsive to the problems they create. No national bureaucracy has ever evidenced the capability for this required sensitivity.

Participatory democracy is a real force reflecting the need of the individual to have some voice in matters that affect him most. It is no passing fad. Nor is the desire for community control of essential public services such as schools, police, health facilities, welfare, employment agencies, pollution control and garbage collection. There is no other way for the individual to influence his own destiny, no other way for him to make a difference in activities that concern him directly and significantly.

For Jefferson it was largely an intellectual exercise to query whether man was capable of governing others if he wasn't first capable of governing himself. Government in his day had comparatively little impact on the individual. For modern man, some power to affect government actions is essential to overcome total personal impotence. Unavoidably in the years ahead government will intrude more intimately in the individual's daily life. There can be no other reasonable expectation. There are few places remaining where the individual can escape the influences of mass population. Soon there will be no such places. To affect the quality of his own life, the individual must be involved in the control of services that concern him most.

The involvement will reach few functions more critical than law enforcement. In a society where at least thirty-eight persons could watch Kitty Genovese slowly stabbed to death on the streets of New York City and not one of them call the police, local citizen participation in law enforcement policy is the only way—excepting self-defense—for the individual to know he will be safe, that protection is possible, or if not, why not. The alternative, self-protection, is dangerous to self and to others. If everyone's safety depends on his ability to defend himself, there is anarchy.

To be effective and efficient, law enforcement must be close to the people and must serve their particular needs. However professional, in the climate of our cities and a nation of our size and diversity a general police agency controlled from a distance cannot be effective. The support, the confidence and the personal familiarity of the public are necessary for the police to do their job. These qualities can be developed only on the streets where people live. Anyone who has been through the frustrations of seeking action from Washington or the state capital on a local project can conjure the limitations of a national or statewide police force. In major urban areas even city hall is too remote. Local precincts alone can know and sensitively meet the needs of the people.

A reason more than adequate in itself to avoid a national police is the immense concentration of power it would pose. The FBI today has as high a concentration of power as people who want to be free should permit. The diffusion of federal civilian investigative and enforcement authority among numerous agencies, state police with a cumulative manpower greater than the federal force, and the dominance of local law enforcement are essential to liberty. The risks of concentration of police power in America today exceed those of any earlier time, because the disparity in power between the individual and the state is so much greater. The dependence of the individual on government approaches total. The development of the computer, the penetration of electronic equipment into the innermost recesses of our private lives, and the anonymity of the individual even in his own neighborhood make the risks inherent in a national police force intolerable.

The prevalence of science fiction distracts us from the unbelievable things that science is doing today and the peril and opportunity it holds for law enforcement. The imaginings of Jules Verne are now old-fashioned. Captain Nemo could not dream of things Admiral Rickover has done. Our astronauts have completed in eighty minutes the trip around the world that took Phineas Fogg eighty days. Buck Rogers' twenty-fifth century will be reached four hundred years ahead of schedule. The incredible today is ancient tomorrow. The fears of George Orwell's 1984 are being realized in many parts of the world. Strict adherence to clear basic principles encased in a wisely proportioned structure of government with firm traditions against their violation will be needed if they are to survive.

At this time the jurisdictional proportions are badly blurred and largely creatures of historic chance. The President's Crime Commission estimated in 1967 that local governments made two-thirds of all expenditures for criminal justice. This outlay was not prorated evenly among the several disciplines. Nearly 80 per cent of all police expenditures are local compared to only one-third of the total correctional costs.

Gross figures in millions of dollars for 1967 were as follows:

	Local	State	Federal	Total
Police	2,201	348	243	2,792
Courts	173	51	37	261
Corrections	343	632	59	1,034
Prosecution	110	—	15	125
Total	2,827	1,031	354	4,212

The federal government has a role in law enforcement and an important one. But that role must be clearly and sensitively defined and the definition carefully adhered to. The role starts with protecting the integrity of its own operations. Customs law enforcement, federal tax collection, agricultural, postal and drug inspection are essential to performance of the federal function. Federal agencies must also reinforce local law enforcement in the channels of commerce—the interstate theft, transportation of a kidnap victim across a state line—and liberate local criminal justice agencies from organized crime. Because of the neglect of criminal justice, the most important federal activity is to provide leadership, financial resources, research and models of excellence in its own performance—the FBI, the U. S. Attorney, the federal courts and the Federal Bureau of Prisons.

State governments, too, have an important role, but except in sparsely populated rural areas they are no substitute for local law enforcement. Some of our states are as populous today as great nations once were. California and New York approach 20 million people. A state police under such circumstances poses most of the risks of a national police.

State law enforcement experience has been limited. A majority of the states have no significant police jurisdiction beyond highway patrol. Seventy per cent of all state expenditures for law enforcement are for traffic regulation. States too must maintain the integrity of their functions, provide model laws and systems of criminal justice, set standards, train personnel and service rural areas. This done, the major law enforcement task of the nation—urban police service—must be left to local government.

If we are to simplify government, to make it responsive to local needs, provide it the flexibility to adapt with reasonable speed, every activity cannot be directed from Washington, Albany, Sacramento, Springfield, or Austin. It is more important for more reasons that we retain law enforcement in local hands than any other government service.

Unless local government can meet its responsibilities, find adequate sources of revenues, attract skillful people, and provide excellent service, the federal government will be drawn into the field. With every major and stubborn problem of the last half century—transportation, social security, welfare, education, housing, agricultural surplus, labor relations, race relations—we have seen the people turn to Washington for resolution. We can no longer afford this.

While it is essential that police functions remain under local control, different considerations govern prosecution, courts and corrections. Offices of prosecution, court systems and correctional services have been created within different political jurisdictions to meet different needs arising from their different functions.

The number of prosecutors and judges is small compared with police. The significant criminal laws they enforce and interpret nearly always apply statewide. Effective case management and efficient use of judges' time require the availability of a number of judges who can be used interchangeably and assigned where the work is. Unless judges are part of a state system this is impossible outside the largest cities, and the largest cities, nearly always afflicted with huge backlogs, lose the assistance of judges who can be transferred temporarily from less busy areas. In prosecution, career development and opportunities to advance are enhanced by larger district attorneys' offices. A statewide system can attract and retain more competent attorneys. As nearly as possible prosecution policies within a state—Buffalo and New York City, Philadelphia and Pittsburgh, or Phoenix and Tucson—should be the same. The laws are the same. The same legislatures enact them. If offices of prosecution are not at least coordinated, prosecution is likely to be discriminatory. There is also substantial waste of resources and loss of opportunity where there is a city, county and district attorney in the same metropolitan area. Often a single office could achieve equal justice and with greater efficiency. There must be a major state participation in the judicial system and at least a significant state coordination of prosecution if there is to be effective performance of those functions with reasonable efficiency and a uniform application of the laws.

Corrections, like other government activities, grew through history to meet needs or fill interests that usually have completely disappeared or drastically changed. Most city and county jails, often situated across the street from each other, offer no hope for programming rehabilitation. They manufacture criminals. Consolidation into agencies that have the ability to rehabilitate is essential to crime control. Generally, strong state systems offer the best opportunity for rehabilitation. To offer the range of medical, psychiatric, psychological, educational, vocational, and other skills required and to provide flexible community services, correctional agencies must be large enough to attract and fully utilize personnel appropriately trained for such a range of services. It is the state correctional systems we should work hardest to perfect.

The Federal Bureau of Prisons, which is chiefly responsible for federal civilian corrections, averages 20,000 prisoners in its institutions on any given day. This is less than 5 per cent of the total daily national prison population. For youthful offenders, federal conviction usually means incarceration hundreds of miles from home. At some federal youth centers 70 per cent of the inmates never have a visitor during their entire stay. With fewer than seven hundred female prisoners in federal prisons, most in Alderson, West Virginia, the others at Terminal Island, California, it is doubtful that the correctional service provided to program women back into a stable environment is meaningful. Federal women prisoners should be placed in good state systems under contracts providing for federal reimbursement for services, or located in small community centers near where they live.

The Federal Bureau of Prisons can provide leadership. It can engage in research and demonstrate new techniques. But because the vast majority of all prisoners are, as they should be, in state custody, the states must be the focus of efforts to improve corrections. Someday the quality of performance at the state level should enable states to assume responsibility for federal prisoners. But this will not be soon.

Only two federal prisons have been built since World War II. Both are outstanding institutions. The adult institution at Marion, Illinois, closely affiliated with the University of Southern Illinois, is recognized as a research center throughout the nation. The Robert F. Kennedy Youth Correction Center at Morgantown, West Virginia, opened in 1969, should soon be the world's most advanced institution of study and demonstration in the field of juvenile delinquency. Despite the quality manifested by the Federal Bureau of Prisons, new support for desperately neglected state services should be found before a new federal building program, which could include jails for pretrial and transfer detention, imbeds an undesirable expanded federal service in concrete. Prisons are durable institutions. Once built, they last for generations.

A careful and continuous review and reformation of jurisdictional lines between federal, state and local offices of police, prosecution, court systems and correctional agencies is important to overall and individual performance. We must adhere to those principles of federalism and self-government that provide both essential protection and best performance. We must recognize that agencies of criminal justice are part of a system, that each jurisdiction is dependent on others, and that all must function effectively or none will.

9

POLICE: THE URGENT NEED
TO PROFESSIONALIZE

N EGLECT has permeated every aspect of the police function and left law enforcement unable to provide its essential services effectively. Jurisdiction, organization, definition of service, personnel and performance are all inadequate to present needs.

The fragmentation of police jurisdictions alone makes excellence impossible and effectiveness limited. The nation has a crazy-quilt pattern of 40,000 police jurisdictions—remnants of history. Major urban areas need a single police service with strong local ties tailoring local action to local need. Yet many major urban countries have scores of police jurisdictions within their borders. St. Louis County has more than a hundred. To have a number of police departments in a single county or urban area rarely makes sense. How does the small police force handle a big parade or major disorder, a riot or a thousand protesting students? How many jurisdictions will a fleeing bank robber or drunken driver pass through in five minutes? How well coordinated can police radio networks be? If gamblers can choose among dozens of police departments before locating illegal operations in a community, how much are the risks of corruption increased? What is the career opportunity for a bright and ambitious young officer in a twenty-man force?

Where police jurisdictions are fragmented because there are

local governments that are otherwise desirable or politically difficult to change, police services can be provided for all jurisdictions by the major law enforcement agency in the area through contracts. The Los Angeles County Sheriff's Office provides police service for more than a dozen municipalities in this way. Rural areas should be serviced by large departments with extensive geographic scope.

In the age of the automobile a huge county with a small population cannot afford the manpower needed to control highway traffic, transient crime, a campus, or vacationers and campers visiting the area. The fleeing felon, vandals in the old farmhouse, the drunks by the lake, the careless cookout that starts a fire, the lost child—not all can be adequately handled by a sheriff and his deputy. There should be no more than several thousand local police jurisdictions in the United States. Organized in such a way, law enforcement would have a rational base on which to build.

Today the average police jurisdiction has ten officers while many have only one: the sheriff, the constable, or the chief without a lieutenant. What happens there twenty-four hours a day, seven days a week in our mobile society is beyond the control of law enforcement. Without manpower or professional skills, these old jurisdictions delay development of effective law enforcement.

The organization of police districts and departments has but slight relation to present social conditions. The average police department has paid little attention to its system. But police administration is big business. Huge budgets covering thousands of employees performing a vast range of services over an entire city require modern administration, a science that has bypassed the police in most municipalities. Administrative skills in police departments can increase effective manpower by more than all the additional patrolmen likely to be provided over a period of several years. When a group of twenty chiefs of police attended a seminar at Harvard University's School of Public Administration in the late fall of 1966, their eyes were opened to the potential of administration. Few had attended college or been exposed to any study of administration. Most had begun police work as young rookies. They had watched their departments grow by simply adding more personnel to old divisions and occasionally by dividing old precincts or adding new sections. The idea of total reorganization was unheard of. Once considered, though, it became clear to most of the chiefs attending that departments organized to serve nineteenth-century needs were inadequate.

We do not have careful analyses of the appropriate content of police activity. What services should police provide and what should they not try to provide? The issue is important. When the wrong kind of work is assigned, performance is poor, important police work is neglected as a consequence, morale of the force is impaired and relations with the public are damaged. When police are not assigned duties that only they can effectively perform, major public interests may be largely unprotected.

How is public intoxication, for example, to be handled? Except for controlling the belligerent or violent drunk or the intoxicated driver, do the police have a meaningful role? While charges of drunkenness declined from one-third of all arrests in 1961 to one-fourth in 1968, they remained a very great burden on law enforcement.

In major cities police make tens of thousands of arrests annually for intoxication. The police time consumed, the diversion from other duties, and the resulting police friction with families and friends of those arrested are very substantial. Because police pick drunks off the streets, from homes, and out of parks and bars, the public has a sense the problem is being handled. Perhaps, in fact, one problem is being aggravated and several others created in this process. Police action in arresting drunks will never prevent drunkenness, nor can it cure an alcoholic. What beneficial interest is served by picking winos off the curb, throwing them in the lockup to dry out for ten days, releasing them when their term is served, and then several days later picking them up again? Is this the way America wants to handle a major health problem afflicting 7 million of its people? This obligatory practice, imposed on the police because they are there, is not only cruel and senseless—it is harmful. It hurts society and law enforcement. It fills jails and impairs the performance of vital police services. It wastes the lives of alcoholics who need medical help. An ambitious, well-trained, professional policeman will not believe for long that he is performing a useful service when night after night he hauls drunks to the precinct station.

Society has thoughtlessly dumped the enforcement of unenforceable laws on police with tragic consequences. Legislatures blandly pass and retain such laws, knowing they are honored most in the breach. Our hypocrisy in refusing to face the truth catches police in the middle. The alcoholic, the bookie, the whore, the homosexual, the unmarried pregnant teenager and the addict fear—and come to hate—the police. Society sends the police against them to do what cannot be done by force. Under many conditions people will drink prohibited alcoholic beverages, gamble, seek illicit sexual relations, incur unwanted pregnancies, take dangerous drugs and borrow money badly needed at any rate of interest. History shows that these practices will not be stopped by mere force.

One reason the British bobby is held in great respect is that he is not asked to enforce the unenforceable. He is spared the anger and hatred of people who would otherwise see him act unjustly. To the child of the black ghetto what theory can justify the policeman who stops and frisks him when he is running home from a movie at night after he has seen that same officer joking with prostitutes, watching a bookie make a sale, and passing the junkie taking a fix to a desperate addict—without acting? The police are not wholly responsible; society sends them on this hate-engendering, corrupting, impossible mission. The law poses the quandary, and society refuses to resolve it.

Police work grew like Topsy—the result of historic chance. Nationwide we average 2 policemen per 1,000 citizens. Boston, in recent years, has had 4 policemen per 1,000 population, and San Diego 1.2. This does not mean that Boston necessarily has too many police, San Diego too few, or that law enforcement is more effective in Boston. Nor does it mean that police coverage or function should be precisely the same everywhere. We are a diverse and varied people with differing local traditions and history. Too often, though, we are unaware of the reasons for these differences and can explain what we do today only by what we did yesterday. Each police department, its city government and the citizens they serve need to look at the content of police services against the national experience and the local need and ask what police services should include.

Some cities rely on police to enforce health and safety ordinances. What is there in the police function or in the training of officers that qualifies them to inspect buildings for structural soundness, fire escapes for adequacy, forty-year-old electric wiring or overcrowding and filth in tenements? What does it mean to the people who live in the slums and know or deeply sense the pervasive noncompliance with building codes about which the police do nothing, when they are charged with such enforcement duties? Slum dwellers may be arrested merely for being on the street at 3 A.M., but they see the illegal conditions of the tenements that blight their lives ignored.

It is imperative that we move to enforce ordinances that can protect safety and health. We recoil in horror at violent crime that kills thousands annually, but we largely ignore violations of law, as inexorably murderous as the gun, that condemn hundreds of thousands annually to death in fires, home, industrial and automobile accidents, and by disease and poisoning. We then tell the slum dweller that he must obey the law, that all progress depends on law and order. We send police to maintain order, to arrest, to jail—and to ignore vital laws also intended to protect life and to prevent death both slow and violent.

Enforcement of a broad range of laws such as building-safety and health ordinances is essential to respect for law. People will not respect the law because they are told it is the right thing to do if their whole existence tells them the law is an oppressor and the police an enemy. Well-trained, adequately staffed teams of professional inspectors, engineers, electricians, plumbers and health officers should work continuously to bring slums into compliance while we build new cities. Government must supply the vast resources required to do the job. The police should work at crime prevention and crime control involving human conduct—and not divert their efforts by endeavoring to enforce regulations better left to others.

Often police operate animal pounds and handle auto, bicycle, pet and other registrations. These functions have no real relationship to the policeman's central purpose. To use officers for such purposes impedes professionalization. This is true of most aspects of urban traffic control, such as regularly assigned rush hour intersection direction and giving parking tickets.

The police mission these next several years may be the most important in public service. The reason is not that we are likely to be overwhelmed by crime, though we will have plenty of that. The importance of the police has to do with divisiveness among our people. Social turmoil that threatens life or property or violates laws is confronted chiefly by the police. Turbulence arising from youth and racial unrest will often require law enforcement intervention. How police perform will have a major effect on the dimension of our internal divisions. A prime way to hasten radicalization of substantial segments of our people, to assure an irreconcilable division between government and the masses, is excessive police force.

Police killings at Newark, Detroit and elsewhere during the riots of 1967, the student massacre at Orangeburg, South Carolina, in February of 1968, police violence at the Democratic Convention in Chicago that summer, and Black Panther raids in 1969 demonstrate the potential. Because of the massive repressiveness of those incidents, thousands, and for generations other thousands through them, will doubt our desire for justice. Society cannot cultivate a climate of violence and then expect to contain it solely by force. Such a course can only escalate tension, hostility and ultimately violence itself.

Except for the possibility of a vast polarization caused by violent police action, there is little chance of widespread revolutionary conduct in America. We are too comfortable. Even the most aggrieved of our people are overwhelmingly placid. Only minor fractions of our young, our poor, our blacks and browns, and other alienated groups are revolutionary, even to the point of civil disobedience. Most are unconcerned. The larger question is whether human nature can stand affluence.

Police performance will be exceedingly difficult. The combination of pressures on the present-day urban police department is immense. From within stem such frustrations as poor pay, inadequate training, limited opportunity, long hours, public antipathy and difficult, sometimes dangerous work. There are intense pressures from hard-liners, from other officers, the wife and wives' associations, as well as from business and civic groups frightened by crime. There is frustration caused by the press, the civil libertarians, the courts and the bureaucracy. There is public demand for greater use of force, there is police isolation from the people of suburbia, from students and from minorities—and there is fear. All of the emotionalism of the public concern over crime engulfs the police.

To combat crime amid the prevailing social unrest that changes constantly in its form and content, we dispatch the police, who are undermanned, undertrained and usually from backgrounds and with attitudes that are not sympathetic to or understanding of the people or the issues they confront. To be disciplined, cool and even-handed under such circumstances is exceedingly difficult, but these traits are essential to effective performance—and to justice.

Law enforcement was once a relatively simple task, but today no activity in our society is more complex or requires a greater bundle of professional skills for effective performance.

Law enforcer and lawyer, scientist in a whole range of physical sciences—chemistry, physics, electronics—medic, psychologist, social worker, human relations and race relations expert, marriage counselor, youth adviser, athlete, public servant—these are but a few of the many skills a major police department must exercise daily. Individual policemen must personally possess many of them—and perform them with excellence. Safety, life and property, equal justice, liberty, confidence in government and in the purpose of our laws will depend on it.

When police do not know the laws they enforce, there can be no government of laws. On one hand citizens may be prevented from doing what they have a right to do, and on the other hand permitted to violate laws. And some people will be permitted to do what is prohibited to others.

Nor do the rights of the individual under many vital and controversial Supreme Court decisions mean anything if the police do not implement them. Many important rights go unenforced. The *Miranda* decision, widely blamed as a major cause of crime, requires police at the time of arrest to warn suspects that they need not make a statement, that if they do, it can be used against them, that they are entitled to a lawyer and that one will be provided if requested. These requirements are generally ignored in many jurisdictions, sometimes ignored in others and misapplied elsewhere. If the police are not familiar with the law, there is no law—there is only arbitrary force. Police ignorant of the law risk destroying important prosecutions in a number of ways, as when evidence is obtained illegally or wrongful arrests are made.

If government is to be more than an arbitrary and capricious power, police must be thoroughly familiar with the laws they enforce. This is a difficult intellectual undertaking. It must rest on a solid educational base. It requires continuing and sophisticated education to keep current.

By self-conception, organization and training, the police function is paramilitary. It virtually ignores the vital interpersonal relationship between police and public. Such a view scoffs at the suggestion that the nation's policemen should be skilled in family counseling. But what are the actualities of violence in America? One out of five police killed in the line of duty from 1960 through 1968—ninety-three out of four hundred and seventy-five—died from wounds received answering disturbance calls. Thousands of officers were injured. Many of the disturbances, perhaps most, were marital disputes. How often have we sent a strapping untrained and uneducated officer to answer a police call—man and woman fighting—only to cause violence? Husbands and wives do fight. Who can prevent violence in family disorders? Who is to control an enraged, psychotic or drunken father or husband when he tries to murder his wife or son?

The sound of a siren, heavy footsteps on the stairs, the sight of a blue uniform in a moment of anger, the confrontation between a psychotic or a drunk and an officer who knows little but force as a means to settle disputes—here are the human ingredients for violent responses. An officer tries to wrestle a husband into submission, and one of them is shot. An officer arrests a husband, and his wife, just brutally beaten by her husband, stabs the officer. For their own protection, police should be trained in the psychology of family disputes.

One-fourth of all murders, and, if we knew, probably a greater fraction of all assaults, occur within families. Perhaps as many homicides and assaults are committed against the family friend, the neighbor, the paramour, the in-law, and the daughter's boy friend as against family members. The family breakdown that such violence reflects is in turn responsible for a large part of all violence and property crime committed outside the family situation. More than 75 per cent of all federal juvenile offenders come from broken homes.

In the light of such evidence, it is not unreasonable to believe that if social agencies can deal with family tensions and prevent some violent crime within families, the police can be trained to play a role. Police have three opportunities to be effective in such circumstances. First, they have the best chance to learn at the earliest possible time of the existence of mental disturbance and family tension. Second, when the crisis comes, the police are called. Their conduct on the spot may determine whether there is an assault or homicide, then or at some later time. Finally, police, if knowledgeable, can guide the troubled family to existing social agencies for help.

Under the Federal Law Enforcement Assistance Act of 1965, the United States Department of Justice financed in part a project of the City College of New York to test the meaning of training police for family crisis intervention in New York City. The project was under the direction of Professor Morton Bard, a psychologist.

Eighteen police officers of more than three years' experience each were given a hundred and forty hours of carefully planned training in family crisis intervention. The program included classroom lectures, films and reading assignments, and laboratory demonstrations in such areas as mental health, the nature of family violence and the influences of early childhood, risk evaluation in confrontation with violent persons, techniques of emergency intervention, patterns of self-destruction, family organization and interaction, disordered-family case studies, family court and social agency functions, cultural and marital style variations, alcoholism, addiction, and the marital relationship and police conduct under stress.

The demonstration period ran for nearly two years, from July 1, 1967, to April 30, 1969. New York's 30th Precinct was chosen for the test. A low-income, high-crime area on the West Side of upper Manhattan, between 141st and 165th Streets, it contained 85,000 persons, largely Negro. The eighteen specially trained police—the Family Crisis Intervention Unit—on twenty-four-hour duty, seven days a week, were assigned regular patrol responsibilities plus intervention in every family disturbance call within the precinct they were able to service. They were equipped with a specially marked squad car, and the community came to know of the project. Operational support included clinical psychology consultants and continuous training and evaluation.

During the twenty-two-month period the eighteen officers intervened in 1,388 family crises—more than 2 a day. In all, 962 families were helped, 30 per cent of them more than once, and chronic disorder was indicated among an even larger percentage of the families. The rate of intervention was twice the rate of reported family disturbances for the three months preceding the test period. This fact reflected both more accurate reporting by police and a higher incidence of citizens reporting to the police. The clear implication is that comprehensive training of the police would reveal a much higher incidence of family disorder at an early stage of its development. The study indicated a probable participation in family crisis intervention of 18,000 officers from the 30,000-man police department during the course of a year. Their impact—if they were adequately trained—would be immense.

The 24th Precinct, with a history of similar crime patterns, was selected for comparison with the 30th Precinct. No officers were specially trained there. During the test period, police in the precinct reported only 492 interventions, barely one-third the number reported by the special unit. In the 24th Precinct only 13.8 per cent were repeat interventions. The disparity between total reported assaults and homicides and police interventions in family disputes was even greater. In the 30th Precinct there were 1,932 assaults and homicides reported, or 3 a day, of which 403 were within families, compared with 1,388 family crisis interventions. In the 24th Precinct, the total was 2,759 and the number within families 508, compared with 492 family crisis interventions. Thus, in the test precinct, police were servicing three family disputes for every family assault reported, while in the 24th Precinct, family assaults outnumbered family disputes serviced by sixteen. Obviously police in the 30th Precinct had a much greater opportunity to prevent assaults by prior resolution of family crises.

No officer in the Family Crisis Intervention Unit was injured in performance of his duty, and no homicide occurred in a family where an intervention occurred.

Excluding family court referrals, the Family Crisis Intervention Unit referred over four hundred families to a wide range of public and private service organizations, including the Catholic Charities, Alcoholics Anonymous, the New York Psychological Center, hospitals and doctors for both physical and psychiatric care and legal aid. Only thirty such referrals were made by police in the 24th Precinct.

The project evaluation found that the police themselves were initially cynical and skeptical but developed a professional pride in their ability to handle situations. Police-community relations were greatly improved, benefiting the entire precinct. Homicides, assaults and violence arising from family disorders were reduced in terms of both immediate violence and prevention of future violence. Crises were handled with much higher professional skill, affording protection to families and officers alike. Earlier identifications of potential problems were made and the opportunity for social service agencies to perform effectively enhanced. The project—18 officers out of 18,000 in the department called upon to perform family crisis intervention services —shows what can and must be done in terms of professional police skills if we are to do more than wrestle with the frustrations of modern urban living. If we could measure, we would find most crime comes from chronically disturbed and broken families. Professional police could direct agencies with preventive skills to these families in time to save their children from lives of crime.

To do anything well, you must understand what it is you are trying to do. For the police this requires no less than an understanding of the dynamics of our people. They deal with every aspect of society and often at times of highest emotionalism. Officers, black and white, policing a black ghetto must be thoroughly familiar with life in the ghetto—its patterns, its habits and needs, its personalities and powers. Somehow police must understand the motivations of youths who commit most crime and the family disorders that start children toward lives of crime. Anything less than sensitive understanding is dangerous —dangerous for the police, dangerous for society.

Never doubt that tensions are high in urban slums—a spark and there is violence. The right combination of high tension and sudden friction and there is a riot. It will be this way until we eliminate the urban slums. This is simply human nature. You cannot cram so much misery together and not expect violence. A racist policeman—and the strains, so often subconscious, of racism in America are pervasive—is a threat to the peace when he patrols the ghetto. Years of careful effort to develop close relations with the community can be undone by his single act.

Only extremely sensitive, skillful and well-trained officers can work that volatile environment effectively and develop the firm neighborhood ties that are essential if preventive services are to be utilized, crimes to be known, criminals identified, fugitives found. Without such professionalism, police will most likely continue to precipitate incidents that ignite the highly flammable fabric of compacted urban frustration.

Every major riot of the 1960's prior to the widespread violence following the murder of Martin Luther King arose from a police incident. At Watts it was an arrest for drunken driving, accomplished only after an "officer in trouble" call, and following a long argument on a hot Wednesday evening while a crowd gathered and a mother berated the police. At Newark a cab driver was arrested and hauled, some thought with unnecessary force, to a precinct station. A crowd gathered, rocks were thrown, a riot started. At Detroit, a "blind pig," an after-hours drinking place, was raided by the police in the early hours of a summer Sunday. Though the place had been raided on earlier occasions, this time insufficient numbers of officers were used. Following hours of delay in which police scuffled with party revelers and drunks, a crowd slowly gathered and the worst riot of the decade had begun. These three riots visited more death and destruction than all others of the 1960's combined. The price of unprofessional police conduct in our times is beyond measure.

Much police activitity is relatively simple and does not require extensive training. Included are such routine matters as guarding school crossings, opening bathroom doors to free children locked inside, getting pet cats off rooftops, checking parking meters and directing traffic. Such work may in fact be good training for those who will become professionals. The nature of police work, however, so interweaves the easy and the difficult that an officer today must be prepared for both, even spend much time doing things that could be done by less skilled people.

Family shooting, automobile accident, lost child, noisy party, traffic jam, burglar alarm, belligerent drunk, desperate psychotic, parade, vandalism, holdup, mugging, numbers sale, boy in tree, tavern brawl, dope ring, riot, frightened wife, student sit-in, civil rights demonstration: all call for the police to perform, usually at once and often under conditions of highest stress.

Police helpers, apprentices, cadet corps and practice training can develop professional officers and can perform many subprofessional functions. If police helpers are used in sufficient numbers with clear demarcation of their duties, professional skills will be released for use where badly needed and professional competence will not be diluted by boredom, waste and inefficiency. Salary differentiation between the apprentice and the professional officer will offer advancement, status, and a better chance for rising pay scales that are the foundation of professionalism. No police department has fully developed the use of nonprofessional police helpers or established adequate professional standards for officers.

To be truly professional, police must have high standards of education and personal competence in a wide range of subjects with continuous and developing training. Some idea of what professionalism in police work means can be gained from the FBI. Before World War II, FBI agents were required to either have a law degree or be certified public accountants. At the time, most local police had not finished high school. Probably one-fourth had not finished junior high school. Personnel standards in large measure earned the FBI its reputation for excellence. By contrast, in 1965 there were only twenty states with colleges or universities offering any police science course, yet the need for police science skills was overwhelming. Where would they be learned? The police departments themselves had little capability to identify the skills needed, much less develop them. Departments characteristically have been headed by chiefs who began on the same force a quarter of a century earlier and supervised by men who began there as rookies and worked slowly up, learning from their own limited experience and by experience alone. Most never attended college. Many never finished high school. They and their departments for the most part have not experienced the vitalization of entry into their ranks of experienced people from other police departments or from related disciplines of science, education, business or administration.

In three years following passage of the Law Enforcement Assistance Act of 1965, thanks to public concern and federal stimulation, the number of states with colleges and universities offering police science courses more than doubled and the number of persons enrolled tripled. Still, only a small fraction of the need was being met. While most major police departments were requiring a high school diploma of recruits, many were not. Only one department—the Multnomah County, Oregon, sheriff's office—experimented with a requirement of a college degree for rookie deputies, but nationwide the great majority of all rookies never went to college and many did not finish high school. In many departments, even major ones, 10 per cent or more of the officers had not finished junior high school.

To send those men to the local college campus to control a crowd or remove sit-ins from the president's office can cause a predictably violent confrontation. The police, ten or fifteen years older than the students, know they will probably never have the chance to develop themselves or to make a contribution to society that compares with the potential of the students. They suspect the student will make more money his first year out of school than a policeman makes during any year of his life. They think of the wife and three kids at home and of the extra income they must make by moonlighting to care for them. They see the student's beard and his provocative actions and they cannot control themselves.

The existing educational gap between the police and the public is adequate reason itself, badly needed professional skills aside, to require college training for police. Half of our college-age population is now in college. We need to draw more than half of our police from colleges merely to begin to reflect a common experience with the public served.

Advanced research in physical, mechanical and social sciences must be greatly expanded to aid police. Exchanges of personnel between police departments and other professions in business, industry, education and government in a broad range of areas including security, management, personnel, business practice, science, research, electronics, medicine and law will vitalize both parties to the interchange. New ideas, competences and techniques will enrich police work. A substantial interchange of personnel among police departments and with related nonpolice activities will provide enlarged opportunities that can help police attract the best people the country is producing.

The police have an important role in the education of the public about crime and its prevention. Teaching young people about dangerous drugs, merchants about protective alarms and devices, and public officials about police requirements will make for better enforcement. Only professional police will be convincing instructors.

To fail to provide adequate protection for life and property is to fail in the first purpose of government. A police department must have enough officers to enforce the laws and perform the services entrusted to it. Police manpower must be increased in many places, but to seek the fulfillment of law enforcement needs by the mere addition of more police can escalate tensions and violence. The basic shortcoming of police service today is in its quality, not its quantity. Personnel standards must be constantly upgraded. The day is not far distant when major parts of the entire officer complement will need extensive college training or degrees. Specialists should have advanced degrees in criminology, police science, public administration, law, medicine, chemistry, psychology, sociology and other disciplines. In times of change all personnel need to train constantly in their areas of performance, developing new techniques, anticipating new problems.

The average policeman makes only three-fourths the money the Bureau of Labor Statistics estimates as necessary to raise a family of four at a minimum standard of living. In a day when we need better-trained police and, in places, more police, tens of thousands of policemen hold one or more additional jobs to support themselves and their families.

In cities of more than 500,000 where salaries are generally highest, half of all new officers started at salaries below $6,556 in 1967. Half of all patrolmen, men who have not been promoted to at least a noncommissioned officer rank regardless of length of service, earned less than $7,591. It is burden enough to start at a salary inadequate to meet your needs. To start there and know that officers serving ten years or longer are making only a thousand dollars more is to abandon hope for a decent living or college for the kids, not to mention comfort.

On the average, Americans pay about fifteen dollars per person for all police services, federal, state and local. Since police work is basically human activity, 85 per cent of all police budgets are for salaries. To double national expenditures for police would cost about one-thirtieth of our annual federal expenditures for national defense. Are the internal danger and the worth of liberty so slight that we will not do this? Decades of neglect and the unrest of our times make this step essential to our domestic tranquillity.

Higher salaries will attract well-educated people, provide opportunities for intensive, continuous training, eliminate the need for police to moonlight and make enforcement of its prohibition possible. Better salaries will attract men with professional skills, standards of competence and personal qualifications consistent with need. They will attract the people who will see the reforms that are needed and make them.

Disregarding the human and social price, the economic cost of crime is tens of billions annually. Better salaries can provide an increased efficiency and improvement in the quality of personnel that would more than compensate for the increased cost. Without fundamental improvement in the salaries of police and other public servants, nothing we do to improve their service will be long or significantly successful. To obtain excellence in police, prosecution, courts, corrections, education and other services we must attract the people that can bring excellence.

If we think in terms of old conditions—the constable, the rural sheriff, the service rarely needed—we will never bring ourselves to act on the scale required. The leisurely adaptations of yesteryear are inadequate to the stormy present. Our interdependence is so great, and the service that police provide so important, that their calling must be among the foremost in our society. This means we must establish new priorities and begin to provide resources for vital public services that can begin to do the job that must be done.

The job itself constantly grows more complex. Beyond the many faces of crime, the police confront the leading edge of attempts to cause change outside the system of law. The pressure for and resistance to change create high tensions that sometimes erupt. In a mass society there are few ways for the individual or the group to effectively express themselves. We have few opportunities to affect issues or decisions of vital importance to us and to those we love. Demonstrations, protests, sit-ins, riots and campus disturbances are efforts of the powerless to influence or to exercise power. Suppress the chance for protest, for speech that can be heard, and our troubles can only increase.

Open dissent and acts of civil disobedience arising from youth and social unrest require a law enforcement presence in the most difficult confrontation between public and police that a nation can experience. The nature of that confrontation, whether violent or permissive or clear, firm and fair, may well determine the future course of our country. If we are divided by hatred and paralyzed by fear, we will not go forward despite our immense capability. If police are effective, we will have the time needed to educate, house and employ our people; to bring health, relieve tension and anxiety, reduce injustice, offer equality, provide for each of us his chance for fulfillment.

The policeman is the man in the middle. It is imperative that he stay in the middle. For him to move right or left will widen the gulf that divides us. A government can endure only if those who enforce its laws have the confidence and support of the public they serve. Without that support, law enforcement is a contest. Crime is unreported. Criminals are concealed. Prevention is impossible.

Tomorrow only a highly professional, broadly skilled, sensitive, temperate police force, deeply traditioned to be fair, to adhere strictly to the law itself and to enforce it firmly, can assure safety, liberty and human dignity. We must start to professionalize our police now and build fast. The control of every type of crime depends upon it.

10

SERVANTS OR OPPRESSORS?

I F too many Americans believe the police do not follow the law; that they do not really warn the ignorant of their rights and question unfairly and relentlessly; that they arrest and hold without significant evidence and bring an exhausted, confused, injured and frightened victim to witness a line-up and then urge an immediate identification of a suspect; that they stop and frisk on bare suspicion or to intimidate; that they tap phones and bug rooms and perhaps worse; that they care more for order than justice; that a pay-off is possible and the rich will never have serious problems with police; and if Americans harboring these beliefs live in mass urban society where police are always present and must be; where you see them every day; where you feel powerless against them and do not trust them—then there is trouble. Then we have become a nation in which the breakdown between the public and the police is complete, in which we govern by force and fear while denying freedom.

The police relationship with the community served is the most important and difficult law enforcement problem of the 1970's. Effective law enforcement depends not only on the respect and confidence of the public but on a close, direct and continuous communication between the police and every segment of the population. Indeed, one is not possible without the other. Strong community ties provide the base for police prevention, deterrence, detection and control.

Only where such ties exist do police have the chance to work effectively. School authorities can then learn how to watch for, identify and report the presence of narcotics peddlers and student addicts. Students are more likely to understand the risks of LSD and refuse to joy-ride with friends in a stolen car. Slum dwellers who know police can complain of consumer fraud in the hope that action may result. Addicts, alcoholics and the mentally ill may find treatment through police who are in contact with friends, family or those in need themselves. The thief and the dangerously violent, frequently unrestrained in the ghetto, will be identified and apprehended when the people trust the police.

Strong police ties with residents in every block of densely populated slum areas are the only opportunity for law enforcement to measure the dimension and the nature of our vast unreported ghetto crime. Police presence can cool rather than heat angry street crowds where officers are known and respected. On campus, police can placate rather than provoke. Organized crime cannot reap the profits of gambling, narcotics traffic, loansharking and prostitution, which account for most of its income, where police-community relations are strong and there is law enforcement commitment to eliminate such activity. Extortion, blackmail and strong-arm tactics cannot then be safely used.

Runners, peddlers, pimps and their sources are readily known within the community. There is no more effective, efficient, dependable or inexpensive way to curb dangerous drugs than through community contacts. In truth, there is no other way. The people of a neighborhood know the addicts and they know the suppliers. A consensual crime in which the victim will not willingly reveal the seller, narcotics traffic poses perhaps the most difficult of all investigative challenges. The people who live where criminal activity flourishes risk most from its presence. They see what is visible, suffer most of the crime that occurs, and are the sources of leads and evidence of criminal activity.

A police department with strong community contacts has the best chance of anticipating incipient riot conditions. Measurement of tension can be made accurately only from within a community. People there, concerned for their own safety and welfare and that of their neighbors, anxious to avoid a riot, to control narcotics traffic or to alert police to a fight, are the foundation for effective police action.

"Police-community relations" is a facile phrase that is difficult to define. A cryptic term, it conjures so many different meanings that we often miss the real one.

Police-community relations are not public relations. They are the farthest thing from mere appearance or "image," as we have come to call it. Police-community relations measure the substance of the most significant quality of police service—the total bundle of all the communications and contacts, of all the attitudes and points of view that run between the police and the entire community they serve; what every element of the city knows and thinks of police service—and most important, what is done in the light of that knowledge and opinion.

If police are alienated from the public, they have mistaken their very purpose and lost their chance to succeed. Is the relationship between police and community one of confidence, of respect, of understanding of the importance of the mission, of full support and free interchange? Or is it a relationship of fear and mistrust? Or perhaps there is no relationship at all, but rather a void, an absence of communication or simply a community's awareness of a foreign force characterized by a specially painted automobile with an unknown person behind the wheel.

Police-community relations cannot be analyzed in a vacuum. The policeman is not a scientist working in a quiet and isolated laboratory. His laboratory is a whole city with all of its people and all of their needs. Relations between police and the community mirror the social structure and the quality of the lives of the people within a city. If there is poor communication between police and public, then that is not the only inadequate communication within that city. It merely reflects other isolations, other alienations and other estrangements. But when segments of the city cannot communicate with the police, the problem becomes critical; for the police, who must serve every part of the city, cannot perform effectively unless they have full and reliable information concerning crime. The police bear most of the pressures, tensions and strains that result from a general lack of communication. It is important, therefore, that they recognize this problem.

The need for close ties, mutual confidence and respect, and open communication is greatest between police and poor and powerless people, young people and minority groups—because this is where the preponderance of our police action has been, is and will be until society addresses itself effectively to the injustices these groups suffer and the rush of change which affects them so vitally.

After the rioting in Watts in August of 1965, it was found that the forty-five-square-mile section in south-central Los Angeles placed under curfew during the disturbances contained less than 15 per cent of the city's people but that historically more than 60 per cent of the city's arrests occurred there. The inhabitants of Watts realized, as no one else in that city, the burdens of crime and the hardships that it inflicts on the poor. Most of the people there, as with most of the people in every area of every American city, believe in this country, respect its laws and want to live at peace, with their own rights and those of their neighbors fully protected. They saw the police, however, not as their protector but as their oppressor. They saw arrests made more frequently as a means of intimidation than a method of law enforcement. They feared and distrusted the police. In Watts they also knew "When the sun goes down, there ain't nobody here but us and the police."

Perhaps the clearest indication of national inadequacies in police-community relations is the fact that most crime today is not even reported; that fact speaks volumes. Why should people against whom most crimes are committed not report them to the police? What is behind this critical lack of communication? The consequent loss not only to the people who suffer the crime but to the community as a whole is immense. Where police-community relations are poor, the police cannot effectively control street crime. Organized crime will flourish. Juvenile delinquency will spawn criminals.

Commissioner Howard Leary of the New York Police Department says he has 30,000 police community-relations officers, because he knows that the total relationship of his force to the public is the measure. Every individual officer must understand that he serves the public and he must conduct himself in a way that secures the public's confidence and support. He must realize that he protects their safety and defends their liberty. This is a difficult assignment in our trying times.

The reasons for the frayed quality of police-community relations are many and complex. Public unrest inevitably leads to friction with police, because police are the law's principal agents of social control. When unrest causes serious disturbances, student confrontations or riots, lasting antagonisms are born. That the police are so frequently untrained, inept and emotional compounds the aggravation.

The automobile has played a major role in the process of deterioration. It has made us the most transient and urban nation in history as neighborhoods swiftly change and individuals live in ever increasing anonymity. It has created enormous traffic control problems. The police cite millions of citizens for traffic violations—people who will have no other direct contact with police and no other arrest in their lives. The trauma of the speeding ticket followed by an appearance in traffic court does not often make good police relations with the public. To many unthinking drivers the police become the enemy and the traffic laws a game. They see no harm in speeding, making illegal turns, ignoring signals—unless they are caught.

The car provides a most attractive source of youth crime. As one ghetto youngster was heard to say, "A car is like part of your wardrobe, man. You can't go nowhere without one." On more than 750,000 occasions a year that part of the wardrobe is obtained by stealing.

Car theft ranks third in frequency among all index crimes and second in financial loss—$750 million a year before recovery values are deducted. It consumes a major portion of law enforcement's efforts and finances. The State of California alone spends an estimated $60 million on law enforcement activities related to car thefts. More harmful, 64 per cent are committed by people under eighteen.

Police techniques for controlling car thefts, which are mostly joy rides, cause constant friction with the young. Few youngsters who drive regularly haven't felt themselves accused of car theft by the demeanor of an officer who has stopped them. Nearly 90,000 youths are arrested each year for car theft. More than one-half of all federal juvenile and youth offenders sent to prison are convicted of car theft. More than one-fourth of the federal prisoners of all ages are serving sentences for interstate transportation of stolen motor vehicles, and most were initially arrested by highway patrol and local police who turned them over to federal authorities.

Good police-community relations would greatly reduce car theft. Perhaps 80 per cent of all car thefts could be prevented by manufacturers and owners. Doors are left unlocked in four out of five cars that are stolen. If the doors are locked, a car is obviously much more difficult to steal. Keys are left in the ignition of 42 per cent of all cars stolen—an invitation to a young boy to drive off into a life of crime.

Police working closely with social organizations, students, churches and other groups can effectively impress on the public the importance of locking cars and other preventive practices. Police can enforce laws penalizing people who fail to lock their cars where such laws exist.

Of all the effects of the automobile on police-community relations, the most significant was the introduction of cars for patrolling. The car took the cop off the beat where he knew the people in the neighborhood. It removed him, for the most part, from friendly and direct contact with the public. It made him anonymous to the people he served. The drive for efficiency forced by inadequate financial resources brought more and more squad cars and finally the one-man squad car. Physical separation of the police from major segments of the public was soon complete, and the consequences grave. A major portion of the American public, for a variety of reasons, feels a little shudder when a squad car goes by.

The scarcity of officers from minority races in nearly every major police department in the nation creates another severe barrier to good relations between police and the community. There is no major police department in which the proportion of Negro officers on the force approaches the proportion of the city that is Negro. The proportion of Negro officers on the force is rarely one-third the proportion that Negro citizens represent in the city population as a whole. The impact of this disproportion is heightened by the much higher crime rates in the black ghetto.

With our history of racism and the deep tensions among minorities living in the high-crime areas of the slums, the use of poorly trained, undereducated, economically insecure white officers to police central city makes effective performance virtually impossible and frequently inflammatory. Society has slowly wrung the joys of life from those who live in the slums, leaving a high concentration of psychotics, the sick, addicts, alcoholics, vagrants, delinquents, rampant crime—and intense hostility toward authority. To this volatile mixture add a law enforcement element of a different race, often with a Southern background or from a recent immigrant group, nearly always lower middle class, and you increase the difficulties and provocations on both sides.

There are few major police departments in the nation that

have not sought Negro and other minority recruits vigorously. None has been wholly successful. We have permitted conditions to deteriorate to the point where it is very difficult for the young black man to accept law enforcement work. The police have seemed the enemy to him, his family, friends and neighbors for too long. Indeed, black officers often do not want their neighbors to know they are police. They ask for assignments far from their homes. They wear ordinary clothes in the neighborhood where they live, changing into their uniform at the precinct station. They may tell friends and neighbors they work for the telephone company.

We cannot expect to maintain order in the black ghettos with white officers. The hostility toward them is not unlike that toward a foreign army of occupation. Today, while an uneasy order generally prevails, crime prevention, crime control and crime solution are hopelessly ineffective in many parts of the slums. Criminal investigation by white officers in black or Mexican-American slums is greatly inhibited. Undercover work is impossible in a segregated society. When the community fails to report narcotics, theft and violence, and undercover activity is impossible, there is nowhere else for law officers to turn besides the informer.

If we fail to move toward integration and if slums continue to decay, it may become impossible in time to have a white police presence without the display of massive force. When Mayor Carl Stokes ordered only Negro officers into the Hough area of Cleveland in the July 1968 disturbance, following the slaying of several policemen, he may have prevented widespread violence. If property was lost, lives were saved. But in the long run the use of segregated police forces—black in black areas, white in white areas—will divide rather than unite. That it worked as an expedient in an emergency in 1968 should serve to warn us that we are drifting toward even greater segregation.

Police departments must be thoroughly integrated in command and in operations throughout every part of the city. Officers of minority groups must be enlisted in great numbers, for until this is done strong police-community relations in the areas where they are most essential will never exist.

Good techniques for building police-community relations are becoming well identified. Highly successful efforts by such pioneers as Chiefs Herbert Jenkins of Atlanta and Curtis Brostron of St. Louis have shown the way. Youth-police athletic leagues are invaluable. It is difficult to overestimate the impact that a few policemen playing with a bunch of kids may have not only on those kids but also on their friends and their families and later their children. Police need to work with youth constantly. Once a child comes to think the policeman is his enemy, he will be hard to reach. Too many youngsters come to think that too early. The police have to be involved with youth because young people account for the increase in crime.

Cadet corps, scouts, boys' clubs and schools are important police opportunities. A major crime prevention opportunity is lost because police, already undermanned, rarely have the trained personnel with the time to do a fraction of the work needed with young people. A high priority for any city that wishes to reduce crime is a comprehensive effort to involve its police officers in activities with youngsters who need their help most.

Community storefronts that really afford citizens the chance to report crime, make suggestions or complaints, or just talk are important. The disorganization of society in ghetto areas is so complete that merely a place to complain releases tension and, skillfully handled, creates understanding. Block organizations and community committees established to communicate with police can be very valuable. If they really began to open relationships so that crime was reported, they would make a vast difference in the police potential to control ghetto crime.

Police must reach what former Chief Tom Cahill of the San Francisco Police Department called the "unreachables." Committees of citizens in slum areas, realizing how important law enforcement is for them and having the opportunity and sense of responsibility to discuss the communities in which they live with the police department, can tie police closely to the people they serve.

Perhaps the most difficult and troublesome procedural issue in police-community relations is arrest. Arrest standards must be clearly understood by the police and uniformly applied. The public must also understand the rules and believe they are equally enforced. Citizens must respect arrest procedures as being firm but fair; too often the authority for arrest is vague, capriciously applied and inadequately reviewed. Arrest has been used as a technique of intimidation to maintain ghetto order. "Law and order" sounds ominous to the ghetto dweller, because it implies force and he has known order without law.

Police stop and frisk suspicious persons in some parts of some cities as a regular enforcement technique. A careful search of persons arrested on probable cause will be necessary sometimes for the safety of the officer. But if the technique is used without probable cause to believe a violent crime has been committed and if it is used excessively—if it is abused—it will undermine the very purpose of the police department. It will negate their opportunity to communicate, to relate, to serve the public, because there will be a loss of respect, there will be fear and no confidence. In parts of some cities most males over ten years old have been frisked by police, often without cause.

A prompt arraignment—presentment to a judicial officer as soon after arrest as is possible—is an absolute requisite in a free society. In most of our cities we should have the facilities and court personnel to provide arraignment at any hour. Because no magistrate was available in 1890 until the day after tomorrow is no reason why in a great metropolitan area today a magistrate should not be available at all times. The disappearance of a husband or son or friend being held in jail for hours or days pending arraignment is a source of great anger toward the police. Anxieties have been heightened for thousands of poor families by our failure to provide this essential right to prompt arraignment. Many held incommunicado have lost their jobs and some important prosecutions have been forfeited or made more difficult through the failure to arraign in time.

Central booking—one place in a city where everyone charged with crime is listed—is a clear need in most cities. For the already frightened family of a person lost in a riot, an unsuccessful effort to locate him is terrifying. In the wake of some of the most severe urban riots of recent years, hundreds of people have gone frantically from precinct to precinct to find out what happened to their husbands, wives or children. In light of reports and rumors of death and destruction, such anxieties add immensely at a critical time to the tensions and frustrations of the city. It is a situation the police can avoid. Police must understand the need and manifest a desire to perfect their service. Citizens have a right to know immediately if a loved one is in police custody.

Every complaint about police performance is important to the police, and none must be ignored. Nothing will give more confidence to the community than to see not only that police are fair but that they recognize the possibility that even they can err, that an officer may be guilty of misconduct, and that if he is, the laws and regulations will be applied firmly and fairly. Citizens must know that the police will act in complaint matters. Police review boards—in which citizen panels finally determine allegations of police misconduct and appropriate penalties—are desirable in most cities. Some civilian review of police conduct, whatever the form, is always essential. Ultimately the police are responsible to the public, not to the chief of police.

Repressiveness is the worst kind of police-community relations possible. No one likes to be pushed around, to be denied his rights, and few will readily forget or forgive it. Police brutality, sweep arrests, roundups of people when there is no probable cause to believe they committed a criminal act, and the unnecessary use of deadly force—these embitter beyond all other acts.

Many chiefs have taken the "tough" line and found that they can then visit some parts of town only at their peril—and these are most likely to be precisely those parts of town they most need to visit if they are to do their job. Chief William Parker of Los Angeles would not visit Watts after the riots in August 1965. His reception would not have been friendly had he tried. Chief Walter Headley of Miami, who launched one of the most widely publicized tough policies—special forces stationed in slum areas with orders to shoot looters—did not return to Miami from his vacation during the major violence of August 1968. His tough line may have comforted the people on Lincoln Boulevard and in Coral Gables, but he had created intense bitterness where the real problems existed. His mere presence would have been a provocation.

The tough line may maintain order temporarily and may even reduce crime in the places involved for a time, but a heavy price is paid. We must ask ourselves what the police were doing yesterday that causes them to get tough today. An even-handed, firm, fair and effective policy is all that will work.

If people have the capability of committing crime, we cannot long deter them by talking of tough police action. The country is too big, the opportunity for crime too vast to rely on police toughness to thwart criminal intent. It is basically a bullying technique, implying force, even unfairness. It should comfort no one interested in his safety or his liberty. It demeans human dignity. Even if the tough line worked—and it does not—it still should not be used, for it causes greater cunning.

The need is for police who by every action show they understand that their mission is service; police who by the strongest institutional conviction would not impinge on the rights of the weakest or the most despised and helpless individual.

The strength of law enforcement cannot come from the club and the gun. It must come from devotion to duty executed with high skill. Any contest with law enforcement must be uneven not because police are bigger and stronger and more numerous, but because they have the best of every skill needed to perform their many roles and the confidence of the people they serve. Nothing else will give stability, confidence and security.

In the stormy years of change ahead we should recognize what is really involved in the relationship between police and the people they serve. It measures the differences between a social order based on force and one based on the will of the people —the difference between authoritarianism and democracy. Only where the police serve with the wide cooperation of the public is there government of the people, by the people and for the people. Where the police maintain order by force, there is totalitarianism. The difference is between a government that subjects its people and one that serves them. One brings fear—the other, freedom. One is a police state—the other, a free society.

11

POLICE IN TIMES OF TURBULENCE

CONVENTIONAL problems of crime prevention and control are exceedingly difficult today, the burdens of police staggering, but new manifestations of social unrest impose even more dangerous assignments.

Riots are not new to our nation. We were born in revolution. Mob violence threatened the Constitutional Convention in Philadelphia in 1787, causing that convention to provide in the Constitution itself for a federal place of government and other places as needed to safely conduct the activities of the new republic. We witnessed mass violence over various issues in most parts of the country before the Civil War. Riots resulting from draft and racial protests caused five times more deaths in New York City in July 1863, one week after the battle of Gettysburg, than all the deaths in all the riots of the 1960's throughout the nation. In 1919 and in 1943, the nation suffered major race riots. Few decades in our history are unscarred by riots.

The rest of the world—free nations and totalitarian, permissive societies and authoritarian—is experiencing vast unrest. Every continent is affected. Youth, minorities, oppressed and sometimes just frustrated people have protested, demonstrated and rioted. In the last half of the 1960's death and property destruction stemming from social unrest have occurred in Canton, Paris, Tokyo, Warsaw, Sydney, Prague, Mexico City, Rome and Madrid.

In America after World War II protest first strongly manifested itself in the civil rights movement. Racism, the treatment of the Negro, the one huge wrong of the American people, was the most morally outrageous fact of our lives. As the movement began in the mid-1950's, it offered little threat to order or power. Bus boycotts, freedom riders, street rallies only slowly began stirring people. To most this activity seemed remote, undignified, unintelligible and a little bizarre. Gradually the truth emerged and the enormity of the social injustice afflicting one-tenth of our people was seen, at first darkly but soon, and with increasing light, by all Americans. Despite the great lethargy of the years following the war, civil rights legislation that was intended to achieve equal justice was considered and enacted. Among the major Congressional acts of the epoch were the civil rights bills of 1957, 1960, 1964, 1965 and 1968. States and localities also legislated to achieve equal opportunity in housing, employment and education.

Institutional change came slowly, and while promising much it delivered little. For the poor, newly aware of their own deprivations and with higher expectations to reinforce their anger, rage finally overwhelmed reason, apathy, indifference and resignation, and in 1964 the reverberations shook whole cities. At Watts in August 1965, we witnessed the loss of control. Until then order had prevailed, albeit a violent order. Then even order was lost.

Riots are the antithesis of humaneness, individual dignity, reason and reverence for life. They manifest an abandonment of faith in a system and of hope that it will right wrongs. Irrational and convulsive, they are as if society were having a seizure. The damage and death they inflict are chiefly to self. Rarely does substantial violence extend beyond places that the rioters know best and the people who live there.

The people of Watts knew they suffered far greater misery than any other part of the city. To many there it seemed as though white society intended to keep them in poverty, on relief, uneducated, unemployed, out of the way. Everything they

had seemed to have been handed to them, uncertainly and begrudgingly. There was nothing they could do for themselves.
Welfare was forced upon them as a necessity for survival. Education was a sham. All power, wealth and opportunity were absentee. They paid more for food, clothes, liquor, whatever they
bought, and they got less. They had no rights. Success and
money fled from the area. They lived amid a new colonialism—
a colony of poverty, ignorance, sickness, unemployment, vice
and crime—isolated in central city.

Order had been maintained by white police through force.
Nearly all blacks in Watts believed the police were brutal, deliberately brutal, as a technique of control—though not without
some psychological satisfaction. So Watts blew wide open one
day and rocked America to its foundations.

Only a week before the explosion in Watts, President Johnson, the nation's most powerful political figures and the united
Negro civil rights leadership had gathered under the dome of
the Capitol in Washington to witness the signing of the Voting
Rights Act of 1965, promising reform through the democratic
process. But for the blacks of Watts voting was not the issue.
There had been no outright prohibition and little systematic restraint of their right to vote. It seemed irrelevant in the hopeless
urban environment. The great moral crusade led by Martin
Luther King seeking change through nonviolence and exempli-
fied by the Selma-to-Montgomery march in the spring of the
year lost its luster with the explosion in Watts.

When the flames died down in Watts, thirty-four people were
dead—twenty-eight Negroes, three Mexican-Americans, one
Japanese and two law enforcement officers. Eight hundred and
seventy-five were injured. Nearly four thousand were arrested.
Two hundred and ninety-five buildings were destroyed, five
hundred and thirty-six damaged, more than a hundred and fifty
looted. The destruction was not entirely capricious. Patterns
could be detected, reflecting community attitudes toward certain businesses—the absentee owner, the no-credit merchant,
the usurious lender. Soul brothers were spared.

When order was restored in Watts, Los Angeles was polarized and frightened. Gun sales soared to ten times normal for more than a month. Rumors of new violence were rampant for weeks. Detected instances of arson were high for months. The people were stunned.

As with every other major riot to date, there has been no massive repetition in the same place. It hurts too much. But did we learn anything from Watts?

The white community was outraged and called for repressive action. The week following the riots a police attack on a Black Muslim mosque near Watts injured several and destroyed the interior of the building but aroused little protest. They were searching for guns, the police said, but none was found—or likely to be found encased in panes of glass deliberately broken. Between August 13 and noon of August 27, the office of the Chief of Police received 17,864 letters and telegrams, 99.13 per cent of them commendatory in tone and expressing an insistence on order. Americans fear riots more than most peoples in the world because our lives have been more secure and comfortable than most.

Tensions remained high and the potential for riots widespread through the end of the decade. The largest and most tragic riots occurred at Newark and Detroit in July 1967. In every instance of riot, it was the police who were called on to restore order. Often untrained, frequently without adequate manpower, police on occasion could not effect control until the riots ran their course.

By the end of 1967 deaths resulting from all riots in the 1960's exceeded two hundred, 90 per cent blacks. Fewer than fifteen law enforcement officers had died as a result of riots. While the National Guard had been mobilized, placed on riot duty and in direct contact with mobs, the Army had never really been effectively deployed in the streets until after a riot was over. The main burden fell on the police.

Slowly the police departments in the major cities of the country trained and prepared for riot prevention and control. It was not easy. Understaffed, fragmented, untrained, unequipped and emotional, many police did not want riot control responsibility, viewing it as a military responsibility.

Intensive efforts by the International Association of Chiefs of Police with financing and support from the United States Department of Justice slowly led to the development of effective techniques of prevention and control. The best police leadership soon realized that riot prevention was possible and that police conduct itself was a major factor in prevention. In week-long conferences of police chiefs at Airlie House near Warrenton, Virginia, in January and February of 1968, followed by regional meetings in California, Georgia, Oklahoma and West Virginia for key police personnel, 90 per cent of the effort was devoted to analyzing and developing methods of riot prevention. Police-community relations were seen as the key. Only clear lines of communication with the ghetto could provide notice of and the opportunity to relieve tension. This rapport was considered indispensable.

Few public servants are more aware of the emotional environment in which they must work—and frequently of their own emotion—than chiefs of police. Caught in a constant barrage of rumors that sometimes seem to be a form of psychological warfare, most learn to be skeptical, to check carefully, to act with caution. Rumors of wild violence, of coming riots, of police and public assassinations are now almost routine for police.

After the riots it was human nature to look for a conspiracy or to assume concerted action as their cause: such a widespread social explosion could hardly be spontaneous. The police and the public saw conspiracies in a thousand forms. Raids were made on empty tenements, and helicopters searched for barns in Alabama said to be full of automatic weapons and armored cars. As with the tragic assassinations of the decade, it was too cruel to think there was not some foreign conspiracy responsible. The conspiracy theory provided the happiest answer: it implicated only a few evil people, people we could all hate. It

could not be ourselves and our fellow citizens who were responsible; it had to be strangers, alien and dangerous. The remedy
was easy—find the guilty few. Nothing was really basically
wrong with us—no need to rebuild slums, educate, employ,
give health. Everything in our nature wanted to find a scape-
goat. Conspiracy alone could relieve us of a sense of national
guilt. The most unpleasant fact could be ignored, that the ghetto
is rampant with crime and that black rage is real.

People without facts were discovering and proclaiming all
sorts of conspiracies. Governor Spiro Agnew of Maryland as-
serted in a statement carried on the front page of many newspapers that he had evidence that the riots of that month, July
1967, in Newark, New Jersey, and Detroit, Michigan, were
caused by the same conspirators. He never presented his evidence to the governors of New Jersey and Michigan or, though
asked, to the Attorney General of the United States. He had
none. Nor did anyone else come forward with evidence of conspiracy. There was none. And if we yield to the belief that a few
conspirators can cause turbulence of such dimension, we divert
ourselves from the truth and from the wretched who plead for
justice. We fight phantoms while the forces of violent potential
continue to grow.

That we have had no concerted effort to cause riots or to
rebel does not mean it cannot happen here. A clear lesson of the
1960's is that the nature of events changes quickly. New frustrations burst forth. New violence occurs. Unrest spreads to new
groups and interests, and police must constantly adapt to deal
with new types and new techniques of protest and new potentials for mass violence.

While the underlying causes of social unrest exist, the police
will have to cope with violence. Their conduct will be critically
important to the nature and dimension of violence. Repression,
desperation, the coincidence of outrage and psychosis can cause
planned violence. Guerrilla warfare is a possibility in America.
It is evidenced in many parts of the world today. America has

no natural immunity. We have witnessed nothing at home that approaches the inhumanity experienced in Nigeria or of Americans themselves in Vietnam. As violent as our climate is, it does not yet give rise to emotions that cause men to cut out and eat human hearts or carry heads on poles. If planned guerrilla violence ever does come, it will have been spawned, if not created, by brutalizing conditions that we have failed to end. Revolution never sprang full grown from the mind. It is nurtured for years in an unjust environment where fundamental changes are occurring that bypass the deprived until they finally realize the possibility of reform—and act.

Police training and preparation for the summer of 1968 was just under way when Martin Luther King was assassinated on April 4. In the immediate aftermath of that tragic murder, the nation witnessed something we should clearly understand and never forget. People feel. Their feelings are interrelated. All of America was stunned, though not all in the same way. Black Americans felt a wide range of emotions: emptiness, frustration, hopelessness, anger, hatred. And they expressed their emotions in many ways. Some wept. Some came out into the streets and waited. Some who claimed not to care for Dr. King did wild things. Some sought violence, some the chance to loot or burn. There was a clear causal connection between the acts of tens of thousands of people separated by hundreds of miles and Dr. King's death. A great man was dead, an apostle of perhaps the most important lesson a mass society can learn—change through nonviolence. People in scores of cities across the country understood that a powerful leader, a persuasive voice demanding social justice, a great unifying force, had come to an end just as had so many of their own dreams—and they reacted.

Until Dr. King's death, riots had sprung from a single incident in a given locale, with police nearly always present. But on the night Dr. King died, people came walking out of their homes in many parts of many towns and cities across the country. Crowds gathered over widely separated areas. Police control problems exceeded anything ever before experienced. Traffic stopped, stores closed, windows were smashed, there was looting, arson and finally deadly violence—all to honor the fallen prophet of nonviolence. In recurring waves for several days, as if we had been seized by a nationwide fever, there was more rioting, looting and arson. Over one hundred cities were affected. In a vague way they tended to delineate areas where Dr. King had labored. Little reaction was felt in the Far West, and the black South responded with its conditioned caution. Federal troops were committed in Washington, Chicago and Baltimore.

Police conduct was far superior to that of 1967. With a potential for violence many times greater, there were fewer deaths than in the Detroit riot alone and less property damage. Generally the police acted with balance. They did not use excessive force. The number of Negroes killed by police was far lower than in previous riots. Law enforcement prevented looting and property damage where they had adequate force to control the crowd, but did not risk the lives of the public or police officers by acting without adequate force. They avoided both the risk of overreaction, which ignites a counterforce, and of inadequate action, which permits a small disturbance to grow into a riot. They acted with awareness that we would have to go on living together tomorrow. They demonstrated that under the most difficult circumstances riots usually can be prevented and, when prevention fails, controlled with minimum loss of life and property.

The summer of 1968 was not scarred by renewed outbreaks as expected. Perhaps the April riots reduced the intense emotional build-up that generally precedes a major riot. The number of small disturbances—riots in the making—actually grew —unless the improved system of reporting such incidents was misleading. Instead of severe riots, the summer of 1968 passed nervously and turbulently, but without devastating outbreaks. The Department of Justice counted forty-six major and serious riots in June, July and August of 1967, compared to twenty-five in the same months of 1968. Minor riots, however, increased from ninety-two to ninety-five. More significant, there had been eighty-seven deaths in riots during the summer months of 1967, but only nineteen in 1968. The National Guard was called eighteen times in the summer of 1967, but only six times in the summer of 1968.

The fever of repression was present throughout the presidential election year, but the police rarely succumbed. In the dog days of 1968 we heard much loose talk of shooting looters. No civilized nation in history has sanctioned summarily shooting thieves caught in the commission of their crime. China, India, Japan, Brazil, Mexico, France, Italy, Poland—nations throughout the world have experienced wild rioting with physical assaults and property crime. None has used shooting as a control device. Could America be the first?

Police have learned to deal more effectively with riot potential. Prevention efforts have succeeded, and control methods have avoided scores of deaths. But the security afforded by better police efforts has lasting value only if full advantage is taken of the time it affords to remedy the underlying causes. It is a delaying game.

Meanwhile, adequate numbers of police must be trained to prevent and control riots and looting. Where prevention fails, rioters must be arrested whenever arrest can be accomplished without causing excessive violence. When police manpower is inadequate, or attempting arrest risks massive violence, rioters should be identified so they can be formally charged at a calmer time.

The first need in a riot is to restore order. Police have learned the price of escalating violence. The random shooting of looters will only increase disorder and destroy the possibility of respect for law. The massive shooting of looters may temporarily stop a riot by its terrorizing effect, if government is prepared to resort to such tyranny. But that government must then gird for the next stage of response: revolution.

Adequate police manpower properly deployed can prevent looting on any large scale. A well-trained force arresting, citing or, at least, identifying offenders for prosecution can bring a rioting mob under control. To say that when looting starts, shooting will start means either that shooting is preferable to nonviolent control or that there are not enough police present to bring about control. Whatever the circumstances, we cannot exhort a people to respect the law while we shoot looters, unless we believe lawless tyranny and inhumane use of force by government can be made respectable.

Where a jurisdiction has failed to provide adequate police protection, or the unpredictable nature of a disorder makes arrests impossible, other control techniques, including the use of tear gas, may be necessary to restore order, protect property and save lives. The use of deadly force, however, is unnecessary, ineffective and intolerable. It demeans human dignity—life itself. It is a violation of law in most places and should be everywhere. Anyone who thinks bullets are cheaper than adequate numbers of $15,000-a-year college-trained policemen values life cheaply and misunderstands human nature. A reverence for life is the only sure way of reducing violent death. Where the basic instincts of a nation do not rebel at the excess of summary execution of looters, its people have been deeply hardened to violence as a legitimate method of control. During the 1968 presidential campaign, Spiro Agnew, candidate for Vice President of the United States, supported the shooting of looters. So long as such a position is acceptable to any substantial portion of the public, violence is inescapable.

Far from being effective, excessive force, inhumane action and bloodletting can only lead to further division and further violence. In every effort at control, law enforcement must always remember that when order is restored, we shall have to go on living together, black and white, forever on the same soil. The threat of excessive force leads to the cries heard during the disorders in Miami in 1968—"They want to kill us all." A bystander observed, "The worst part is they believe it." Police violence creates the very violence its advocates claim it is their purpose to avoid. The death of a twelve-year-old looter or the innocent bystander will inflame minds and spirits for a generation.

Persons under the influence of alcohol killed 25,000 Americans in automobile accidents in 1967. Fewer than 250 people died in all the riots of the 1960's. Looters, as such, killed no one. Why not shoot drunken drivers? What terrible fear or hatred causes some to call for shooting looters when no one is heard to suggest the same treatment for a far deadlier crime? Is it that white America understands, even knows, those who drive after drinking, while poor ghetto blacks are incomprehensible and therefore threatening to it? We can prevent most drunken driving. Indeed it is inexcusable not to, but rarely do we hear outcries of indignation, let alone calls for blood, when a family is destroyed by a drunken driver. Most of us have only pity and sorrow, because we understand and accept things common to our own experience. Many believe drunken driving is less controllable than murder, because from their own experience they know an intoxicated person is not rational. But a broader experience tells us most murderers are even less so. The emotional disturbance underlying them doesn't arise from a few cocktails one evening, but from months or years of emotional strain. It is in fact far easier to control drunken driving than murder.

Some have suggested that the real purpose behind the threatened shooting of looters as proposed by a few public officials is intimidation—deterrence by fear of instant bloody reprisal. If so, the purpose is wrong. A system of law must operate with integrity. It must do what it says it will do. The first rule of law enforcement is never bluff. If you announce you will shoot looters and do not, the next time you will not be believed. Police are trained never to pull their pistols unless they intend to use them. This is basic. If you threaten to shoot and do not, you risk the lives of law enforcement officers and others unnecessarily when the perpetrator takes you at your word and shoots in self-defense. Every threat creates danger. The empty threat encourages the lawbreaker to go ahead and do what he will.

A nation that permitted the lynching of more than 4,500 people, nearly all blacks, between 1882 and 1930 can ill afford to engage in summary capital punishment without trial in times like these. Between 1965 and 1970 only three men were legally executed throughout the entire nation for all the inhumane murders and assaults we suffered. Is our determination to achieve equal justice under law so slight that we prefer to imperil the lives of officers, looters and innocent bystanders and risk escalating riots rather than improve the control methods of our police? Is shooting an updated technique of control through fear, much as lynching was scarcely a generation ago?

Leadership and tradition determine the use of deadly force by police. Compare the conduct of federal officers enforcing a court order admitting James Meredith to the University of Mississippi in September 1962 with police conduct during the disturbances at South Carolina State College at Orangeburg in February 1968.

At Oxford, Mississippi, in the late evening of Sunday, September 30, 1962, fewer than two hundred federal officers—deputy marshals, border patrolmen, and Bureau of Prisons guards, none trained for such duty—acting under the direction of Deputy Attorney General Nicholas Katzenbach, confronted a crowd at least five times their number. The place was strange to them, the whole environment hostile. Scores of shots were fired by the crowd toward the university's main administration building, where the federal force stood. While tear gas grenades were used during the many hours of wild assault, no federal officer ever drew his gun. Two people were killed and many injured, but no shot was fired by any law enforcement personnel. National Guard units and federal troops arrived after hours of delay and restored order on the campus. James Meredith was enrolled and completed his course of study at Ole Miss. Many people could have been killed that night, including James Meredith, whom law enforcement was present to protect. The federal court order was executed. Some offenders during the night of violence were subsequently charged, despite the difficulty of identification. A number of students were disciplined by the university. Had the federal officers returned fire, there is every reason to believe dozens of people would have been killed.

At Orangeburg, South Carolina, in March 1968, state and local police and a National Guard company were sent to control students at the virtually all-black campus of South Carolina State College. Protests against a bowling alley which refused to serve Negroes had caused several days of disturbance. The officers knew the campus and environs well. They were trained in riot control and equipped with gas. A few hundred yards away, a National Guard unit stood by. The total police presence outnumbered the students. While a few onlookers said students had fired on the officers, most observers did not agree, including many of the officers themselves. Certainly no officer was hit by gunfire. In a sudden burst, without warning, the police fired on the students at point-blank range and killed three. Thirty were seriously wounded. Many were shot while lying on the ground. Most were hit in the back, several in the bottom of the feet. One policeman emptied his revolver at the crowd. The shotguns were loaded with heavy buckshot—a deadly charge. No gas or other less deadly control technique was used.

The difference was between leadership and disciplined personnel which sought to avoid violence and emotionalized police leadership which reacted with massively deadly violence. By firm discipline, wider violence under great provocation was avoided at Oxford. At Orangeburg unnecessary use of force brought death.

Imagine the public outcry if, rather than a small Negro college in South Carolina, it had been Amherst, Princeton, Clemson, Rice or Claremont. Consider also the anguish and rage that this incident caused for thousands of Americans, black and white.

Present unrest is far too serious to be dealt with superficially, for life to be threatened casually. Throughout the history of law enforcement in our nation, the use of deadly force has been restricted generally to circumstances in which the lives of officers or other people are endangered. Some laws authorize the use of deadly force when it is necessary to effect the arrest of a fleeing felon or prevent his escape. In practice, this action has usually been taken under circumstances where life was imperiled.

The best rule is stated by the FBI:

> The most extreme action which a law enforcement officer can take in any situation is the use of firearms. Under no circumstances should firearms be used until all other measures for controlling the violence have been exhausted. Above all, officers should never fire indiscriminately into a crowd or mob. Such extreme action may result in injury or death to innocent citizens and may erupt into a prolonged and fatal clash between the officers and the mob. The decision to resort to the use of firearms is indeed a grave one. Such a decision must be based upon a realistic evaluation of the existing circumstances. Among the important considerations, of course are the protection of the officer's own life as well as the lives of fellow officers, and the protection of innocent citizens. A basic rule in police firearms training is that a firearm is used only in self-defense or to protect the lives of others.
>
> The firing of weapons over the heads of the mob as a warning is objectionable. In addition to the possibility of injuring innocent persons by ricocheted bullets or poorly aimed shots, the firing may only incite the mob to further violence, either through fear or anger. At best, this is a bluffing tactic and a basic rule when dealing with a mob is never bluff.

In guidelines prepared for law enforcement agencies, the International Association of Chiefs of Police states:

> The use of firearms should be considered as a last resort, and then only when necessary to protect the lives of citizens and officers.

The excessive use of force can have unforeseen consequences. The FBI Manual points out:

> Unwarranted application of force will incite the mob to further violence as well as kindle seeds of resentment for police that, in turn, could cause a riot to recur.

General Robert H. York, commanding officer of the United States Army troops deployed in the Baltimore riots in April 1968, explained his use of the minimum amount of force required to be effective as follows:

> Force invariably produces counterforce. Here in Baltimore we did not have a race riot, as such—and it was my endeavor to prevent that if at all possible. This is what the extremists want, as you know, and I feel we would have been playing directly into their hands if we had created a situation whereby this would have occurred. And, of course, if it had occurred, the loss of lives and destruction of property would have been immensely greater than I feel it has been. No one—your women, children—would have been safe under these kinds of circumstances, and neither would any home in the city . . . we know from experience that when there is indiscriminate firing, more innocent people have been killed than guilty ones.

A fundamental purpose of government is to protect the lives and property of its citizens. This aim requires the maintenance of order under law. We cannot fail to make the effort essential to effective control. We know that riots can usually be prevented and can always be controlled. The question is whether we have the strength to act wisely, or will resort to the law of the pistol.

Even if our only purpose was order, and life meant little, still the most effective control technique would be balanced enforcement, not intimidation. All our experience tells us this.

Intensive police training can bring a new discipline and a new effectiveness to police control efforts. The police must be thoroughly prepared to act swiftly to avoid overaction or underaction, permissiveness or repressiveness. The chance to stop the incipient riot is with the local police and with them alone—unless we retrain and garrison soldiers throughout our cities. By fast, careful, firm action local police can catch trouble before it is out of control.

What do the police themselves believe? After all, they are the ones urged by some to pull the trigger as looters flee toward a crowd. Rarely do the police favor use of deadly force except as a last resort to prevent a direct and immediate threat to life. Few officers want to be haunted always by the memory that they have killed someone. If shooting is required to save a life, it is tolerable; if it is only to prevent looting, or even flight, it is not. Well-trained and well-equipped police can develop techniques for apprehension or identification for future arrest. Killing is an unacceptable substitute.

Who are the rioters and looters in question? Who is it we would shoot? Nearly all have been Negroes. The riots of the 1960's were usually in the black ghetto. Except for color, their backgrounds have differed widely. Data gathered about persons arrested for participating in some way in a riot show that 29.4 per cent of those arrested in Boston held white-collar jobs compared to only 6.4 per cent in Grand Rapids. In Grand Rapids 14.2 per cent were skilled workers, while in Buffalo 3.5 per cent were. In Newark 59 per cent were unskilled but employed laborers, and in Boston 47.1 per cent were in that category. In Boston 48.4 per cent were married compared to 22.5 in Cincinnati. In Grand Rapids 19.7 per cent were between ten and fourteen years old. In Cincinnati 73.4 per cent were between fifteen and twenty-four years old. In New Haven 35.4 per cent were between twenty-five and thirty-four. Of persons arrested for looting in the riots in Buffalo, Cincinnati, Detroit and Newark, 48.1 per cent were between ten and twenty-four years of age. In Detroit 37 per cent of the self-reported rioters were women.

Thirty-five per cent of all riot area residents between the ages of nine and sixty in New Haven and eleven per cent in Detroit are estimated to have participated in rioting.

From so diverse a population in various cities, it would appear that the potential for riot participation includes nearly everyone in the slums. Juveniles and those of mature age, skilled and common labor, unemployed and office worker, male and female. A rioter may be anyone in the part of town where riots happen. It is wrong to assume that rioters are simply irresponsible citizens who take out their frustrations in lawless acts—and are therefore fair game for repression.

Student unrest usually shifts the confrontation from one between police and poor urban blacks to one between police and young advantaged whites from middle class families. This will humanize our attitudes toward use of excessive force, because people with power in America will know the students and show greater concern.

In all likelihood, it will be many years in most parts of America before police can operate without pistols strapped to their waists. This fact reveals a great deal about us and our police. Even in these restless times the police in England carry no guns. Foreign visitors, even people from countries torn by guerrilla warfare, are unbelieving when they see guards wearing pistols in the United States courts and in shrines, museums and memorials of this nation.

Why, in a time of turbulence, is the direction within most police departments toward more firearms and greater fire power? The reasons are many—traditions of force, the brutalization of our participation in Vietnam and the almost total failure to provide better weapons and techniques. But the underlying reason is our insistence on relying on force as a major method of social control and the false assumption that, however ignoble, force can prevail. Compounding the difficulty is the present psychology of police personnel. It is paramilitary, based on force and fear. The level of violence in England is lower than ours, but far from wholly absent. Yet in England there is an understanding, unexpressed, that the game of crime is played without guns. Ways are found to break and enforce laws without the threat of deadly force. Violence does not then beget violence.

The whole role—and prevailing attitudes—of the police changes when instruments of force and death are not their visible sign of authority. When the police carry guns, their power does not rest on respect for the law and confidence that it will be fair, or in the belief that the policeman is a friend serving the public interest, but on the ultimate power of his gun. The best, if not the only, way to challenge police power so threatened is by resort to the same means. This is one of the principal reasons guns play so large a role in crime in America. Without guns public service would become more than an incidental part of the police function. But it will not be easy to reduce police reliance on weapons, even though experiments in the United States have shown it possible, for we have tens of millions of guns lying around this country, a history of gunfights and an atmosphere of violence where unknown and unrestrained psychotics are allowed to possess and are conditioned to use guns.

Guns spell trouble for the police. All but 20 of the 475 law enforcement officers murdered in the line of duty from 1960 through 1968 died from gun wounds. Of the hundreds killed annually by police fire, a small minority were shot by officers defending their lives or the lives of others from direct threat. These deaths have added immeasurably to the climate of violence in America. They destroy the chance of the police to establish any communication with major segments of our people.

A well-disciplined, well-trained, adequately manned police department with effective communication with all segments of the public can successfully prevent riots in America today. That failing, it can meet and contain rioting and violence with superior force. Excessive force, or its opposite, unrestrained lawlessness when riot violence, looting or arson occur, promises the holocaust. To overact—by use of firearms, as an example—may seem at the moment to end a threat. To underact—by leaving the scene where looting is occurring, for instance—may seem to escape harm's way. Neither proves long-lasting. Either is likely to cause violence.

Those who, without understanding or humaneness, encourage shooting do the police no favor. Both overaction and underaction increase danger for the police as well as the public. Balance will encounter fewer risks in the long run. If America has a conscience, if we are to survive as a wise and courageous people, we had best turn away from wild talk of shooting looters and face the reality of our troubled times. Greater effort at prevention, with new techniques developed to meet new challenges, offers the time needed to make essential reforms. By measured action, police can provide us a few precious years to activate the massive effort required to rebuild our cities, to restore faith in our citizens, to begin to offer to every American the promise for his own fulfillment: to be educated, employed, housed and healed in body and mind.

Racial injustice is not the only cause of turbulence in America today, nor is the ghetto the only place police power has been used to maintain order without law.

The force that police currently use in junior high schools and high schools and on college campuses will make it difficult to change their image for decades. Attitude samplings at Texas Southern University indicate that before the student disturbance in the spring of 1967 more than 90 per cent of the students thought the Houston Police Department fair and that it did not use brutality. Following an evening of disturbances, during which a policeman was killed by gunfire, students were routed from their dormitory with or without pajamas and photographed for the national press lying on the ground under police guns. Property damage inside was capricious and extensive—furniture broken, books and clothes strewn, TV sets knocked to the floor, a wrist watch on a dresser smashed. After the incident a poll indicated a complete reversal of opinion. Ninety per cent of the students then thought the Houston police brutal and unfair. Hundreds will remember that night for the rest of their lives.

As a result of the way police removed them from Hamilton Hall, dissidents at Columbia University in April 1968 achieved far greater support for their positions and their tactics than from all their own words and deeds. More severely damaging than the immediate impact of police repressiveness was its long-range effect. Many of those who observed or were involved will never again have a tolerant attitude toward police and the police function. Authority too anxious to win battles can lose wars.

The most dramatic and controversial conflict between citizen and policeman in the 1960's was at Chicago during the 1968 Democratic National Convention. It divided the nation as traumatically as a major riot. Perhaps most Americans who watched the confrontation on television thought force should be used, because they did not like what they saw and heard from demonstrators. But irreconcilable division and intensified radicalization of our people are the only result we can expect from excessive police force. This is the aim of those who seek division. When it occurs, they succeed.

There was no need for police violence at Chicago. It did not maintain order, enforce law, prevent crime or protect lives and property. It did the opposite. Other situations far more volatile involving many more people and equally provocative tactics had been controlled without significant violence. At Chicago police violence was a tactic of control.

The march on the Pentagon in October 1967 brought ten times more people to Washington for protest than came to the Democratic Convention for that purpose. Opposition to the war in Vietnam was at fever pitch in late 1967. Talk of violence preceded the march for months. With tens of thousands of people in front of the Pentagon, some doing their utmost to provoke, the amount of physical violence unleashed was insignificant. Only a handful were injured and fewer than twenty allegations were made that excessive force was used by officers. So disciplined was law enforcement that several hundred of the most determined protesters who remained camped at the Mall entrance of the Pentagon for thirty hours after the major confrontation were removed without a single act of violence.

Violence could have been the technique chosen to control the crowd at the Pentagon. It was not. In such a highly charged atmosphere scores of officers and others had as their sole duty the prevention of any police violence. Ranging behind the front lines to observe police and soldier conduct, to calm and to relieve men under pressure, they maintained discipline. The major concern was professional performance of duty. The most intensive police training in preparation for the march dealt with avoiding violence. If there had been a significant police assault on protesters at the Pentagon in October 1967, it could have caused hundreds of injuries and might have led to widespread violence on campuses over the country and major demonstrations of violent potential in many cities.

Protesters are human beings like the rest of us, and however obnoxious they may seem to many, law enforcement must not deliberately injure them. When it does, it has violated the very principles that law relies on for the order which the rioters seem to threaten. When police exceed their authority, even while making arrests for serious crimes, ours is no longer a government of laws. If law enforcement yields to those who call for violence, only one response is possible among people who believe that what they are doing matters.

At Chicago the belligerent approach was followed. The stage had been set following the riots in April 1968 after the death of Dr. King. Reacting to the vast emotional wave that follows such a cataclysm, city leadership called for the tough line, for maiming looters and shooting arsonists, for repression. Perhaps those least affected and most afraid were assuaged, but the police have had to go on living and working in the South Side and the

West Side. The tactics employed by the police during the April riots had saved lives but were repudiated by the mayor, and the tone of future repressive enforcement was set. The very method of setting that tone—public rebuke of police leadership—weakened the position of the Commissioner of Police prior to the convention and its confrontation between police and protesters.

Police have more reason to be emotional about such events than anyone. And frequently they are. There are deep-seated feelings within departments, pent-up emotions calling for force. Police leadership is sensitive to this tension, lives with it, works with it, endeavors to diffuse and control it. When the word comes from on high to crack skulls, the difficulties of police leadership in controlling its own men are compounded.

The attitude of leadership in Chicago was clear to anyone who tried to work with it. No help was wanted from Washington. The same assistance that was employed at the Republican Conventions in San Francisco in 1964 and Miami Beach in 1968 was not only tendered in Chicago but was on the scene. It was shunned. There was no desire for sensitive handling of the expected demonstrations. The city wanted to show the nation that it would not negotiate with or yield to the rabble. Efforts of the federal Community Relations Service to establish communications between city leadership, law enforcement and the leaders of the protest were rejected by the city.

This strategy was senseless from every standpoint. If you assume the demonstrators are the enemy and bent on violence, you want to stay as close to them and know as much of their motives and moves as possible. You reduce your chances to control them if you do not talk. With communication there is always the possibility that the protest can be shaped and guided to keep violence, and the injuries risked by violence, at a minimum.

It was clear for months that many protesters would come from all over the country to Chicago. The surprise was that so few came. There is no way in an open society to prevent people from coming to a given community. You do not have to invite them, but you must recognize their ability to appear on the scene as a fact of life. Responsible government must prepare to cope with them. Tear gas and clubs will not be adequate. They will only heighten anger and restlessness.

At Chicago, strategically and obviously, Soldiers Field, the huge stadium on the lakefront, surrounded only by parking lots and freeways, was an ideal location for the planned protest. Big, isolated and relatively indestructible, it offered a high control capability. But permission to use it was denied. The result of the failure to communicate and to provide a place and opportunity for protest was crowds in Lincoln Park and Grant Park and confrontation at the worst possible place, Michigan Avenue, where hundreds of uninvolved and innocent people were affected.

When the provocations came—and that they were coming was certain—the police were conditioned in the worst way possible. Having been told how tough they were, they set out to prove it. Leadership was unable, often unwilling, and perhaps sometimes did not even want, to control police violence. It would not have been easy to do so even if city policy had been wise and humane. It is difficult to maintain self-discipline in the face of verbal and physical abuse of the dimensions concocted by angry, wild young radicals. But self-discipline is the only effective antidote. It is all that sets a system of law apart from tyranny. Make arrests as warranted and possible, but never lose discipline. Law enforcement officers cannot wildly break ranks, chasing and clubbing people, and expect no repercussion. When they can do so with impunity, we know we are in a police state. We are a long way from that revolutionary stage where crowd control is not easily attainable without police violence. Provocation calls for professionalism of the highest order. The professional by definition is ready for anything and never breaks the rules of the game.

Protest leaders immediately sense local law enforcement attitudes. They have usually been through such collisions before.

Those who really seek to divide our people know the best way is to get a cop to act like a fascist pig when he is called one. Rhetoric becomes fact.

Coming to Chicago, the protest leadership saw the obvious. The city would follow the hard line. The word was out: be tough. Few of the protesters wanted violence. Time and again they sought real communication, real negotiation, intermediaries. But the city had a different policy—no negotiation, no tolerance for troublemakers.

Thus it was that in Chicago, second only to New York in its manpower capability to control an angry crowd, wild violence occurred. The city had 12,000 officers in its police department, reinforced by strong contingents of neighboring local police, a large county sheriff's office and an effective state police. The Illinois National Guard had begun riot control training over a decade earlier under the supervision of one of the most experienced and sensitive men on the American scene, Governor Otto Kerner. Guard units had effectively prevented riots in Chicago in 1965 and 1966 at times of great tension by carefully balanced actions.

But in 1968, 6,000 federal troops, in an unwise and virtually unprecedented move, were pre-positioned in and near Chicago —largely at the Great Lakes Naval Training Center. Whatever their deterrent effect on the protesters and the public, it was slight on the Chicago police. Against—or because of—such overwhelming force, several thousand people, including at most several hundred really capable of even minor violence, emotionalized the community so that the police humiliated this great nation in the eyes of the world and ourselves. Law enforcement did not follow the law. There was a massive failure of leadership. We saw the grim possibility of a police state. As a result, there are literally hundreds of thousands of young people who will never again look at the blue uniform without some residual hostility. They have seen a raw demonstration of police capability for violence and they will never forget it.

The majority of the public and particularly the people of Chicago may uncritically support the law enforcement policy used at the Democratic Convention. Los Angeles supported Chief Parker following Watts. They reflect the polarization within any community that comes from fear and hateful conduct. Given the opportunity to understand, the public will see the perils of such a policy. Of all violence, police violence is the most dangerous. Who will protect the public when the police violate the law?

Deliberate efforts by the Nixon Administration to emotionalize the public before and after the massive Moratorium March in November 1969 can only divide the nation. To have built up expectations of violence and then to characterize the march as violent after its occurrence, despite the facts to the contrary, may have been good short-range politics—it appealed to millions of affluent, uninvolved and unconcerned Americans—but it overlooked the consequences of tomorrow. We cannot radicalize and divide with impunity.

It is the role of leadership to enlighten and guide, to appeal to the best in us, to manifest the qualities on which survival in the years ahead depends—gentleness, tolerance, humaneness, a reverence for life. We get little of this from our national and local leaders. The popular line is the hard line, and it sinks us steadily into greater turbulence.

12

COURTS AND PROSECUTORS:
BREAKDOWN AND REFORM

THE role of courts and prosecutors in the efforts of government to control crime is limited but critical. Essentially, they separate the innocent from the stream of persons suspected of crime, determine guilt and set penalties. They are both a screen and a conduit between police and prisons, setting the facts presented by the police against the standards of the law to determine whether a person should be prosecuted or freed, whether he is innocent or guilty and, if guilty, whether he should pay a fine or serve a jail or prison sentence. Because the law enforces the rights of individuals, prosecutors and courts have the full and equal protection of those rights as a major responsibility. This role is frequently misunderstood in times of grave concern over crime and has caused most of the attacks on the courts, but prosecutors and courts must protect the individual as well as society from transgressions of the law. To perform their role well they must be objective and nonpolitical, well organized and expeditious, professional and wise.

A district attorney's office reviews facts gathered by police and decides whether a prosecution is warranted. The test is whether, based on the evidence available, there is probable cause to believe a particular person committed a specific crime. To convict, the prosecutor must present evidence of the commission of the crime by the accused that is convincing beyond a reasonable doubt, and the evidence must comply with rules intended to insure truth and fairness.

The power of a district attorney is immense—the public has entrusted many of its most cherished rights to his discretion. While his role in the system of criminal justice is crucial, his office generally reflects the neglect characteristic of the entire justice system. The salaries of assistants are poor and the turnover is high. The typical D.A.'s office is staffed by young lawyers seeking a brief trial experience, a few people with political ambitions, some who found no other job, and often a handful of older lawyers who could not or did not succeed in private practice. With rare exception, there is little chance for career development. Jobs there offer little prestige, a limited future, and salaries set by state legislatures, county commissioners and city councils. The attorneys who head the offices are generally elected to office in state government and are political appointees in the federal system, usually the patronage of a United States Senator, since the appointment requires Senate confirmation.

Rarely can district attorneys attract, develop and retain our best young lawyers, although security for the public, fairness for the individual and justice itself depend on the quality of their public service. In a survey in 1965 it was found that only 18 per cent of the more than six hundred Assistant United States Attorneys in the nation had practiced law for five years. The average salary was 15 per cent lower than that of federal lawyers in Washington with the same length of practice. A career program with good salaries, opportunity for promotion and transfer, and continuing training and legal education will be necessary to develop high professional standards in these offices. Without excellence in them we cannot expect the system to perform well.

Only excellence can assure initiative, and offices of prosecution must initiate if we are to be a government of laws. Their relationship with police, for example, is critical. Police investigative and enforcement priorities and activities necessarily determine the range of prosecutorial discretion. District attorneys can proceed only when they have evidence and must proceed when there is clear evidence of significant crime. To influence the impact of enforcement, to have priorities, to reflect the law's purpose, police must be guided in their investigation and enforcement practices by law. If white-collar crime is to be reduced, if even-handed justice is to be administered to powerful as well as unpopular groups of people engaging in the same illegal conduct, if diversions of police manpower are to be made from arrests of drunks to prevention of armed robbery, the district attorney's office must work effectively with local police, must initiate programs that plan and execute policies, practices and priorities of police activity that follow and enforce the law and devote scarce resources wisely to areas of highest need. Only offices of the highest quality can do this. Today most district attorneys' offices merely receive what police forward, and they act or fail to act uncritically.

Prosecution must proceed on facts and law without regard to politics. Political appointment of the United States Attorneys inhibits the development of a career service and divides loyalties. If we believe in the separation of powers, the executive branch should be independent of the legislative. How independent will some chief prosecutors be when they have associated all their adult life with a Senator, when he secured their appointment, when he approved the selection of their assistants, when the close association between the Senator and the United States Attorney will continue after administrations change and ostensible superiors in the Department of Justice have retired to private life? The United States Attorney and the Attorney General of the United States usually start as strangers, frequently remain distant because of the burdens of their respective positions and often are divided by the different demands of national policy and local interest. Who is likely to learn first of evidence of crime with political implications—a Senator or the Attorney General? Who is likely to be influential in a case, or a grand jury investigation, or if a riot occurs and a judgment must be made as to use of federal troops, or if civil rights or other prosecutions that are very unpopular in the district are necessary?

To assure their independence from local political pressures and their responsiveness to directives from those with the authority and obligation to equalize enforcement nationwide, United States Attorneys should be drawn from the career service without political recommendation. This is an important reform, though the need is barely visible to the public.

An analogy to the FBI is instructive. The United States Attorney has more power than the special agent in charge of a district office of the FBI. Without the United States Attorney, there will be no prosecution, and through him there can be malicious prosecution. He prosecutes nearly all federal cases developed in his district by all federal investigating agencies. He is privy to all investigative reports turned over for prosecutorial decision. Yet he is selected usually by a state or local political figure. If FBI personnel were selected in this fashion, the risks would be clear. But the FBI has effectively prevented political interference with its personnel. It is a fatal mistake for an ambitious FBI agent to seek political support for a promotion. If he does, he will not be considered.

If there is to be justice and a sound basis for confidence in the system, prosecutorial decisions must be based on fact applied to law and, like facts, must be treated alike. Any inference of political influence in a decision deprives the system of integrity. Without integrity in the system of criminal justice, there is no justice.

Pragmatism in decision making by a prosecutor, separating action from fact for the sake of appearance, is an abuse of discretion and a corruption of justice. No matter how difficult or seemingly harmful or unfortunate they prove, the prosecutor must stand on the facts and the law. If the facts say there is no basis for proceeding against a Stokely Carmichael, even if a hundred Congressmen demand it, or against an Adam Clayton

Powell, even if the case is referred by the House of Representatives, so be it. If the facts say there is probable cause to believe Dean James Landis of Harvard or Representative Thomas Johnson of Maryland or former Governor William W. Barron of West Virginia committed an offense, you must indict. If, in his judgment, the facts indicate that a Dr. Benjamin Spock has violated the law, a prosecutor has a duty to indict—or resign—even though he may believe the person accused to be morally right.

The pressures on a prosecutor are powerful and the temptations to bring a case because public or special interests demand it can be great. But making decisions for the sake of appearance is intolerable, and as nearly as humanly possible there must be one standard for all. The public can never know all the facts available to a prosecutor, and what may seem an obvious crime from press reports may prove insupportable in a court of law when investigation reveals the whole story or fails to obtain corroborative evidence of incidents that allegedly occurred or of facts that turned out to be doubtful.

The great difficulty of clearly establishing fact is a burden, inherent in the system, that a prosecutor cannot seek to overcome by public discussion. The information within his possession is far too pervasive to permit him to begin to select arbitrarily from among the pieces to justify what he has or has not done. Revelation of fact made by prosecutors outside the judicial processes of formal charges, indictments and testimony in court is a pernicious threat to freedom. For example, the Department of Justice announced that it was investigating leaders of the Vietnam Moratorium March of November 15, 1969— even citing one by name. This followed a public characterization of the march—the largest peaceful protest in our history— by the Attorney General as generally violent and his accusation that the leadership failed to do its duty after being informed through public statements by Administration officials that Communists were involved in the protest and violence was intended. Such action by the Justice Department was highly improper and can only have a chilling effect on free speech. It is harmful and unjust to the individual accused. If the Attorney General has evidence of a federal crime, he should indict in court, not in the press.

The powers of investigation and the facts and falsehoods that come to the district attorney from the whole range of police, private, and public sources are easily abused and represent a constant threat to the rights of the individual. A prosecutor can never properly divulge facts outside the courtroom without the approval of everyone involved and affected, except when necessary to inform the public on matters of general concern that do not imply an identification of particular persons. During the 1960's we witnessed many wrongful divulgences of fact, alleged fact and inferences drawn from investigative files, perhaps by prosecutors, perhaps by investigative agents or the police. Stories in magazines and newspapers, alleging or implying criminal associations or conduct and citing unnamed "official sources," severely damaged the reputations of such figures as Justice Abe Fortas, Senator Edward Long of Missouri, Congressman Cornelius Gallagher of New Jersey, Governor James Rhodes of Ohio, Mayor Joseph Alioto of San Francisco, Frank Sinatra, Roy Cohn and James R. Hoffa. Perhaps there were no "official sources" for these stories, but if there were, the conduct of such officials was inexcusable.

The question is not whether the figures involved are admirable or comtemptible, but whether the processes of criminal justice can ever be appropriately used to inform or misinform the public about the conduct of individuals. For a people who cherish freedom, the answer must be no.

Moral judgments are not for prosecutors to make. The district attorney so sure he is right—and so bent on convincing the public—that he will leak stories even though he has little or no evidence on which to indict is a menace. Of course, the press and other media render invaluable service to the public by seeking out corruption, but when they obtain and use police information, they corrupt themselves and the system of justice. We are dealing with crucial rights of privacy, reputation and liberty. Under Attorney General John Mitchell, the United States Department of Justice has regularly and often openly placed investigative information from its official sources in the press. Public anouncement of pending investigations and imminent indictments may seem to be good politics, but it slowly destroys justice. It is as dangerous to liberty for the press to use police sources for news as it is for the police to use press sources for prosecution.

America was treated to an incredible display of abusive conduct by District Attorney Jim Garrison of New Orleans during the 1960's. For reasons, or neuroses, that we may never know, he chose to trample on the raw nerve ends exposed by the nation's shock and grief at the murder of its great young President, John F. Kennedy. Three years after the assassination, Garrison launched a sensational, if bizarre, series of public charges of conspiracy reaching even into the federal government. With enigma as his evidence, he played on the profound emotional doubts of not only millions of Americans but people all over the world. For Americans seeking desperately to find some rational explanation for so insane a crime—for anything that would explain away this deed as something other than a product of our society or a reflection of our character—he supplied the hope of an evil conspiracy. As witnesses, he assembled a pathetic group of people—a psychotic, an addict, a convict taken from prison. Garrison finally focused his case on one man, Clay Shaw, chosen quite by chance, so far as can be determined, whom he tried to completely crush. Conceding that Shaw was not in Dallas on the day of the assassination, Garrison brought all of the powers of his office to bear unfairly against Shaw. Gathering the most dubious—even incredible—testimony, much of it conflicting and all remote from events in Dallas, and continuously changing vague charges made to the press, he deliberately prosecuted an uninvolved and innocent man. That the system did not succumb is a tribute to the defendant, his attorneys, the jury and the court, but America paid a heavy price. As a study of injustice and the occult in American prosecution, this sad case will be a classic. We can, and must, learn from the classics.

Courts are the major balance wheel in the system of justice. While they determine guilt or innocence and sentence persons convicted, they also insure fairness and objectivity. They neither initiate investigations or prosecutions of crime, nor execute plans to rehabilitate criminals. Their role is intermediate—to protect the innocent, to assure fair trials, to apply the law, to instruct a jury or, if trial is held without a jury, to determine guilt or innocence, and to fix penalties for those found guilty.

Basically, courts administer case loads. They accept pleas of guilty, which account for nearly 90 per cent of all convictions, but even in so doing they take precautions to be sure that the accused understands the charges against him, that he desires to plead guilty, and that he is competent to do so. In a trial the courts assure fairness in selection of a jury—and determine what evidence is admissible. A jury or, in its absence, a judge will find facts from the relevant evidence, and the judge will apply the law and in most jurisdictions fix the sentence.

Mass population, urbanization, the greater interdependence of individuals and consequent conflict, the increase in crime, and other factors have confronted the courts with major problems of administration. New rules and procedures assuring equal justice have complicated the judicial process. Bail reform, the provision of lawyers for indigents accused of crime, public payment for appeals by paupers, and other improvements in the quality of American justice have prolonged criminal litigation.

At the federal level from 1956 through 1968 there were never fewer than 30,000 or more than 34,000 criminal cases initiated in any year. The nature and complexity of the cases changed, but their number was fairly stable. The number of judges handling the cases, on the other hand, increased 45 per cent, while the number of Assistant United States Attorneys increased only 14 per cent. Simultaneously, the number of criminal cases pending—the backlog—increased by more than 100 per cent. With twice as many cases pending, only a few more new cases commencing, and far more judges to handle them, it became clear that the constitutional right to speedy trials would depend on more than just additional judges. The solution must include better techniques and more supporting personnel, in all activities of the judiciary, civil and criminal. Criminal cases should not be separated from the total operation of the courts.

There are two great arts to the judicial function: determining the rule of law and applying the rule determined—the definition of right and the method of remedy. Excellence in both arts is essential to justice. When Disraeli said, "Justice is truth in action," he meant inert truth has little advantage over active falsity, that injustice results equally from the absence of truth or action.

Long before the law explosion—the vast increase in the body of law, in the number of cases and regulations—John Stuart Mill noted of the judicial function that "there is no part of public business in which the mere machinery, the rules and contrivances for conducting the details of the operation, are of such vital consequence." Indeed, he believed, "all the difference between a good and a bad system of judicature lies in the procedures adopted" to apply the rule of law.

This much seems clear: the most just corpus juris has but academic value except as it is fairly and efficiently applied in disputes between man and man or between man and society. The vital purpose of the judiciary is not abstraction but action.

Of the two judicial arts, procedure is the more difficult and demanding. There is nothing in the Constitution or inherent in the judicial system that compels introspection and self-criticism of procedures which are essential to performance. The more complex the laws and numerous the litigants, the more difficult and demanding the judicial procedures. Today the system fails not so much because of the rules of law as because of their imprecise, inefficient and dilatory application.

More judges are needed from time to time in places of growth and where unusual litigation problems develop, but the quantity of judges is not the key to the quality of justice they administer. The judicial process is an intellectual one. The rule of law must be uniformly applied if we are to achieve equal justice. Inherently, the process cannot stand limitless proliferation of judges, opinions and precedents. The diffusion of power through too many judges will render the judicial branch ineffective and make its product—judgment—poor, inconsistent and unjust.

System must be the answer. Most cases contain no seriously disputed issue of law or fact. These need not consume judicial resources. Lawyers, litigants and other interests who do not want their cases disposed of, or who cannot adequately service their case load, must be forced by an affirmative judicial administration to settle or try their dispute. Vast backlogs are created by insurance companies that save money by delaying payment, by law firms that have more cases than they can handle, by defendants who do not want to be tried. The interests of justice require a judicial method that cuts through such motivations and clears dockets so judges can reflect on the issues that count. Courts should process cases with such dispatch that the most dismayed defendants will concede, as did Polonius of Hamlet's distraction, "Though this be madness, yet there is method in it."

We cannot tolerate conditions in which each jurisdiction is an island to itself, compelled to discover every mistake alone in its own school of experience. What works and what doesn't can be determined for most by the national experience. The judicial branch needs resources to train judges and to provide them continuing legal education in procedural and substantive matters. With the interchange of information, experience and technique, the productive capacity of present judicial resources can be substantially expanded.

A judge's time must be put to its highest and best use. Support in the form of magistrates, referees, masters, commissioners, bailiffs, clerks, legal assistants and secretaries is essential to this end. Major parts of the time-consuming burdens of judges can and should be handled by such aides. To deny such assistance is to impair justice and to deny speedy trials.

Research can also bring benefits. Automatic legal-data retrieval—the storage and electronic recall of pertinent briefs, decisions and legal documents—can save every judge many hours of labor and assure higher uniformity in decision. While the Pentagon and physical scientists spend tens of millions of dollars on computer capability for data retrieval, justice, overburdened with already vast and steadily expanding bodies of unmanageable information, has barely begun to utilize computers. The quality of justice suffers as a result.

As with every activity depending primarily on the personal services of people, as do police departments, district attorneys' offices, courts and prison systems, the quality of judicial performance will ultimately depend on the quality of the performers. Judges should be our wisest, strongest, best-motivated people. Often they are, but there are serious deficiencies in methods of selection. The democratic process does not lend itself to judicial selection. The issues are too remote and esoteric for the general public. Popularity is irrelevant to a judge's qualifications; indeed, he above all must hold a steady course, whatever the emotion of the moment. He must follow the law, however unpopular. Many lawyers who would make the best judges are not suited to political activity. The temperament, experience and personality of the politician are not generally desirable in a judge.

The State of Missouri has pioneered the impartial selection of judges. Under the plan it developed, judges are appointed by the governor from a list of persons selected without regard to partisan politics by a nominating committee composed of members from the bench, the bar and the public. Once appointed, judges have tenure and are subject to recall or to an election only if there is substantial public dissatisfaction with their performance.

Judges must always be subject to removal for serious crimes by nonjudicial power and to control by their fellow judges where incapacitated for any reason. The judiciary itself must assume primary responsibility for insuring the integrity and competence of its own performance if a balanced separation of powers is to be maintained.

Though the federal theory of the judiciary is not perfect, it may be like Churchill's definition of democracy—the worst form of government except for all the rest. Life tenure of federal judges may produce an excessive independence that makes some judges arbitrary and others careless. Where the processes of selection are not thorough and the chief judges and judicial councils empowered to administer much of the work of the judiciary fail to exercise initiative in restricting unprofessional or incompetent conduct by individual judges, the risks to the public caused by an unjust or incompetent judge with life tenure are great.

Senatorial courtesy built upon the constitutional requirement of advice and consent by the Senate effectively places the power of lower court appointment with Senators in most cases. Every President, beginning with George Washington, has had to face this political fact of life. As a practical matter, the size of the nation makes it impossible for the President and his advisers to know who is best qualified for judicial appointment to the lower courts. Mass population increases the risks that politically motivated appointments will result from mere chance acquaintance or repayment for political support. The bar associations generally have not done well in judicial recommendation—or selection. Frequently bar association involvement merely shifts the selection areas from state politics to association politics. Bar associations generally have not devised techniques to assure participation of more than a few lawyers in the recommending or screening process.

The nominations by President Nixon of Clement Haynsworth and later G. Harrold Carswell to fill the vacancy left by the resignation of Justice Abe Fortas clearly illuminated the incapacity of the bar to make its independent evaluation of the nominees. Both nominations were tragically wrong. Judge Haynsworth was involved as a judge in the same type of indiscretion that caused Justice Fortas' resignation. However venial and commonplace the conduct, 1969 was no time to nominate a man to the Supreme Court who had engaged in it. Hopefully, there will never again be a proper time. Judge Carswell had not manifested in his life a quality of performance that could support his nomination to the United States Supreme Court unless the purpose was to downgrade the Court as an institution. If the President of the United States is callous about the quality of the United States Supreme Court, the people will not be encouraged to respect the law. Both nominees had reflected through their judicial careers, and Judge Carswell before assuming the bench, a prejudice against fulfillment of equal justice for black Americans.

Is there so little relationship between the strength of our institutions and the nation's confidence in them—and between injustice and crime—that the President can ignore it in making appointments to our highest court? These nominations told black America that the one institution of this nation that promised equal justice and did the most to give it was being transferred to hostile hands. The American Bar Association through its committee on the federal judiciary was unable to see this, or unwilling to offend the President if it did. It found both men qualified—though not without dissent.

We need to develop a corps of young lawyers who have an interest in judicial service from early stages in their careers, perhaps even before the completion of law school. These individuals can work toward a level of experience and performance at which they may be considered for judicial service. Such a system would provide the opportunity for long observation and sound evaluation of the individual—tests almost totally lacking now—as well as personal preparation and training for judicial service by the person interested. It takes more than the alchemy of the President's appointive power to transform a lawyer, a politician or a bar association activist into a competent judge. Too often no other element is present.

As with so many things in our complex environment, the great need of the law is to simplify. We must reduce laws to basic principles and to numbers of a dimension intelligible to the mind of man. The proliferation of the corpus of law, the failure to distill and refine, to reduce to minimums, can hurl the system out of control. Then we become a government of men and chance, not of law.

Constant criminal code revision to evaluate the relevance of the substantive law, to repeal obsolete law and to organize and codify is essential in our time. It is also important that the proliferation of opinions from case law be curtailed. Opinions should be written only when they focus, expand or shape beyond the present refinement of the law on the subject in dispute. They are not literary exercises. They consume time and all too frequently obfuscate. A simple order or judgment will advise parties of their rights. They do not always need an explanatory opinion.

A fair and efficient system of criminal justice, providing swift resolution of cases, will serve both public safety and individual freedom. Nor can safety be found in unfairness or harshness. Ten-year sentences in lieu of two-year sentences—because we are angry—will not reduce crime. It is not the length of the sentence but the effectiveness of the correctional program that will make the difference. If it is the public safety we are concerned about, the question is how persons convicted of crime can be rehabilitated, not how long they should be locked up.

If long prison sentences deter crime, why is bank robbery the fastest increasing federal crime? Bank robbers receive the longest sentences imposed by federal judges, while most embezzlers never serve in a penitentiary. Bank burglary sentences average less than two years, while sentences in bank robbery cases average seven years. The average sentence for bank robbery increased by two years during the last several years of the 1960's in which we were so concerned about crime, yet the rate of increase for bank robberies exceeded every other federal crime. Bank robberies on the average produce only one-third the dollars per crime that result from bank burglaries and far less than embezzlements. Bank robberies are subject to investigation by the FBI in virtually every case. If good police work is an adequate deterrent, how do we explain the rise in bank robberies? The probability of apprehension for bank robbery would seem, and is in fact, high. Forty-seven per cent of all bank robberies are solved, compared with twenty-seven per cent for other robberies. It is not the fear of severe punishment that deters crime by persons capable of committing it, but an effectively functioning criminal justice system. The speedy trial is necessary not only because it is required by the Constitution but because it is essential to provide effective criminal deterrence.

A number of political leaders and social critics would lead us to believe that courts cause crime. If courts were tough, it is said, people would behave themselves out of fear of punishment. The theory has several attractive qualities. It promises relief from crime and a quick, cheap and easy solution by merely changing the conduct of a few thousand criminal judges. It offers someone other than ourselves to blame for crime, the judges—an escape as easy as the conspiracy theories to explain our political assassinations. It relieves society of both the responsibility for crime and the burden of acting to control it. Judges, isolated by tradition, and dignified, quiet and reflective by training, cannot becomingly answer, much less fight back. They are ideal scapegoats for the demagogue.

There are legions of little men who build political bases attacking courts, appealing to prejudices that cannot abide equal justice, diverting us from very real and urgent problems, leading us toward repression and injustice that would sorely compound our present problems. Of all serious crime in America, only a fraction is ever known to the police. Of the total serious crime known, barely one crime in five results in arrest. Of these, half end with convictions, and nearly nine out of ten of the convictions are on pleas of guilty without a trial. Fewer than one out of fifty serious crimes result in convictions. The direct impact of the courts on the crime rate is extremely limited.

Ironically for all the hue and cry about judicial decisions that have reversed convictions, delay in trials is responsible for failures and dismissals in a much greater number of cases. A survey of the reasons cases could not be prosecuted in the District of Columbia estimated that lapse of time was the cause seven times more frequently than the failure to promptly arraign an accused as required by the *Mallory* decision, the failure to give warnings required by *Miranda,* and violations of other decisions invoking exclusionary rules. With the passage of time, witnesses die and disappear, memories fade, evidence is misplaced and the sense of urgency is transferred to more recent crimes. Inefficiency, not fair rules, reduces convictions.

The truth is that the courts and primarily the United States Supreme Court have done more to right wrong, to perfect the system, to speed the process and to bring equal justice than the legislative and executive branches combined. That a handful of men have been capable of this shows how readily we can overcome, if we truly care.

What single act is likely to have a greater effect on our political institutions—to make them more responsive to present needs and capable of faster adaptation—than the rule established in *Baker v. Carr* and other reapportionment cases? The creaky governmental machinery of the nineteenth century, clearly inadequate to the stormy present, is being reformed by reapportionment to reflect current needs and conditions. The allotment of representatives to areas in proportion to the present population will provide a heightened sensitivity to pressing problems, including urban crime. Who is less likely to understand the nature and causes of urban ghetto crime than elderly Southern rural Congressmen—the very men who seek legislation that exacerbates the already frayed emotions of the urban poor?

The Supreme Court started us toward reforms that will reach major underlying causes of crime when it held public education segregated by government action unconstitutional. The implementation of *Brown v. Board of Education* will do more to reduce crime than police and courts ever can. The deprivation of an equal education for Negro children has been one of the largest single factors causing crime in America. At least 80 per cent of our felons are school dropouts; an even higher percentage received what little education they did get in poor schools. It is a severe indictment of our sense of humanity that it took the Supreme Court to tell the nation that segregated education is inherently unequal.

Equally incredible was the necessity for the Court to tell the lawyers of the nation, as it did in *Gideon v. Wainwright,* that there can be no equal justice unless the poor, the ignorant and the despised are adequately represented by lawyers. If the lawyers themselves do not believe these services make a difference, what is their reason for being? When the *Gideon* rule is implemented, many who otherwise have believed the nation has no intention of securing equal justice may come to believe that perhaps it really does. When rights to pretrial release are enforced and the opportunity for an adequate defense afforded, persons presumed innocent will not have to undergo brutalization while waiting trial in jail. Some will be acquitted who otherwise would have had no chance, and some will detect fairness in a system they previously believed held them purposely in bondage. Crime breeds with great difficulty in a society that practices equal justice.

An important step toward the attainment of equal justice was the 1966 decision of *Miranda v. Arizona,* which provided that the poor and ignorant, as well as the rich and informed, should be afforded a lawyer before they are questioned about their conduct by police. But many would have us think that nothing is more important to crime control than a reversal of the *Miranda* rule. America had ample crime before. The *Miranda* decision can scarcely be blamed after the fact. The best law enforcement practices had largely abandoned reliance on police interrogation as a major investigative technique years prior to *Miranda.* In 1948 the FBI, not because a court or an Attorney General told it to but because it was thought to be good investigative practice, instructed all agents to give warnings containing the essential elements required by *Miranda.* Guilty pleas are obtained in 87 per cent of all FBI cases today. The *Miranda* issues have not affected FBI performance at all.

Indeed the long-range effect of *Miranda,* when old and ineffective habits are broken and emotions subside, will be to compel law enforcement to use efficient, scientific, reliable methods of investigation. *Miranda* was decided in the only way it could have been decided consistent with equal justice. The educated know they need not answer police questioning. Hardened criminals never talk. The rich have lawyers whom they call immediately. It is the poor, the ignorant, the inexperienced and the trusting who are vulnerable to unfair police interrogation. Their awareness of this condition does not enhance their respect for law, for police or for the system.

We cannot wait for the courts to point the way to justice. All agencies and institutions must exercise initiative in the quest. Nor can we fail to implement court decisions. They are not self-enforcing. Unenforced decisions reflect a lawless society. Important constitutional rights are continuously denied by our failure to fulfill the word of law. It is imperative that we enforce such decisions as *Baker, Brown, Gideon* and *Miranda* if our system is to have integrity and our people are to respect the law. The courts alone cannot achieve enforcement of decreed rights any more than they can cause crime. Their reach is far too limited. If rights are to be fulfilled and crime reduced, society will have to act comprehensively.

The trial of the Chicago Seven, accused of crossing state lines to incite a riot at the Democratic Convention in August 1968, contained a concentrated dose of the raw stuff of our times. There was not much quiet, order, reason, dignity, art, or faith, hope and charity in that courtroom. Such qualities were not totally lacking. They shone brightly from their turbulent setting, but their supply was desperately wanting. A handful of personalities—defendants, judge, prosecutors, defense attorneys, jurors, witnesses, clerks and spectators—participated in an intense little drama subjected to the full forces of the major dynamics and emotions of the day. The strains and tensions of such powerful currents were clear in the conduct of the participants.

A vital slice of distilled truth, the trial can tell us much about ourselves and our times—but like all important messages it is not easy to understand. It is a valuable case study for examination and thought, but the student must bring as much attention to the matter between the lines as to the printed word if he is to do more than observe a wild and sometimes seemingly bizarre episode.

The principals came to court with their prejudices, of course. Consider the impact of these on the trial. Suppose the defendants believed the trial was purely political—that the court had neither the purpose nor the capability of sifting facts to find truth and applying clear and uniform rules of law to those facts. Suppose the judge, trained in law and religiously committed to respect for the system of law and the court as its highest priest, believed there was a deliberate, preconceived, continuing and contumacious effort to humiliate by revolutionary forces? Might much of what happened flow from such attitudes? Add the sudden emotionalization from courtroom conduct appearing to confirm such prejudices on both sides, and you may glimpse why what happened happened.

If there is to be a judicial process as we conceive it, there

must be reason, objectivity, fairness of purpose, diligent preparation and presentation of evidence, clear and just rules, an orderly proceeding and at least a modicum of efficiency. We know
of no better way to seek justice in contests between the individual and the state. These elements are essential to the administration of courts as we have theorized them. But courts cannot operate in a vacuum. There is no way to check the action and
passion of the times at the courthouse door. While we can strive
to imbue the judicial process with special qualities of dignity
and rationality, we must recognize that issues and personalities
come to court with antecedent history. The impact of that history is inescapable. Those who participate in writing it must be
conscious of its meaning to judicial administration and justice.
Compared to what is possible, even reasonably foreseeable, the
Chicago Seven trial was sweet reason and placidity personified.
There were fifty trial days—two months—without even allegedly contemptuous conduct. This record does not indicate an
ardent and immutable intention to disrupt. We can bring desperate, irrational, uncontrollable emotion and cunning to the
courtroom. Chains and gags can never contain it.

This test—the trial of the Chicago Eight, then Seven—which
was relatively easy, was failed miserably. We should ask why.
The capacity of the judicial system to cope with existing conditions is in question, and, ultimately, government by law. We
must look deeply for the lessons of Chicago, then, and strive to
avoid its mistakes.

This trial of torment raises many questions. Their answers
can guide us toward effective justice.

Why this "Rap Brown" statute, prohibiting crossing of state
lines for the purpose of inciting a riot—creating a new federal
crime for 200 million Americans? Was its genesis only fear and
hypocrisy? Is the trial the price we pay? Without the new law,
only several months old in August 1968, the conduct of the defendants would have been judged by state laws as had always
been the case theretofore.

Why was no permit to speak, assemble, march and petition

granted the protesters at the Democratic Convention? Soldiers Field stood empty, as did a dozen other places. What of the constitutional rights of free speech and peaceful assembly? Were they violated? Had the permits been granted, might violence have been avoided?

Why did a federal study refer to several episodes forming part of the basis for these indictments as "police riots"? Did civic leadership emotionalize police? Did the police violate the law? Could the defendants have believed they were victims of officially sanctioned repression?

Why did the state government not prosecute if defendants were guilty of acts of incitement to riot? Was the alleged conduct not a violation of state law? Did not the federal law recognize the primacy of state jurisdiction over riotous conduct?

Why was a federal prosecutor closely identified with Mayor Daley permitted to try the case? Must we not remove prosecutors personally involved—witnesses to parts of the activity complained of—from participation? How objective and fair might he seem to defendants?

Why were the cases brought? Was there really evidence giving probable cause to believe a crime was committed? Why these eight defendants out of scores who participated? Might the defendants feel persecuted?

Why was conspiracy alleged? Is it not enough to allege illegal acts of violence and incitement? Does acquittal of all defendants on the conspiracy count indicate it was a prosecution ploy? Had conspiracy not been alleged, this trial would never have occurred, and the defendants would have been tried separately.

Why was Bobby Seale indicted? Did the other defendants know he had nothing to do with planning the protest? Had he attended only at the last moment and made speeches made hundreds of times by scores of black militants, never a one indicted? Was it a sense of persecution and injustice that caused Bobby Seale to insist on his own lawyer? Was nearly all of the disruptive conduct in court caused by Bobby Seale's inclusion?

Why did the court permit Judge Julius Hoffman to try the

case? Was the inherent volatility of the trial not apparent? Was he temperamentally suited for such a trial? Was there no one on the federal bench who could have tried the case better?

These are only some of the issues that may have contributed to creating attitudes of contempt or respect for what happened in the courtroom. Respect does not come easily these days. It is not always accorded even when earned. But we must never value decorum over justice. If the rule of law is to prevail, it must proceed wisely, deliberately, fairly and rationally. It must never react in emotion. If the system is so frail that it cannot cope with events like those in Chicago, the days ahead will be turbulent indeed.

The failures at Chicago were failures of men and emotion. From that trial one could conclude that the greatest threat to judicial administration is the method of judicial administration itself. We cannot and should not judge the facts while the rights of the defendants remain before the courts, but even now we must see that Chicago offers no substantial evidence that our institutions of justice are inadequate. The principles of our judicial system will suffice if reason can conquer emotion.

The contempt power of courts must be used with wisdom, fairness and restraint. It perhaps poses a greater threat to respect for the judiciary than any courtroom conduct to which it might address itself. It is not necessary for effective performance of the judiciary; the powers of the courts to proceed are more than ample without it. If it is used unfairly, then only the courts can be faulted.

At the very least the summary conviction of the defendants and their attorneys for contempt in Chicago at the trial's end by the very judge involved and the cumulation of separate citations of contempt to impose sentences up to four years is impermissible by any standard of justice or law.

The story of government in America, of how we solve our pressing social problems, has been told in large measure through lawsuits. Sooner or later most of our critical issues and social tensions find their way to court for resolution. When the power of government impinges on the rights of the individual, judicial action is inescapable. Thus we add new chapters in the history of freedom and new names to the rolls of the little people whose stories, tragic and happy, tell the tale of liberty in our peculiar American way: J. M. Near, publisher; Newton Cantwell, Jehovah's Witness; the Society of Sisters; Edward and George Boyd, importers; Thomas E. Kepner, lawyer; Thomas Lee Causby, chicken farmer; Linda Brown, schoolgirl; George M. Bain, Jr., bank cashier; John T. Watkins, labor organizer; John A. Johnson, United States Marine; Clarence Earl Gideon, drifter; Danny Escobedo, laborer; Loretta Stack, bakery worker; Bobby Seale, Black Panther; David Dellinger, pacifist.

This is not to say our courts are perfect—far from it. They desperately need reform. The right to a speedy trial was viewed as essential to protect individual liberty when the Bill of Rights was written. Today a speedy trial is essential to protect the public and to the very meaningfulness of the system. Unless there is a clear, direct and swift connection between the commission of a crime and apprehension, trial and sentencing for the offense, the criminal will never be deterred by the fear of conviction. Swift apprehension is the greater part of the deterrent force because anxiety is highest at the moment of crime and the relationship between antisocial conduct and deprivation of liberty is then forcefully clear. The lapse of months between arrest and conviction dissipates any significant deterrent effect and reduces rehabilitational probabilities.

We cannot panic when trials are long delayed. But we must recognize that the system is not working and its purposes are frustrated. Speedy trials are essential to justice. The long, careful effort to reform judicial administration—to insure speedy trials, to enlist informed and fair-minded prosecutors, and to select wise and humane judges—will measure the quality of American justice.

13

PRISONS: FACTORIES OF CRIME

No activity of a people so exposes their humanity or inhumanity, their character, their capacity for charity in its most generous dimension, as the treatment they accord persons convicted of crime. Here are individuals who have offended, who have done those things society holds to be most abhorrent. Are not criminals the least deserving and the most dangerous of people? We owe them nothing. They owe us their liberty, perhaps their lives.

The history of penology is the saddest chapter in the history of civilization. It portrays man at his worst. His cruelty, brutality and inhumanity are unrestrained through most times in most places. Virtually absolute power over nearly helpless people has often wholly corrupted.

When Dostoevsky wrote of his years in prison in Siberia, he called it *The House of the Dead*. The title told the story. Living there was like death. Of the bathhouse—filthy, stinking, hot, filled with dense steam and hundreds of naked bodies—he wrote that if he died and awoke in hell, he would expect it to be no worse. On his last night in prison, while walking the fence that had confined him for four years, he concluded that, on the whole, the men there were no better and no worse than people generally. Among them were exceptionally strong and gifted people; the waste of their lives was an intolerable cruelty. From this experience he defined man as "a creature that can become accustomed to anything."

It sometimes seems that prisons try to disprove Dostoevsky's definition by brutalizing beyond the ability of man to bear. Jails and prisons in the United States today are more often than not manufacturers of crime. Of those who come to jail undecided, capable either of criminal conduct or of lives free of crime, most are turned to crime. Prisons are usually little more than places to keep people—warehouses of human degradation. Ninety-five per cent of all expenditure in the entire corrections effort of the nation is for custody—iron bars, stone walls, guards. Five per cent is for hope—health services, education, developing employment skills.

A glimpse of prison custody at its worst is afforded by investigations begun in 1966 of the Cummins and Tucker prison farms in Arkansas, where discipline was basically maintained by prisoners themselves—trustees with shotguns—with only a handful of paid employees supervising. Allegations, at least partially verified and largely credible, included the murder of inmates, brutal beatings and shootings. Shallow graves with broken bodies were uncovered. Food unfit to eat was regularly served. Forced homosexuality was openly tolerated. Extortion of money by wardens and sexual favors from families of inmates to protect their helpless prisoner relatives from physical injury or death were alleged. Torture devices included such bizarre items as the "Tucker telephone," components of which were an old telephone, wiring and a heavy duty battery. After an inmate was stripped, one wire was fastened to his penis, the other to a wrist or ankle, and electric shocks were sent through his body until he was unconscious.

Many American prisons include large dormitory rooms with a hundred beds or more where guards do not venture at night. There is no way of controlling violence in such an area. Beatings, deaths and suicides are frequent. Rape and homosexual cultures involve most of the inmates by choice or force. When riots and fires do not occur in these prisons, it is only because no one feels like starting them. They are breeding places of crime, violence and despair.

It would be difficult to devise a better method of draining the last drop of compassion from a human being than confinement in most prisons as they exist today. In a climate of fear and violence many wardens work only to avoid the general disorder that can wreck their prisons. They hope only to release the most violent inmates before they cause trouble inside and are so relieved to see the dangerous ones go that they disregard the public safety—and the fact that most will be back before long.

Meaningless or obsolete work is the best that prisons generally offer. More often no work is available. There is no chance for most young dropouts to continue school while they are in prison. Nearly all of the prisoners in federal youth centers are school dropouts. The offense for which they were convicted nearly always occurred after they dropped out. Youth corrections often deprive young offenders of their last chance for an education—and today that may mean their last chance for fulfillment. When that chance is lost, the probability is great that they will turn to lives of crime.

The opportunity for treatment of the mentally ill in prison is virtually nonexistent. Most prisoners suffered from some mental disturbance at the time they committed crime. More have mental health problems on leaving prison than on entering. Psychotics are frequently left for the inmates to control. Sometimes it is the psychotics who control.

Simple physical illnesses generally are poorly treated in prison if treated at all. Most prisoners, for example, need dental care. Because they are poor, they have never had any dental work, but few get adequate attention in prison. Personalities are shaped by such factors as the loss of teeth. When that loss is but one of many disadvantages and part of a dehumanizing existence, it adds its measure of brutalization. Human dignity is lost.

Drug addiction is common in prison. Many become addicted there. Even with close surveillance it is nearly impossible to keep drugs out of prisons. Guards are bribed. Some visitors with the slightest opportunity for physical contact attempt deliveries. Packages contain hidden drugs. Prisoners who get outside on work release programs, to attend funerals, visit sick relatives, or for court hearings smuggle dope in even where body searches are routine. Many have swallowed rubber or plastic packages before entering the institution and retrieved them inside.

In the light of existing conditions, knowledgeable observers find it incredible to hear those less knowing say that we coddle prisoners—that penitentiary life should be harsher. Such people do not know the facts. Much of our crime is caused by the inhumanity of our prisons and by our failure to rehabilitate those we send to them.

It is one of the larger ironies of our time that, concerned as we are about crime, the one area within the whole system of criminal justice that offers the best opportunity to prevent crime is the most neglected. In fact, neglect in the criminal justice system reaches its zenith in the neglect of corrections. There may be no comparable neglect within the whole range of government service. Yet, until the underlying causes of crime are relieved, corrections is by far the best chance we have to significantly and permanently reduce crime in America.

The most important statistic on crime is the one which tells us that 80 per cent of all felonies are committed by repeaters. Four-fifths of our major crimes are committed by people already known to the criminal justice system.

We know further, indeed we have demonstrated, that recidivism—the repetition of crime by individuals—can be cut in half. It can be cut far more than that. But if only one-half of the repeated crime we now suffer could be eliminated, society would be free of 40 per cent of all serious crime. If we are really concerned about crime, if we really care about our own character, how can we fail to make a massive effort?

Corrections in its entire range of services includes pretrial and postconviction detention in jails and prisons as well as a variety of community-based activities, among them probation, parole, work release, halfway houses and prerelease guidance centers. Neglect debilitates corrections efforts across this whole spectrum of activity. Probation and parole are rarely what they profess to be—few if any prison systems have adequate manpower to give meaningful supervision. The personnel available rarely have the training or professional competence to provide the service needed.

Jails, generally located in cities and towns, house prisoners awaiting trial and persons convicted of minor offenses and sentenced to short periods of confinement. They are manned by untrained people with no professional skills. Prisons, where serious offenders serve penitentiary sentences, are usually located in remote areas where it is difficult to obtain personnel with professional skills or to retain those that do have them. Salaries are so low, working conditions so unpleasant and opportunity for advancement so limited that few want to work in prisons. Many who might help, affected by our general fear of prisons and prisoners, would not work there whatever the conditions, while others seek the power and authority over people offered by guard duty. Many prison guards are slowly brought to brutality by the environment of the prison itself. It can happen to anyone.

We spend less than 1.5 billion on all corrections—federal, state and local—although the process offers us the chance to save many billions of dollars through reduced crime and more in terms of human suffering. As public concern over crime rises, prison budgets are cut while police budgets swell. Governor Ronald Reagan caused the best leadership in the California prison system to resign by cutting already inadequate budgets while he simultaneously sought increases for the state police.

The Federal Bureau of Prisons is probably the most effective corrections system in the nation. Its directors, Sanford Bates, James V. Bennett, Myrl E. Alexander and now thirty-seven-year-old Norman A. Carlson, are among the most sensitive professionals in the history of penology. It is responsible for 20,000 federal civilian prisoners, yet its budget for 1968, including the cost of owning, maintaining and operating expensive prison facilities, was $77 million. By contrast, the FBI, one of the more than twenty substantial federal investigative and enforcement agencies, has a budget of nearly $200 million. Every year the prison budget is the first of those in the Department of Justice to be cut by the Congress. The FBI budget is often increased above its own request. The Bureau of Prisons struggles to keep old facilities operational. Only two federal prisons, one at Marion, Illinois, the other at Morgantown, West Virginia, have been built since World War II. As recently as 1965 the only all-female federal prison had no toilets in many units—the inmates used jars.

Fewer than twenty psychiatrists are available for the entire federal corrections system, though most prisoners need mental health services that the Bureau is unable to provide. When Congress reviewed the Manpower Development Training Act program for budget savings in 1968, the first cut—and the only 100 per cent cut—was for prisoner training. That training might have kept hundreds or thousands of young men from further crime.

During Congressional consideration of the Omnibus Crime Control Act of 1968 designed to provide federal funding for state and local criminal justice needs, the issue of corrections caused a major battle. Nationwide, corrections receives about 25 per cent of all funds provided for the criminal justice process. Self-styled tough crime fighters like Senators John McClellan of Arkansas and Strom Thurmond of South Carolina wanted to limit funds available for corrections under the bill to 5 per cent. They joked in public hearings about raising it to 7½ per cent. Could the reason have been that they knew the jails and prisons of their states and many others are full of Negroes? Fortunately, such a tragic limitation was avoided. Instead, up to

20 per cent of the grant funds were expendable for corrections. This compared with a 30 per cent allocation for police to combat organized crime and an additional 30 per cent for police to control riots. Corrections remains the stepchild of the criminal justice process. The hard-liners have no interest in corrections. They want punishment.

Philosophers have debated the purpose of penology since organized societies first began killing, maiming and confining individuals for conduct or expression they did not like. In early and simple times, vengeance was the major motivation for such responses to criminal acts. Among small closely knit groups, always threatened by nature and warring tribes, vengeance may have been thought to balance accounts. From today's perspective, such acts seem cruel, as they were. But life was cruel, a bare existence often, scratched from the earth with crude tools and fiercely protected with feeble weapons. In a way, too, vengeance shows how much, how emotionally, a people care—no nonsense here, an eye for an eye. Vengeance evokes a violent response. Vengeance as a motive for punishment evidences outrage, hatred, fear and self-righteousness.

The day—if there ever was one—when vengeance could have any moral justification passed centuries ago. Vengeance, at most, can be only a private balancing, not an atonement between the individual and the state. Sheer multitudes of people in a modern society make balancing between one and so many a meaningless form of retribution. Slowly civilization came to see that action by the state could not be compared with action by individuals. The state must act justly, coolly, rationally, deliberately and systematically. No human emotion or disability, no intoxicant can overwhelm it.

Centuries before vengeance as an admitted motive passed from general practice in the most advanced nations, it was recognized as an aggravant of crime. It caused crime. Society, in its quest for justice, sought vengeance through the action of a major social institution to which the people could look for leadership—government. At a time when civilized men could hope to create a gentle, nonviolent, humane society, vengeance served as a brutalizing throwback to the full horror of man's inhumanity in an earlier time when he contended unequally against nature for survival.

The modern penitentiary grew from another theory of penology. The very name is rooted in the Latin word that gives us "penitence." To seek divine forgiveness, to repent, to be sorry for one's sins, to be alone to contemplate the pity of one's own wrongdoing—this was the theory, if not the practice, of the early penitentiary.

For the Puritan conscience, penitence may have been a powerful regimen. In our mass culture it is rarely relevant. Some who commit crime are stricken with overpowering remorse. They are tortured by their own acts. These few pose little threat to society. Remorse comes from within. No prison will create it. But for those who pose America's crime problem penitence has little meaning. By and large, their lives are so empty, they are so full of frustration and despair, they are so sick in mind and body, and their entire life experience providing them grist for thought is so totally lacking in charity that contemplation is more likely to cause anger at society's sins than remorse for their own.

Punishment as an end in itself is itself a crime in our times. The crime of punishment, as Karl Menninger has shown through his works, is suffered by all society because punishment has regularly given rise to subsequent criminal acts inflicted on the public. The use of prisons to punish only causes crime.

We cannot say we practice any theory of penology in America today. We do what we do. And what we do has practically no relationship to what we say we do. Essentially, we use penology, without saying so, to confine—as inexpensively as possible—and thus separate for a time people who have committed crime. Simultaneously, if incidentally, we punish by providing an unpleasant experience. The combination tends to turn the prisoner from any sense of compassion that he may have and from concern for anyone but himself. Where he has lived, abuse of the individual's integrity and personality has been almost total. When he comes out of prison, no other individual seems very important to him. He will try to take care of himself. He will take what he wants or needs. He will be a threat to society.

Rehabilitation must be the goal of modern corrections. Every other consideration should be subordinated to it. To rehabilitate is to give health, freedom from drugs and alcohol, to provide education, vocational training, understanding and the ability to contribute to society.

Rehabilitation means the purpose of law is justice—and that as a generous people we wish to give every individual his chance for fulfillment. The theory of rehabilitation is based on the belief that healthy, rational people will not injure others, that they will understand that the individual and his society are best served by conduct that does not inflict injury, and that a just society has the ability to provide health and purpose and opportunity for all its citizens. Rehabilitated, an individual will not have the capacity—cannot bring himself—to injure another or take or destroy property.

Rehabilitation is individual salvation. What achievement can give society greater satisfaction than to afford the offender the chance, once lost, to live at peace, to fulfill himself and to help others? Rehabilitation is also the one clear way that criminal justice processes can significantly reduce crime. Those who are sent to jail and prison commit most of our crime. We know who they are. There is no surprise when they strike again. Unlike some crimes, theirs were predictable. All we had to do was act. Our failure to act demeans our character and tortures our lives.

The end sought by rehabilitation is a stable individual returned to community life, capable of constructive participation and incapable of crime. From the very beginning, the direction of the correctional process must be back toward the community. It is in the community that crime will be committed or a useful life lived.

Prisons create the starkest possible segregation from the community—distant, isolated and full of subcultures strange to urban life. Months or years in a prison environment followed by sudden release and full responsibility for one's self—for food, clothing, shelter, associations, employment, handicapped by a criminal record and in a new, strange and emotional environment—is enough to unsettle the most stable individual. We could not devise a more traumatic social experience. Hanging over most who are released is a deep self-doubt and a long-pent-up desire for the old ways—whisky, women, cars, money. There lingers a personal disorganization, an emotional instability and the threat—almost the expectation—of returning to prison. So most return. We almost seem to want it to happen this way.

From the moment a person is charged with crime, corrections personnel should work toward the day he will return to unrestrained community life. Accused people should be released pending trial; we say they are presumed innocent, and that presumption should be respected. They may need help and can be given it, including supervision that will protect the public and that is not inconsistent with their presumed innocence. Many of the personal problems tending them toward crime were visible long before a first arrest. They were having trouble in school—and dropped out—or were unemployed, running with a gang, drinking too much, taking dope, or obviously mentally unstable. Counseling, guidance and treatment can be offered to them immediately. If the suspect is on parole from an earlier sentence when arrested, there is a high risk that earlier correctional effort has failed. Parole supervision should be so effective that a quick estimate is possible. A hearing can be held to determine whether the conditions under which he was placed on parole have been violated. If they have been, the parolee should be fitted back into his program or into a revised program more carefully tailored in the light of his apparent failure.

Following a conviction, an analysis of the individual, his background, his history and his personal physical, mental, emotional, family and social condition must be made. Its accuracy should be tested by the prisoner's review of its content. This study, with continuing observation and treatment, will be the basis for designing his individual program. It should be available to the judge and carefully analyzed by him before sentencing.

If rehabilitation is the goal, only the indeterminate sentence will be used. Such a sentence sets an outer limit beyond which the state may no longer restrain the liberty of the individual. Depending on the offense and the condition of the prisoner, the sentence may be for a period not to exceed ten years, or six months, or thirty days. The prisoner may be unconditionally released or gradually released under restrictive conditions designed to assure rehabilitation at any time within the period of the sentence. The sentence contemplates a rehabilitation program specially designed for each individual convicted. Professionally trained correctional authorities can then carefully observe a prisoner and release him at the earliest time within the limits fixed which his personal situation indicates, and under conditions reasonably calculated to protect the public. Techniques of release may begin with family visits of a few hours' duration. Later, part-time or full-time employment may be possible or public or private schools attended from a community correction center. Overnight visits with the family may follow and finally a release, requiring continued schooling with good performance, employment at a productive level, or a stable family situation. Close communication, personal counseling and assistance, and regular phone calls or appearances will help the individual and improve chances for the program to succeed. Excessive drinking, associations with an old gang, staying out late in the evening without explanation may justify changes in supervision. An intensive supervisory effort for a period of months will get prisoners through their most difficult times and achieve a high level of rehabilitation.

The indeterminate sentence is premised on the fact that a judge has no way of predicting how an individual will develop or what he will be like in one year, or five, or ten. Fixing a period of years in advance during which a convict must be confined in jail cannot be rationally explained if rehabilitation, not punishment, is our goal. An immutable sentence for years is largely arbitrary—a guess or reflex—reflecting a judge's habit or frame of mind. The sentence to a fixed term of years injures beyond its irrationality. What motivation does a prisoner condemned to prison for seven certain years have in the first, the second or the fifth year? He is waiting. A program designed to rehabilitate him is waiting, too. There is no incentive. The cost and waste and harm are immense. If even in the early months of an indeterminate sentence for a maximum period of ten years the prisoner can see the chance to work days, to attend school, to learn a trade, to visit home, to move to a community correction location, he has the strongest motivation to try, to work with his supervisors and to prepare for the future. For many prisoners such efforts may be sheer cunning—an effort to appear to be what they are not. But the light at the end of the tunnel is visible, and it always looks good. It can be a goal—perhaps the first goal of a lifetime. Sometimes cunning may fool even professional correctional personnel. We can afford that risk. We are not fooled now. We know most prisoners who are released will commit more crimes. Sometimes the cunning will be entrapped by their own cleverness and the game they played will become their way of life.

Judges dislike sentencing intensely. It is the most difficult part of their whole job. No sensitive person can easily make a critically important decision for society and, without rational guidance, the most important decision in the life of another human being. Many judges dread the day they must impose sentence. It may look easy for them in the courtroom. They may seem stern, even indifferent, but some judges will tell you they sleep little the night before they impose sentences. They are, after all, exerting a greater influence on the life of another man in a single moment than most men do in a lifetime. Asked to do the impossible—to foresee the effect of a sentence on the life of a person for years into the future—how can they be just? They must try to guess what period of confinement will rehabilitate someone they will never know, under unknown future conditions they cannot control or even affect.

Some judges sentence long, some short. Illustrations of the inequality in sentencing occur every day, often in different courtrooms in the same courthouse. Two boys fail to report for military induction—one is sentenced to five years in prison, the other gets probation and never enters a prison. One judge sentences a robber convicted for the third time to one year in prison, while another judge on the same bench gives a first offender ten years. One man far more capable of serious crime than another and convicted of the same offense may get a fine, while the less fortunate and less dangerous person is sentenced to five years in the state penitentiary. One judge, because of his personal values, thinks homosexuality the most heinous of crimes and gives long sentences. Another hates prostitution. A third judge would never jail juveniles for either offense. Some judges regularly give juvenile offenders prison terms for first-offense car theft, while others turn them over to the custody of their parents.

Indeterminate sentencing affords the public the protection of potentially long confinement without the necessity that long sentences be served. It gives the best of both worlds—long protection for the public yet a fully flexible opportunity for the convict's rehabilitation. It provides the chance constantly to adapt correctional programs to personal needs even as individuals develop.

The day of the indeterminate sentence is coming. Less than fifteen years old in the federal system, indeterminate sentences are given in more than 20 per cent of all convictions in which imprisonment is ordered. The number of indeterminate sentences given in the federal system doubled between 1964 and 1969. Still, many federal judges have never given an indeterminate sentence, while others give little else. There remain whole federal judicial districts where an indeterminate sentence has never been given. The greatest deterrent to the use of the indeterminate sentence is the slowness with which the judicial system adapts to obvious and urgently needed changes.

No correctional system in the United States is yet staffed to make effective use of the indeterminate sentence. In some prison systems benefits would be immediate because professional skills are available. In all, however, even those with no skills, the change to indeterminate sentencing would be for the better. The judges would at least be relieved of committing acts that inherently cause unequal justice. The prisoner would have the chance, however remote, of release at any time. The correctional system would have its opportunity to rehabilitate.

There are risks, of course, in the use of the indeterminate sentence, as there are in any technique. The method does not, obviously, guarantee rehabilitation; it is only the beginning—only an opportunity. Parole authorities and prison personnel can abuse this additional power, use it arbitrarily or fail to use it through timidity. But we must reform personnel standards and techniques in the system, anyway, and there is the opportunity for judicial review. Due process in the administration of indeterminate sentences can be assured. If there is arbitrary administration of indeterminate sentences, appeals can be taken through the correctional system and subjected to judicial scrutiny.

Under any system most prisoners will be released someday. Very few will be held until maturation, senility or death itself has stilled criminal instincts. If we release persons who have the capacity for further crime, only temporary safety has been afforded. In the meanwhile, imprisonment has often increased the individual's capacity for crime. If nothing but selfish interest impelled us, then rehabilitation is worth the effort, for when it works, it reduces crime, reduces the cost of handling prisoners, reduces the cost of the criminal justice system and even relieves pressure to provide the basic and massive reforms that are necessary to affect the underlying causes of crime.

One billion dollars would nearly double our entire expenditure for corrections. Spent for the right purposes, a billion dollars could show immediate results. Correctional expenditures protect the public and should therefore be more readily acceptable to the public. They lack the charitable qualities of the purely preventive expenditure. They are direct, practical and effective.

No set program of corrections can fit the needs of more than a small number of the prisoners in any system. The backgrounds, experience, deficiencies and needs of inmates are as diverse as our total society. For many offenders a program of rehabilitation should be only the effort of society to communicate clearly the reasons for its rule of law and the purposes of its penalties.

Young men who refuse induction into the military service because they oppose war often believe they adhere to a higher moral standard. Many do. Certainly from the standpoint of their potential for violence or property crime, there is no quality in their character requiring rehabilitation. But they should understand that the rule of law is not mindless, that it has a purpose, and that if the system is to have integrity, the purpose must be fulfilled. The question is not who has the higher morality, but shall the system of law do what it says. For society to consume years, or even days, of the lives of these young men in prison idleness and brutality or blight their personal potential through social stigma is tragically wasteful and desperately wrong. Until laws can be reformed, sensitive corrections systems must afford the hundreds of young men serving sentences for violations of the Selective Service Act the chance to make constructive contributions outside the prison environment. We should not make criminals of those who oppose war.

The young boy convicted of smoking a marijuana cigarette and the young girl in prison for having an abortion present difficult challenges, as does the drunken driver who has caused a fatal accident. The latter may never drink again and, sober, be incapable of antisocial conduct. Merely to confine such people in prison or place them in an irrelevant program designed to rehabilitate persons who have deliberately committed serious crimes against others is senseless. Special programs for such offenders can protect the public without the waste and injury risked by imprisonment.

Some crimes are acts of momentary irrationality by people who will never commit another serious crime. Murder—a crime of passion—is often such an act. Occurring most often within families, and between friends and neighbors, it is sometimes the result of an uncontrollable impulse, of sudden overwhelming anger or hatred, spontaneous, unpredictable and nonrecurrent. To place the tormented people who have committed such a crime among hardened criminals who lead lives of crime can be cruel and senseless.

The preponderance of all efforts by correctional agencies must be directed at the youngest offenders, those from backgrounds and with personal histories and conditions that indicate emotional instability and the probability of continuing and increasing antisocial activities. Numbering in the tens of thousands, they commit most common crimes of violence and most burglaries, larcenies and thefts.

Many coming to prison are so disorganized, so confused and so lacking in self-control that they cannot focus on any subject more than a few moments. Their span of any intellectual effort is too short to permit training. Before they can begin their rehabilitation, they must live in a calm, orderly, organized atmosphere in which they can learn to concentrate. For many this is the highest hurdle. It is something they have never known. Born in bedlam, physically abused in infancy and childhood, they have lived amid chronic violence, fear and confusion. Their physical and mental illnesses—alcoholism and drug addiction among their most common manifestations—must be professionally treated and dealt with as the medical problems they are. Major portions of the population in every prison have such needs.

At the earliest possible time schooling should be resumed for those capable of it. In federal youth centers, probably 90 per cent of the inmates are high school and junior high school dropouts, the great majority years behind their appropriate grade level. Special tutoring is essential if they are to advance. If they do not advance, if they do not get back in school, with their history and handicaps their chances for a life free of crime are slight.

Meaningful vocational training in high-employment fields will be the best program for many. Learning a skill is more than a possibility for most prisoners. It is what has been missing in their lives. Often they absorb skills quickly and take pride in their workmanship. From there the opportunity for rehabilitation is great.

Throughout the history of federal corrections most prisoners have been faced with two alternatives—the total custody of a prison or release to the community with insignificant parole supervision. For decades dormant skills were largely undeveloped. While Federal Prison Industries trained and meaningfully employed some, its programs were located in a prison environment. The skills learned were minimal and often in trades in which employment is hard to find. In the early days it was agriculture, still a dominant occupation in some state prison systems. Later textile work, bricklaying, tire recapping, auto repair and metal work were offered some. Now automatic data processing and white-collar training are afforded a few.

In 1965, in what seemed a bold step at the time, supervision of prisoners in normal community employment situations was first attempted. A work release program authorized by Congress permitted prisoners to leave prison in the morning for a place of employment, work there during the day, and return to prison when the work day ended. The potential was immediately apparent. Jobs were found. Prisoners were cautiously selected and assigned to the program, nearly always during the last months of their incarceration. Other prisoners often made it clear to those chosen that they had better not abuse the opportunity, for nearly every prisoner wanted work release. If those who were released failed, others would never have the chance, and they all knew it. Bricklayer, carpenter, automobile mechanic, tire recapper, bookkeeper, college student: these were among the first jobs offered prisoners in the program. One young man traveled sixty miles a day by commercial bus from the federal institution at Seagoville, Texas, worked a half day in the dean's office in a state college, took three courses and made three A's.

The strain was great on these prisoners. The meaning of imprisonment had never been so clear. Freedom had new meaning to them. Some admitted the great difficulty of returning to prison at night, and the contrast between liberty and detention seemed much sharper. But by the end of 1968, thousands had been in the program, and more than 500 of the 20,000 federal prisoners were always on work release.

Fewer than one in twenty failed to comply with all the conditions of work release. Alcohol was the cause of failure in nearly two-thirds of the cases. In most of these the tavern looked too inviting after work and the prospect of the prison too dismal. We should not be surprised that 5 per cent failed. After all, before the program was launched, 50 per cent were failing when finally released. The real surprise was that there were so few failures. The policy was far too cautious and the supervision inadequate, but a good beginning was made.

Since we know that better than one-half of all the people who leave prisons return convicted of a subsequent crime, it is clearly worth risking six months on work release after a convict has spent many months or years in prison. Among the 95 per cent who did not fail in the work release program, perhaps only a third will return to prison. As to the 5 per cent who failed to meet the conditions of release and sought to escape, all were caught and returned to prison, where they served more time. People do not really escape from prison successfully. In the history of the Federal Bureau hundreds of thousands have been imprisoned and thousands have escaped, but fewer than twenty have not been recaptured or otherwise accounted for. It is only a matter of time—usually not very long.

Perhaps the most discouraging thing about work release is the timidity of the program and the opposition it arouses. It is a small, late and uncertain step in a direction in which we must move forcefully. Even so, the hard-liners—those who would control crime by long brutalizing penitentiary sentences and the fear of eternal damnation—have attacked work release as if it caused crime. Blind to the fact that prisoners will soon be released anyway, they prefer six more months of incarceration to a chance to test the personal stability of the individual in community life. What perversity so deprives such critics of compassion that they will not give a prisoner any chance, as a job will do, or see that by failing to give that chance, they assure more crime? The worst that can happen when work release begins only six months before a prison term ends is that the length of the term is shortened six months if the prisoner flees and is never caught. Perhaps some crimes may therefore be committed six months earlier, but if we are not willing to take that small gamble, what do we expect will happen six months later when the inmate will not return to prison at night and authorities will not know what he is doing? We are admitting the total failure of the rehabilitative power of penology.

From work release men can move back into society with a job and a history of work at it. Many have said they feel human again—for the first time in years. Of all the loneliness of our mass society that of the former convict is greatest.

A typical releasee in the very first group that began in the late fall of 1965 worked on a construction crew in Texarkana, Texas. He liked the men he worked with and they liked him. A camaraderie developed between him and his co-workers. They became buddies. He was kidded: "How about going fishing with us Saturday?" and he said, "Wait until spring." They slapped him on the back—it had been a long time since anyone had done that. He said he felt like a man again. Before, he had been alone against the world. His family, on relief for five years, was off relief and moving to Texarkana. He was supporting them. He could send them money. He was going to live and work in Texarkana. He would be the best carpenter there, he said. He would work hard and raise his family. He may.

Work release, halfway houses, prerelease guidance centers— these are only the beginning. Community supervision is the future of corrections. Work release affords a good test of the ability of a prisoner to relate to other people in an unrestrained environment. It is in society that the individual must master his frustrations, temptations and weaknesses. When a young offender who can continue schooling is placed in a regular public school, he often need not be identified to his fellow students as a prisoner. The greatest difficulty that the former prisoner confronts in establishing relationships with people is they tend to think of him first, last and always as a convict—not as a person. We tend to be what people expect us to be. Few things are more important to us than the regard of others. Identified as a troublemaker or a criminal, we tend to be troublemakers and criminals. We want to live up to our reputations.

As soon as their condition indicates that it is consistent with safety and rehabilitation, prisoners should be moved from conventional prisons to community facilities such as a floor of a YMCA, a wing in an apartment building, or a house. Special plans for security and supervision will permit easy control. In such settings they can learn to live in an environment approaching the kind they must adjust to before they will be released. They can attend school and return after school, take the vocational training their aptitudes and experience indicate, or work at jobs that test their ability to make it on their own. Their freedom, their associations, their schedules can be controlled as needed to help achieve rehabilitation. Family visits can begin, followed by church attendance if desired, perhaps a movie or a date, and later a whole weekend. This is what they must learn or relearn. Who will say they cannot? And if they cannot, what then? We should stop deceiving ourselves with sentences for a term of years; we might as well lock up offenders and throw away the keys.

Like all pioneer endeavors, our experience with community corrections is hardly definitive. There have been successes and failures. Those close to the experience know it will work if sufficient effort is made. It will work because it has to work. We can neither abandon these people nor permit them to injure society.

The California Youth Authority experimented with young offenders chosen at random—pure chance determined the selection—from all except those convicted of the most serious crimes. One group was confined in conventional prison facilities. A second was sent to the celebrated California Forest Camps, initiated in the 1930's. Somehow, perhaps because of the dignity and solemnity of the forests, the fresh air and nature, it was thought that the big trees would make decent citizens of kids from the slums of Oakland. A third group was treated in small community centers near areas they would live in when released. From there they were slowly worked back into the communities.

The test began in 1960 in three counties. Hundreds of youngsters were involved. By 1967 recidivism among conventional facilities and forest camp inmates ran about 54 per cent. For the community correctional program the recidivism rate was 29 per cent.

In the years to come millions of boys and hundreds of thousands of girls throughout the United States will be confined in prisons. They will be the youngest offenders, representative of the American child in trouble. They will come, in the main, from poor families and broken homes. they will be school dropouts. So little loved are they that in the federal system, 70 per cent will never have a visitor—relative or friend—while they wait in prison. No one cares. Most will be afflicted with mental and physical illnesses, and many will be addicted to drugs.

How many crimes are committed by persons with congenital brain damage and chemical imbalances in body processes? How many slum children with brain injuries will get the medical and psychiatric help they need? How many crimes are caused by the neglect of mentally retarded children of the poor? When mental retardation afflicts wealthy families, for all the sadness it may cause, the children at least are well cared for. But when this tragic handicap strikes the poor, it can overpower their remaining will to cope with life. Families and individuals disintegrate. When we know that mental retardation may be five times more common in the ghetto and that 25 per cent of the prisoners in state penitentiary systems such as Texas' are mentally retarded, we may know more than we care to know about the causes of crime. Had we known and cared, the physically or mentally deficient youngster could have been helped. Instead, because he was different, a handicap that did not of itself make him antisocial alienated him from all love, and he became antisocial. In time, he committed criminal acts. Should we treat him, then, like a worthless life, penning him up and dismissing his case as hopeless? We do not need to go on like this.

If we permit history to repeat itself, most such youngsters will commit crimes after they are released. Nearly all who live lives of crime, who repeat and repeat, began with insignificant crimes when they were kids. Here then is our major opportunity and high duty.

We know that corrections can rehabilitate. We know that the younger the offender the better his and society's chance. We know that when we fail it is all of us who suffer. America is a nation with the skills and resources to provide the necessary elements of rehabilitation: physical and mental health, all the education a youngster can absorb, vocational skills for the highest trade he can master, a calm and orderly environment away from

anxiety and violence, living among people who care, who love
—with these a boy can begin again. With these we can restore a
reverence for life, a sense of security and a self-assurance amid
all the pressures of modern community life. These attitudes will
not be developed in a laboratory. They must be developed in the
community itself: first, sometimes, in the prison community but
finally in the open society in which the individual must make his
way by himself.

To youth corrections we must bring the most advanced research and best techniques. We must provide ample resources to
implement both. We must assure funds and professional skills
to guide a boy when he may need it most—on the hard return
home. Every prison can be just another manufacturer of crime
—just another place to hold bad boys out of sight, out of mind.
Better that we tear them down now than that we let that happen.
What nobler work could involve us than to save one boy from
the horror, for himself and for all who sense his empty heart, of
a life of crime?

One of the unanswered questions in modern mass society is
whether institutions, organizations and associations can meet
the challenge of change effectively and efficiently. Can they
adapt to new conditions with reasonable speed? Can they serve
present needs rather than old habits? There is substantial evidence that most such institutions do not have the inner force or
motivation for the task.

Prisons are a classic illustration. Some 125,000 full-time employees are scattered through an impossible maze of jurisdictions throughout the country. Jails across the street from each
other—one run by the county, the other by the city—are still
commonplace. The time spent moving prisoners from one facility to the other and the risk involved each time are reasons
enough to abolish one. But the waste in manpower and resources available for rehabilitation effort is outrageous. Re-

sources for corrections are so grossly inadequate to begin with that continued waste and inefficiency are intolerable.

Even in the biggest city there should be but one jail system. It will need many facilities and varied programs, but it should manage all correctional activities in the area. Persons in pretrial detention, whether charged with federal, state or local crime, can be boarded in the facility best suited to their need and most convenient to the courts and other agencies that may require frequent contact with them. By such methods reasonably efficient use can be made of facilities and manpower.

A single agency serving all jurisdictions—federal, state, and local—will have greater resources and be subject to the scrutiny of several masters. Different courts can insist on good performance, as federal courts have often demanded that a county jail provide regular and decent meals, beds for every inmate, and separation of youngsters and first offenders from hardened criminals. The manager of the overall agency will be involved with other agencies, which will be more likely to complain about his performance than they would of their own.

Federal jail standards assuring adequate care and custody by local jails holding federal prisoners have done much to raise the overall conditions for other prisoners in the same jails. Federal inspectors make sure the standards are enforced. Other political jurisdictions can do the same. Excellence can be attained with one comprehensive service, if properly funded. Now there are usually several bad ones, none with enough qualified personnel or proper rehabilitation programs. Someone mugged by a teenager just released from county jail can derive little comfort from the news that the federal youth center is doing a marvelous job. Unified service can bring quality to all.

Prison administration is an extremely complex business. It includes most of the problems known to guard agencies, hotels, restaurants, schools, hospitals, infirmaries, mental institutions, psychologists' clinics, small businesses, vocational and athletic training departments, employment bureaus, libraries and law offices. To provide all the services needed, and the size necessary to attract, train and retain professional excellence, a statewide system is required. City and county prisons or jails rarely look beyond mere confinement as their purpose. They are restricted by geography and finances to large old brick buildings downtown. An occasional county prison farm will teach slum boys how to cultivate crops that their families left the South ten years ago to get away from growing. Local prisons do not, and in the nature of things cannot, have the staff, the range of skills, or the numbers of prisoners necessary to provide all of the services required. They are even less able to provide the special services needed by female and juvenile offenders. A basic reorganization of corrections is necessary in nearly every state if we are to have any hopes of achieving rehabilitation.

The federal system has too few women prisoners to offer needed services to them. Coming from all over the United States, federal female prisoners number fewer than eight hundred. How far from their homes are the women's reformatories at Alderson, West Virginia, and Terminal Island, California? How many will have visitors while in prison? What will happen to their children, whom they will not see during the entire time they are in prison? What does this deprivation mean to the child and the family—and to the crime rate? It is doubtful that confinement is meaningful for 10 per cent of the women prisoners, but there they are, in penitentiaries in the hills of Appalachia and on the harbor at Long Beach.

The whole system of corrections for women needs analysis. Prisons for women began by analogy to male prisons after the penitentiary system developed in the nineteenth century. Techniques have been refashioned only slightly to reflect the very great differences in the conduct of male and female prisoners. Women are rarely violent in prison. They are not a threat to the public. Confinement will not break a drug habit or train a girl for employment or make less likely her return to prostitution. Mental health services are a need of most women inmates, but prisons rarely provide them, nor are penal institutions the best environment for treatment. The only benefit possible for many is the calming influence of what can be, but in most women's prisons is not, a quiet, orderly, attractive environment. Regular meals, never experienced before, and a clean private room can be shown as life possibilities. Such amenities—and the habits they imply—can soon become desirable, but iron bars will not speed the process. The community is where life will be lived out.

There is a need to reallocate manpower between prison and community services. Eighty per cent of all corrections manpower guards jails and prisons. The larger number of criminals on probation—800,000 out of 1,200,000 serving sentence on the average in the late 1960's—is serviced, theoretically, by one-fifth the total national correctional personnel. The community-based officers have additional duties that add to the impossibility of meaningful supervision. Surveys have revealed federal judicial districts where probation service officers carry four to five times the case load of forty persons that the National Council on Crime and Delinquency considers desirable. Some such officers devote up to 85 per cent of their time preparing presentence reports for judges and are therefore left with only minutes a day to supervise hundreds of persons recently released from prison. In those districts, as is the case nearly everywhere, probation and parole supervision is negligible if not meaningless.

When a prisoner is released on parole after prison confinement of perhaps many years' duration, he needs help desperately. He may not know it, and he may not want it, but he needs help, careful supervision, a steady hand, a voice with his employer and fellow workers, a friend to eat dinner with once in a while, a visit with a family. The early months are the hardest; once he gets through them, his chances for making it all the way are much higher. But instead of help most of his supervision now takes the form of routine office visits, spot phone checks, pointless report writing, all of it often surrounded with an aura of mistrust.

The allocation of manpower between custodial care in

prisons and supervision in community settings must be reversed. Only when we devote 20 per cent and less for institutional care and 80 per cent and more for community supervision can we begin to rehabilitate. Only a dedicated community supervision staff properly trained with high skills can cut recidivism substantially.

There is no effort within the criminal justice system that holds a fraction of the potential to reduce crime offered by a vigorous, thoughtful corrections program. Not even efforts directed at the underlying causes of crime, such as health services, education, employment or decent housing, offer the same immediate potential at near the cost. Corrections focuses directly on the highly distilled mainstream of criminal conduct. Three of every four persons that it deals with have a potential for antisocial conduct. Here are identified offenders. The risks are clear and substantiated by statistical evidence from over the entire country. If all of our research and learning about human behavior, if all the teaching in our great universities about medical science, mental health, psychiatry, psychology, sociology, hereditary and environmental influences has any applicability to real life, here in corrections it has an immense and critically important role. Yet, divorcement of all those lessons and skills from the people who need them is almost total.

If America cares for its character, it must revolutionize its approach to corrections.

14

THE YOUNG, THE POWERLESS AND
DISSENT: NEW FRONTIERS FOR
THE SOCIAL COMPACT

BEING young was never very easy. Today it is harder than ever. The confusion, complexity and irrationality of modern mass urban society provide the adolescent with few solid bases for understanding his environment and what it all means. Our senior generation grew up in a world of trees, farm lands, and neighbors they knew. Communication was people talking to one another. Young America, however, has grown up with the bomb and the television set.

There has been more change between the birth of a father and the birth of his son than in the preceding millennium— atomic energy, supersonic flight, television and Telstar, Apollo 8, Hiroshima and Vietnam, and 1 billion more people. These and other forces have caused vast migrations of people, high mobility, total anonymity, steady urbanization and a fivefold increase in college population. One-half the college-age population is in college now compared to one-eighth when Dad went to State U. twenty-five years ago. We've moved from Glenn Miller past the Beatles; from the Katzenjammer Kids beyond Barbarella.

The generation now managing our major institutions matured as mankind finally gained the upper hand over nature. This success bred a self-confidence that was short-lived in the face of the difficult, sometimes sinister questions: Can man control the technology with which he mastered nature? Will nuclear energy, the computer and electronics destroy or liberate?

The young seek to know themselves in a world permeated with noise, pollution, movement, communication, strangers and gadgets of great complexity. The task is formidable. We live in an environment mostly of our own making but largely beyond control. Young America senses the immense opportunities this country offers, but is desperately aware of the difficulties and frustrations in achieving them.

Most crime is committed by minors. Nearly two-thirds of all persons arrested for serious crime are under twenty-one. Minors were arrested for 79.9 per cent of the car thefts, 70.7 per cent of the burglaries and 68.5 per cent of the larcenies in 1968. Kids between eleven and seventeen, constituting 13 per cent of the population, were arrested in one-half of all cases of serious property crime.

Though sentiment resists it, reason and fact tell us crime will most frequently be committed by the young. Youth is a time when character is forming, a time when an individual begins to know himself. It is difficult for many adolescents who see hunger and deprivation around them to understand why property should not be taken, or why sensitivity to the feelings of others is necessary. They do not yet understand.

Young people who steal will find it as hard to change that habit as any other they acquire. When stealing is frequent it becomes a part of the style of living. Ostracized by society for conduct it condemns, the individual turns against society. It is human to defend one's own actions. As the protest of society is voiced, the conduct becomes more antisocial. For some, society itself becomes the enemy.

Nothing accelerates this dehumanizing process more quickly than jails and prisons that merely cage young wrongdoers together where they inevitably do wrong to one another. Milton L. Luger, the Director of the New York State correction system's Division for Youth, has observed, "It would probably be better for all concerned if young delinquents were not detected, apprehended or institutionalized. Too many of them get worse in our care." This is literally true. The best chance we have— rehabilitation of the youthful offender—is usually the greatest failure. Our heartless efforts only harden criminal capability.

Youthful crime is less violent than adult crime. In 1967, 9 per cent of all persons arrested for murder were under eighteen, compared to 64 per cent of the same age arrested for car theft. Only 37 per cent of the persons arrested for murder were under twenty-five. Persons under twenty-one accounted for 30 per cent of all arrests for aggravated assault, while the proportion of the same age group arrested for burglary, larceny and theft was two and a half times greater. Robbery, which brings property crime and violent potential into close proximity, entails higher youth involvement. Fifty-four per cent of all persons arrested for robbery were under twenty-one in 1967, a figure still well below the percentage arrested for serious property crimes who had not reached twenty-one.

It takes longer for society to brutalize, to dehumanize and so unhinge people that they can murder. The deep psychosis, profound instability, sickness and cruelty essential to premeditated murder develop slowly. Children are rarely capable of it. They start out wanting things. Later they become insensitive to human feelings. Some finally rage at society.

For serious crime the age of most frequent offense is between fifteen and sixteen years old. The crime curve rises rapidly from age eight and nine to peak in the mid-teens and then describes a long decline—first rapidly, then slowly—toward the limits of life expectancy. Violent crimes reach their rate of most frequent commission a decade and more beyond the peak for property crimes. The median age of murderers is near thirty, while most petty thieves are under seventeen.

Young people will be around longer than their elders. Their character is our character tomorrow. If we care about the future and ourselves we must help today's young.

To prevent crime we must begin with young children of preschool and primary school years. We know where children most likely to commit crime live. We know how to find them. With a few instructions even census takers could provide the names and addresses of at least those children who have no parents, have been beaten and abused, are not sent to school regularly, cannot read, or share a room with four people. Professionals could find 90 per cent of the children likely to become delinquent. We may have to live with the rest; we do not have to live with most. That we do tells us much about our character. It means that, knowing we create criminals, we continue. Later, frightened, we seek to control them by force.

The children who will become criminals live mostly in the slums. Their older brothers and sisters are dropouts—unemployed. Their mother comes around some, but grandmother raises them, more or less. Father, they never knew. Uncle is an addict. The neighbors are alcoholics and fight every night. The food they eat dulls their whole perception as do the effects of malnutrition incurred before they left their mother's womb. Prenatal measles or tuberculosis afflicted the boy next door and his mother. Big sister is a prostitute. They live in a place where violence is common, where a few, finding power in no other way, achieve it with a gun.

The Head Start teacher sees the one who can never sit still, who pushes other children down, who cries frequently and for no apparent reason, who sits by himself and talks to no one. A good first-grade teacher can name most of the children in her class who are destined for lives full of trouble and trouble making. She knows which one cannot learn to read. His eyes move from right to left. He cannot concentrate two minutes. He is dull or frenetic. He desperately needs help. His chance in life is swiftly passing him by. These are his days before delinquency, when effort can avoid the misery of a wasted life or a life of crime.

It will never be easy to help a child while the filth, disease, ignorance, poverty and vice of the slums permeate his existence. Those conditions must be changed. In the meantime an intensive effort to reach the children of high delinquency potential must be made. The Juvenile Delinquency Prevention Act of 1968 was intended to provide federal funds for the whole range of youth crime. The concentration of effort must be in the predelinquency years. Child care centers, health services, Head Start, concentrated primary education programs, youth centers, summer camps, athletic leagues, Vista volunteer efforts, broad-scaled youth recreation programs, planned constructive activity for gangs, apprentice and vocational training, Job Corps, after-school, weekend and summer jobs available in ghetto areas can reach tens of thousands of children who otherwise may never see a chance that looks better than crime. Such programs can create the strength of opportunity tempered by adversity. Children can be reached and many saved from an environment that otherwise teaches inhumanity.

The effort will have to be comprehensive and massive. We will need clean, orderly, integrated schools with good teachers —more teachers in the slums than in the easier neighborhoods —and specialists to work with disturbed youngsters. Teachers will have to work closely with children from ages three or four until the last dropout. Hospitals, health clinics, medical, dental and nutritional services must be provided. Instructors will be needed to staff recreation, health and physical development programs while exhausting the immense energies of youth from the toddler to the teenage athlete. Above all, we must open two-way communication and transportation that bring in the outside world to see the slums and provide the chance for bridging the gap between the ghetto and the suburb.

Professional guidance can help every child achieve his maximum development. Pursuing aptitudes and overcoming individual handicaps, we can reduce the numbers of dropouts, tailor programs for those who fail in school, extend their capabilities, all the while releasing energies, creating opportunities and preventing crime. Nearly all youthful offenders who are imprisoned drop out of school before the crime for which they were convicted was committed and years short of absorbing the education of which they were capable. Schools must also be prepared to work constructively and realistically with behavioral and disciplinary problems that arise, fully aware of the consequences to individuals involved and to society when they fail.

Most youthful offenders who are imprisoned come from broken families. In Watts in 1965, 50 per cent of the population under eighteen lived with only one or neither parent. An intensive effort in family support, counseling and crisis assistance, including not only guidance but essential economic aid, will be necessary to ameliorate one of the major causes of crime in America—the pressures of modern society which destroy families.

For those guilty of serious antisocial conduct we must provide correctional programs for rehabilitation. Long and patient treatment will be required for many. A woman's presence and influence, so often missing for the young male offender, an education, a skill, a job and a helping hand back to a community—these are the methods of juvenile rehabilitation that will work.

We will have to do all these things—and more—simultaneously. We must be willing to experiment and explore, constantly refine, strive to improve and greatly increase the money and manpower applied. Delinquency prevention must be a major commitment of our people if we are to reduce crime.

The young of such intense disadvantages are only a few million. Most Americans do not worry about them. It is the legions of young, the tens of millions who seem so wild and uncontrolled, that trouble most. High school riots, junior high fights, drugs, sexual immorality, the longhaired college kids and the common view of the hippie—violent, dirty, thoughtless—these frighten the older generation.

There has always been a difference between generations, but the difference has increased more in the last generation than in all the preceding ones. Today it is far more than questions of individual maturity, the conflict between parental authority and youthful desire, or the reaction of son to father. It is the difference between the environment in which parental attitudes and understanding developed and the environment in which today's children are forming their character. This is why it is so difficult for the young to understand their parents, or the parents their children. The very nature of the generation gap also means that the young will usually be right. Children live in today's truth while parents cling to yesterday's.

For the blacks the generation gap is even wider than it is for the whites and the frustrations it creates are greater. Poverty is more widespread, urbanization has moved faster, the broken family is far more common, education is significantly inferior and jobs are harder to find. History holds fewer torments greater than that of the young black in the slums and his Southern-born grandmother discussing the Christian Church. Never have two who needed to love each other so much so violently disagreed on what to one has been the article of faith that made life bearable and to the other often a symbol of resignation to injustice.

We can bridge the generation gap, but not by leadership taking sides—by seeing in one all truth and in the other all error. Leadership must take that difficult middle ground in the gap and extend its hands both ways. It must stimulate the efforts to understand. Escalating emotions, calling for the use of force, ousting students who protest, cutting off federal scholarships—these tactics will only divide.

Today's youth, on the average, are the best-educated, best-motivated, most idealistic and socially concerned generation yet produced in America. If we can be tolerant and understanding, they will show us much and we can help them. Their road will be far more difficult and dangerous than ours. We will have to assist them patiently, compassionately and diligently if it is to be successfully journeyed. If they seem to dramatize ills without proposing remedies, we should be tolerant. How well have we done? The young, even when uncertain, usually carry the germ of inarticulate truth. That germ will grow. Its force is irresistible.

Young people sense all the turbulence, anxiety, frustration, fear, hatred and insecurity around them. They see the horror of Vietnam and Biafra, the insanity of nuclear missiles and the ABM, the impotence of Czechoslovakia and the violence of our society. Our vast hypocrisy, 7 million alcoholics, 40 per cent of the blacks in poverty in the wealthiest nation in history, 4 million serious crimes reported and violence everywhere —these things profoundly affect their being. They wonder whether we can change.

In grammar school they are taught the three R's but not how to live together. Many of their high school courses were developed in the 1930's and have not been updated. More than a few colleges are administered by men who have lost touch with the needs of students and society. Law students memorize the rules of bills and notes, while whole areas of cities have no law.

The young seek change in the most effective way the powerless have devised in mass society where institutions—governmental, educational, social and religious—are unreachable and unresponsive. They act in mass. Undignified and aggravating as mass action is, it sometimes works. Too often the only way in which young people have been able to effect change is by confrontation. We need to open old ways and create new ways of communicating between student, teacher and school administrator. We must involve students in decisions that affect them and distribute power so they can participate. We need better ways of achieving change. They can be devised and institutions can be responsive.

Until they are and while some people care, we will have mass demonstrations with their potential for violence. Methods of nonviolent protest and techniques of police control must be carefully refined. Police should not be armed in confrontations with students, and troops should never carry rifles. Nor can we constructively focus only on the violence that has occurred. For all the damage done, youth achieved more change for the better in university performance in the 1960's than had been achieved theretofore this century.

No university will be destroyed by student violence. Places that call themselves universities and men who claim to head them may fall, but a university is an open place of reason, an uninhibited seeker of truth, a unifier of life, a tolerant, gentle, humane, compassionate place that will survive any violent force, however scarred the buildings may become. It will never abandon its principles or close its mind. It will face violence with the unconquerable spirit of nonviolence. We have seen great universities at the eye of the storm come through unscathed.

There are millions of powerless people in America. You are powerless if you live where there is no hospital, and psychoses, drug addiction and alcoholism go untreated; where poor health and retardation are commonplace and infant mortality is many times more frequent than elsewhere in the same city; where the people die young; where you pay more than the rich in suburbia for rancid meat and stale bread, both sold in violation of food ordinances; if your house is a firetrap, the only stairwell unlighted and unsafe and the wiring is forty years old, its insulation chewed off by rats; if you share a two-room flat with the remnants of three families, and an addict sleeps on the landing, all despite building-safety and health codes; if your schools are old, overcrowded and dilapidated; if the teachers are frightened, supplies are scant, students are segregated by race and the system is run by an administration that has hundreds of thousands of pupils and no time for anyone; if you cannot get a job because you are black and employers and unions discriminate against you, violating state and federal laws; if when you buy a twice-repossessed television set with cash savings from a man who knew the tube was broken, you cannot afford to sue; if the risk of assault is real, robbery is common and murder frequent; if your property, little though it is, may be taken or destroyed and you can do nothing about it; if all around you gamblers make book, addicts peddle, whores hustle and high-raters loan cash and are ignored by the police, who maintain order by arrests on suspicion of people who are on the streets late at night, by frisking and searching without cause and by beating some persons arrested who are never even charged. You are powerless.

Powerless people live by their wits. For them, rules of society are alien in spirit and in fact. The law is irrevelant except when it comes after them or their loved ones. The law and government pretend to give men rights. Hospitals are built, but the poor and powerless cannot get to them. The law protects citizens against assault and reveres the sanctity of property, but it works for the wealthy, not the poor. The law says you can sue the used-car salesman if the motor block was cracked when you bought the car, but the poor cannot afford a lawyer. It says the landlord must provide a fire escape and only one family may occupy a flat. And when you get food poisoning you can sue the grocer who sold you the week-old egg custard pie—the law says. And you can call the police and run off the addicts and prostitutes and bookies—the law says. Only you cannot. Because you have no rights and you have no power. You have what you can get away with and take care of by yourself.

The law may leave you without any rights, but it does not ignore you altogether. You saw the body of the fourteen-year-old boy the police shot to death when he tried to run away. You will never forget that. You have been arrested twice and put in jail, but never convicted. You were stopped and frisked last night coming home from a movie and a cop this morning said, "Move along, boy," when you were watching Crazy Charlie being wrestled into a paddy wagon. Many of your buddies say the police have beaten them up. Your younger brother is in prison and you know how difficult it will be when he gets back this time. You are always aware of the police standing by the call box, walking together down Main Street, circling in the squad car. You hear sirens every night: fire, ambulance, police. This is the law to you. You are told to respect it.

Anatole France observed of nineteenth-century French justice that "The law in its majestic equality forbids the rich as well as the poor from sleeping under bridges, from begging in the streets and from stealing bread." The law imposes little inconvenience on the rich when it prohibits these acts. For the poor it may prohibit survival. Can there be social justice where there is poverty? In an interdependent, technologically advanced, mass society the answer is no. The elimination of poverty and the diffusion of power are essential to justice—and justice is essential to the reduction of crime.

Communications between the ghetto and the outside world can do much to give power and establish rights while we act to eliminate poverty. The slums, usually near the heart of the city, are its most isolated sections. Few communicate effectively with people in the slums. The power of knowledge and human compassion, not inconsiderable forces, can be released by communication of the truth about poverty.

The risk to organized crime operations increases when the people among whom the criminals do business, though powerless themselves, have contact with institutions of power. A slum dweller complaining to the police is no threat. The pastor of a large church, the president of a major social organization, a businessman, a member of the Chamber of Commerce, or a city councilman complaining presents a more urgent problem. The illegal moneylender, landlords who maintain unsafe and unhealthy tenements and merchants who sell bad food at high prices will have to be more careful then. By opening communications, the hold of organized crime can be loosened.

If the suburban dweller really knew the facts of life in the ghettos that seem so strange, hostile and dirty to him, he would be aroused to action. He would see the causes of crime and realize that in our interdependent society his own well-being depends on relieving the intolerable conditions that exist there. Then he would know what he could do for his country and his own character.

Lawyers in America work feverishly with an immensely complex and growing body of law to adjust relationships between interests with money. Ninety per cent of the time of the nation's lawyers—and time is their stock in trade—is devoted to fulfilling the rights of ten per cent of the people. Expensive as it may be, monied might will usually find ways of doing its will, sometimes by merely wearing out the right. There will be few common nuisances in the suburbs. The cesspools, the dumps, the factories belching smoke and stench are where the poor live or will live. But the odor reaches outside. It can no longer be contained. Industrial air pollution from Hamburg drifts over Stockholm, and municipal waste from Des Moines pollutes the Mississippi at Memphis.

Law schools train bright and ambitious young people in esoteric theories and overrefined rules of corporate, tax, commercial and business law. Slowly they shift their focus from courses developed for propertied classes of nineteenth-century America —contracts, agency, partnerships, bills and notes—to new studies such as rules and techniques of law applicable to science, technology, mass population, space, nuclear energy, rural and urban poverty, education, health, housing, public administration and institutional change. All the while there are millions without rights to whom the law is irrelevant except as a clumsy technique for maintaining order.

Until slum dwellers, who live where we breed crime, have rights, we will only further test their patience by admonishing them to respect law. While society ordains order without law, how can the poor believe in law? The poor see how affluent America lives. For the first time in history, they understand their own misery, know that most do not share it—and realize that inequality need not be. What delusion would make the law of the jungle respectful? The poor may want law, but they cannot be asked to respect its absence. We are too rich, too well educated and informed, too interdependent and concerned to expect sentient people to be resigned to substantial poverty, misery or injustice. This is not regrettable. The regrettable fact is our failure to exercise earlier initiative to end such intolerable conditions. Only when the poor have rights will they respect the law. It will then be worthy of their respect.

Those who have no rights will, given time, not respect the rights of others. Crime will exist while people do not respect the rights of others. Only when the individual cannot bring himself to injure another will we be free of crime.

Not everyone is satisfied with the way our system is working or with the course of human events. Some shrug and go about their business. Others, having no business, merely shrug. Some try alcohol or drugs, others protest once in a while. A few work most of the time organizing, demonstrating, engaging in acts of civil disobedience. They are the young, the poor—powerless people—who care enough to act. Of these, most have believed in change without violence. Violent ones have emerged. More can come.

The major effort of dissent has been to cause change through speech. How does an individual communicate in mass society? How does a person affect things that are important to him? He can no longer escape, go West, or stay on the farm. He is overwhelmed by the numbers of people in his environment. His college courses are not relevant to what he wants to know. His children go to a school that prepares them for nothing. The police do not protect him. Industry pollutes his air and water. Electronics and the metallic commotion of technology deprive him of silence. Inadequate public transportation robs him of hours every day. His last place of recreation is yielding to bulldozers. Employers and unions ignore him because he is black. Welfare strips him of dignity. He is compelled to fight a war he doesn't understand or want. Billions of dollars that could improve the human condition are diverted to capabilities for mass destruction. Millions of people are suffocated by violence, noise and ugliness.

He should vote? Forty-seven million qualified to vote in 1968 failed to vote for a President, while only thirty-one million voted for Richard Nixon. He should write his Congressman? How can a Congressman serve half a million people? He should go to the employment commission? He waited there three days last week. He should complain to public officials? They are so harassed they cannot answer their mail, or, worse, they answer in platitudes. He should talk to the superintendent of schools? It's easier to see the President of the United States.

How can the powerless influence power in our times? This question has been studied chiefly by those without power, in the hard school of experience.

The early pioneers of confrontation were the civil rights leaders in the South. In the mid-1950's efforts patterned on those used during Reconstruction were resurrected. How bizarre it seemed to most Americans that people would boycott buses. Why would those who need public transportation most not use it? What is so bad about riding in the back of the bus? Will America ever understand its debt to Rosa Parks?

Later, Freedom Riders sought by the force of bodily presence to desegregate public facilities segregated in clear defiance of the Constitution. When buses were burned and federal authority was needed to protect those who sought change, no one was really surprised. In the spring of 1963, hundreds, even thousands, rallied nightly in the streets of downtown Birmingham for weeks to desegregate lunch counters and secure the first sales job for a Negro in a downtown department store, years after most whites shopped in the suburbs and the central city black had become the chief customer of the downtown merchant. Some asked how people could act that way after all we had done to help the poor. Unconcerned people philosophized that you can never accomplish a goal by offending. But how else would you secure the right to sit in the front of a bus or get a job as a sales clerk? Negotiate with the company, or the mayor of Montgomery or Birmingham?

Masses of bodies, a small minority of even the small minority they were a part of, forced society to recognize them by simply being there—by causing inconvenience, parading, singing, sitting in and closing off. They had found a weapon used before but much more effective in a highly interdependent urban society.

Other segments of our dissatisfied society saw the civil rights demonstrations. Students, the poor, welfare mothers, those who opposed the war in Vietnam, even government workers began to protest because, unreasoning as it seemed, it sometimes worked. It often forced change where none would otherwise come. It speeded change where change came slowly. You cannot ignore hundreds of people standing in your way.

The technique of protest by massive presence is clumsy, undignified and, like any technique, subject to abuse. It is, however, a fact of life. It will remain until institutions find means of sensitively identifying and responding to human needs—or until repressiveness endeavors to stop it. Then we will test the volatility and determination of its force.

Leadership will unite or divide this country by the way it deals with dissent. If through weakness it speaks only to the 80 per cent of the people who are basically uninvolved, who are comfortable and do not want to be disturbed, it will risk the radicalization of millions. Americans are a generous and sympathetic people. We may be indifferent or selfish when we act without understanding. But when America finally sees injustice and when it sees force itself revered as the true sovereign, it will be aroused to action.

Every time police are pitted against students and violence occurs, thousands are alienated. Police violence at the Democratic National Convention had a greater polarizing effect than the

Chicago riot following Dr. King's death, which took lives and destroyed property worth millions.

Comparatively balanced police action during the march on the Pentagon in 1967 and at Resurrection City in 1968 prevented what could have caused even more traumatic and tragic polarization. Reverberations from repressiveness could have shaken the nation. Instead dissent was tolerated, energies were spent, and ideas were tested in the marketplace of public opinion. The dissent expressed at the Pentagon and at Resurrection City proved to be an effective agent of change. First Amendment rights were fulfilled and the voices of powerless people were heard.

In turbulent times dissent can risk violence. Where violence occurs, where people's safety is jeopardized or significant property damage threatened, society must act effectively to protect itself. The security of persons is the first purpose of government. While the methods society adopts to prevent injury to persons and substantial damage to property must be humane and carefully avoid excessive force, they must be adequate to the need. Individuals who act to injure and destroy should be arrested and subjected to correctional techniques that will protect society from further wrongful conduct.

Will Durant has said that when liberty destroys order, the hunger for order will destroy liberty. Liberty is not a destroyer. We can enlarge liberty and order. The threat to our order exists mainly in fear and in the repressiveness that results from fear. Fear and repression will cause violence. Leadership must maintain public confidence among the vast majority who have as their chief concern, the safety of life and property. To do so by inciting fear or resorting to excessive force is the most divisive action possible. A peril of the time is the ease and apparent popularity of such a policy. Any temporary sense of safety repressiveness might inspire will be paid for dearly in division, the failure to change and the violence it begets.

Beyond the issue of conduct that causes physical injury is the issue of interference. In a mass society most human conduct interferes with others. This is why we invented the traffic signal and must queue in cafeterias. We accept of necessity substantial interference with our daily conduct because we cannot live together any other way. Much of this interference is unnecessary. Some is a gross impertinence that we barely recognize. Too few elevators, a handful of clerks to handle thousands of persons wishing to register to vote, trucks on the freeways during rush hours wasting thousands of man hours daily, streets blocked for crosstown traffic in rush hours to service merchants who could receive deliveries at other hours, buses and trains off schedule, doctors with too many patients, overcrowded hospitals, sidewalks too narrow to hold all the pedestrians when the factory shift changes, police too few to dispatch a car for two hours while the husband and wife fighting next door get louder and louder—these are daily inconveniences to millions. Most we quietly endure. Some we never question.

We cannot conduct ourselves so as not to interfere with others. The question is what interferences are permissible. The need is to consciously seek to limit unnecessary and undesirable interference. Neighbors' lights and fences and loud talk, horns and sirens, the gas company's causing the street to be torn up half the time, the city's failure to collect the garbage and remove the snow, the bowling leagues' pre-empting of every alley on weekends—all interfere with the pursuit of happiness by others. In mass society one must adjust and accommodate.

It is more important for us to hear dissent than the neighbors' fight, or the teenager's honk. An interdependent people must tolerate many interferences involving communication until we provide ways for dissent to present ideas that must be considered.

There were over 140 cities with two or more newspapers thirty years and 50 million people ago. Now fewer than thirty cities have two wholly independent papers. Three TV networks and several radio networks determine the content of most radio-TV programming. Seven substantial movie producers and a dozen magazine and book publishers provide the greater part of the remaining communications on which 200 million Americans depend. For millions of people caught in the interstices of mass society, deeply opposed to important aspects of their condition, unable to change them and isolated from the booming voices of mass media, except as occasional subjects of coverage from the media's perspectives, it is difficult to articulate loud and clear.

Dissent is the principal catalyst in the alchemy of truth. It is essential to change in human affairs. Treated constructively, it is a major way of preventing the approaching collision between immovable objects and irresistible forces.

Dissent must be viewed with tolerance. It is a creative force when constructively employed. Society and governments must seek ways of providing dissent its forum. This includes an opportunity to be heard—not merely to speak but to be listened to. In our times it is very difficult to focus dissent on the place of complaint and the people involved. If they cannot be reached, the best opportunity for a reasoned change is missed.

If some dissenters are dissent's greatest enemy, society must be wise enough to know this and to deal sensitively with it. Dissent will cause inconvenience. There are few other ways to be heard or to release the frustrations caused by the seeming paralysis of institutions. We must accept inconvenience that does not substantially interfere with the rights of others or disrupt important activities. When we fail to do this, we should ask ourselves whether the reason is that we fear the force of an idea, that we do not want change, or that we dislike and even hate the dissenter.

Where can you protest today if not in the street, on the sidewalks, in the park, on a campus or in public buildings? Can the poor protest in their rat-infested tenements or singly to the commissioner of buildings? The need is to speak in unmistakable language to those who may not want to, but must, hear. Public officials must listen to all of the people; in a democracy everybody counts.

The saddest illustration of our intolerance toward protest is Resurrection City. Even before Dr. King's death, rumors of violence were being spread over the country. The apostle of nonviolence, it was alleged, would bring violence to the nation's capital. There were predictions of holocaust. Strong pressures were exerted to prevent the issuance of any permit for the poor people.

Congressional hearings were held for the purpose of stopping the Poor People's Campaign. Absurdly improbable testimony about clandestine meetings and planned violence was presented. Senator John McClellan, the chairman of the committee, was advised that witnesses were unreliable. He made no effort to avoid such damaging testimony or to inform the public of its nature. His purpose was to stop the Poor People's Campaign.

The nation was led to expect horrible crimes and violence. We were not yet out of shock from Dr. King's murder and the riots that followed. Tourists and conventions were publicly urged not to come to Washington.

The poor people came—three thousand at most, fewer than a thousand on the average day. They built a shantytown in front of the Lincoln Memorial and camped there for two months. Lincoln smiled kindly, but much of the nation was outraged. Why should they be permitted to camp there when no one else could?

Then the American people saw too much of the truth. Poverty is miserable. It is ugly, disorganized, rowdy, sick, uneducated, violent and afflicted with crime. It demeans human dignity. We didn't want to see it on our sacred monument grounds. We wanted it out of sight and out of mind. The demanding tone, the inarticulateness, the implied violence deeply offended us. An emotional wave called for the removal of Resurrection City. The public and most vocal political leadership called for the police to close Resurrection City, to tear it down and run its inhabitants out of town.

The leadership of the campaign could barely hold Resurrection City together. The difficulty of working with groups from all over the country was greater than anything previously attempted. Southern rural and Northern urban blacks, Indians concerned chiefly with fishing rights, Mexican-Americans from half a dozen states, poor whites from Appalachia and elsewhere, college students and militants combined to compound their problems. That so many thought so few posed a threat to the public safety shows how frightened we were. They were a threat to themselves and a few others at most. They are always such a threat. To remove this handful from Lincoln's feet and put them back among the millions where they live does not remove the threat.

The police were in constant contact with the perimeters of Resurrection City, not unlike a small ghetto. They were prepared to maintain order—and they did. But within the City there was little law—much as inside the ghetto itself.

We know that poverty, misery, ignorance, mental and physical illness, violence and crime mark the slums. Is the lesson of Resurrection City that we will tolerate, even contain, such human suffering in the ghetto, but never on the monument grounds?

The poor people presented petitions to most of the major federal agencies. The petitions included many grievances that were remediable, many points that were right. At the federal Departments of Agriculture, HEW, HUD, Justice, Labor and others the poor people speaking in dissent presented their needs. They asked, in tones not always understood or appreciated, for help. They showed their deprivations and often showed ways of reducing them within the capability of existing programs.

Few who watched failed to learn. The poor people themselves framed most of the issues with which our government is still grappling. They spoke of hunger in America, of welfare robbing people of their dignity, of racism and schools that fail to teach. They reminded us that the law spoke of equal justice, while they had no rights.

The police were professional at Resurrection City. Their

leadership was sensitive. Many times a steady head like Deputy Chief Jerry Wilson would come up to an officer about to lose self-control, put his arm around him and walk him back to cool his fury. Officers in direct confrontation with crowds were rotated regularly to help maintain balance through the long hot summer.

When permits expired, many residents of Resurrection City refused to leave. The police, following the orders of civil authority, cleared Resurrection City. They knew there were some psychotics there. They knew there was danger. They performed professionally, calmly, without violence and without division. It was not a happy scene. But, one did not find bitterness and hostility engendered by police action at Resurrection City. The leadership of the Poor People's Campaign was relieved. It was over and perhaps we had learned.

By definition there is no right to violate the law. Rights are created by law. But law is an imperfect instrument of justice, and if justice is to be achieved there will be times when conscience may compel an individual to say, This is wrong and I will not obey. Thoreau, Gandhi, Martin Luther King did. They affected history by doing so and enriched justice. Hopefully we will find ways of achieving change that will make civil disobedience unnecessary. Until we do, those who deeply believe that acts of government are profoundly immoral and who have the courage to act on that belief can justly test the law and its purpose by nonviolent disobedience. Nonviolent because no wrong is so great as to justify the greatest wrong—human violence.

Our system must respond to those who violate its rules, even in civil disobedience, if ours is to be a government of law rather than whim, of principle rather than convenience. The system must have integrity and do what it says. Only if laws are enforced will there be a firm place, a foundation against which forces of change can push. Then reform is possible, unjust and unwise laws can be repealed and the law can assume its real role of moral leadership.

In the days ahead we must not only seek new ways of permitting meaningful dissent, we must prepare to cope with new methods and areas of dissent. As change pervades everything else, it will pervade dissent. New styles, new places, new areas of protest come swiftly. Many will involve danger. Some will touch our most sensitive nerve ends and devoutly held values. Always there will be those who seek to provoke and are good at it. An attitude of calm tolerance, a gentleness and patience will be needed. We must strive to understand, however obnoxious or irrational we find the dissenters. The years ahead will be stormy. Without the strength of tolerance we will enslave ourselves. If the law has no higher purpose than order, it is itself ignoble. Justice is the purpose of the law.

15

TECHNOLOGY: THE PROMISE
AND THE PERIL

THERE is no greater evidence of the total neglect of the criminal justice system than our failure to apply science to the solution of crime. America is devoted to science. We have sought and found solutions to many of humanity's greatest problems through science, yet we have scarcely begun to explore the potentials it holds for crime prevention.

In the main, the several disciplines within the system of criminal justice continue to conduct themselves as they did in the nineteenth century. For the police the automobile is the big change. The squad car may be essential to performance today but, on balance, it has increased the burdens of police. In the courts there are more cases, more judges, more laws and lawbooks—and more delay. For corrections there is no significant development. Prisoners, suffering the fate of the small farmer, do less farming and more labor, though with little more meaning; essentially prison life remains a waiting game.

Thus, while scientific discoveries and their application to our lives through technology overwhelm us with change, the criminal justice system remains largely unaffected in its methods. If we really cared, we would devote the best scientific resources at our command to the prevention and control of crime. There are few, if any, areas of public importance so shrouded in myth, fantasy, fear and ignorance. Our ignorance of crime, its causes and cures, exceeds our knowledge. Yet clearly, science could quickly solve a number of critical problems.

To begin with, there is the basic area of crime statistics. We must know facts about the incidence of crime. Comprehensive analyses of crime by carefully defined category will provide many of the missing facts needed to fashion specific remedies. How much crime is there? Where is crime committed? Who commits it? Is it increasing, or do we torture ourselves with fear of waves of crime, unaware of its real incidence? The unreported assault hurts as much as the assault that makes the newspaper. The unreported theft costs no less because it is not reported. Techniques of assuring the fullest possible reporting of crime must be developed.

The National Crime Commission in 1967 estimated that most crime is unreported. Most murder is reported to police, and nearly all police communicate reported murders in their districts for inclusion in the FBI's uniform crime statistics today, but this was not always so. America is deeply disturbed about violence. Are we a comparatively violent people? Are we becoming more so? Careful scientific studies can tell us whether we were more violent in the nineteenth century than now, whether the depression years and war years spawned violence, whether crime has really increased in the last six years, or six months, whether violence occurs more frequently in our nation than elsewhere, whether violence is as American as cherry pie. We must know more about the days in which Bonnie and Clyde were alleged to have robbed half a dozen banks hundreds of miles apart—an impossible feat—than newspaper accounts can tell us. We must know whether Southern lynchings were such a constant and common threat to black Southerners that they were conditioned to extreme violence by the threat and fact of broken necks. Is black ghetto violence partly urbanized and congested Southern violence? Why is the murder rate in the South twice the murder rate of the nation?

If we have transmitted a terrible history of violence from recent comparatively rural days into urban slums, we should know it. The awareness of that burden may explain what happens in the ghetto and indicate the path to effective prevention. To the demagogue who relishes every ghetto crime as new evidence of the inherent evil of the people who live there such statistical data can reply that it is the slum dwellers who suffer most —and compassion arising from truth can answer that only society can prevent that crime.

Systematic reporting might disclose that most assaults occur within families—not just one-fourth of all assaults, as indicated by our statistics. How many wife and child beatings are unreported and how many children who suffer or see such beatings later administer some themselves? Sympathy and fear often inhibit a person from reporting the wrongdoings of father, mother, son or friend. The realization that drunkenness, psychosis, uncontrollable impulse, or anxiety over weeks of unemployment caused a moment of violence may explain why such crimes go unreported.

Perhaps 90 per cent of all property crime is not reported. How can law enforcement begin to deal with the prevention of crime if its existence cannot even be determined? The poor are far less likely to report property crime. Individual property losses are not great among the poor, because they do not own much property, but the poor are likely to need what gets stolen far more than rich people do. Many ghetto dwellers have become so accustomed to street robbery, burglary and theft as part of life that they see crime as an inconvenience much as the middle class accept car trouble. By its being accepted so widely, crime loses its horror, and children come to see crime as a common fact of life. Many in the ghetto, moreover, do not believe in white man's justice, and crimes often go unreported because of hostility toward the system itself and the police in particular. People would rather suffer violence than pay homage to a system they think unjust.

If distrust or hatred of the police conceals most ghetto crime, we need to know this. We can never deal effectively in ignorance. If ghetto crime is usually not reported, suburban crime is. As a result, the real disparity between suburban and slum crime is blurred. That suburban crime is prominently reported in the press is a factor in shaping public attitudes. How many ghetto murders make headlines? How many murders in the suburbs miss the headlines?

To develop better statistics we must also improve police methods of crime classification. Wide differences in state criminal codes and police practice will make this task difficult, especially since thousands of police departments are reporting millions of criminal incidents. But until there is uniformity, the reports will compare unequals and incomparables. Law enforcement agencies must transmit all reports of crime accurately and uniformly to statistical centers.

The most important and difficult task will be to motivate people to report crime. Until this goal is achieved, we cannot know of crime, much less prevent or control it. Research, opinion sampling, and scientifically developed demonstration projects can tell us how. The close police-community relations essential to full reporting must be developed. Deteriorating police-community relations may cause a decline in reported crime at the very time crime is increasing most rapidly.

There are reasons for law enforcement to misreport crime. A new chief of police may want to show how effective his leadership has been in reducing the crime rate and therefore he may discourage full reporting. Emphasis on other aspects of police operations reduces the care and the effort put into statistical reporting, which takes time and often seems pointless. Officers may fail to turn in reports of muggings and thefts where no solution seems possible. Sometimes they refuse to accept reports of crime in slum areas where successful investigation seems remote. In other circumstances—to exert pressure for more manpower or a pay raise—crimes that are not usually included in statistics may be listed, or crimes defined as petty theft become grand larceny, or three boxes of candy bars stolen by children become three thefts instead of one, or none. Tampering with crime statistics, like their misuse by the demagogue, is a cruel hoax. Crime is too serious to deceive ourselves about it.

Improvement in gathering crime statistics is useless, though, unless we deal with such findings sensitively. If all crime that actually occurs were reported tomorrow, our crime rate would appear to triple, even if, in fact, it was down 20 per cent. The crime was there all along; we just didn't know it. Increased sophistication in interpreting statistics will be necessary as reporting becomes reliable. As an example, consider the matter of data regarding our teenage population, which continues to increase faster than the total population. Infants and octogenarians rarely commit crime; teenagers commit a great deal of crime. Statistical analyses must explain the effect of changes in age groups. There was a 20 per cent greater increase in our teenage population in the 1960's than in our general population, a fact that contributed substantially to the increase in crime per capita—a fact we should not miss.

When we think of research, we usually think of hardware, of physical objects. In the police world we think first of bigger guns and faster cars, but the behavioral and medical sciences offer greater safety than the physical sciences. Crime is human behavior. What more important study could man undertake than the causes of his criminal conduct? Man becomes again the proper study of mankind. Is it not far more important for man to know what makes him capable of strangling another human, of cutting out hearts and dismembering bodies, of gang-raping a young girl, or pack-mugging and killing a dirty, grizzled old vagrant than to know what is on the far side of the moon? Why do we steal, embezzle and defraud? Is the answer beyond the reach of a people who double their knowledge of the physical world in a decade?

Should we not set out to discover why we commit crime and

how we can cure it? Is mental health manifest as a cause half the time? What about brain damage, with its social overlays? We know we can eliminate physical addiction to heroin through chemistry, yet we sacrifice hundreds of thousands to wretchedness because we will not spend one-half the cost of a nuclear submarine to find a cure. How much crime is caused by addiction? Alcohol looms large in the world of crime. How many murders and violent crimes are committed by people under its influence? Injustice itself causes crime, as research could prove. Why should I be just to my neighbor when society is unjust to me? To overcome crime we shall have to learn to detect and eliminate injustice.

We do not know if there are hereditary characteristics that affect criminal capability. We should. If there are, how can they be prevented or, if not prevented, controlled?

What can medicine, psychiatry, psychology and sociology bring to corrections to rehabilitate those who have demonstrated their capabilities to injure others or take property? If these disciplines have any relevance to the real world, they can do far more than iron bars and stone walls. We should make every effort to seek the answers they may provide.

In crime prevention, behavioral science can offer techniques that will reduce crime. How should police act in the presence of dangerous psychotics? What is the effect of street lighting on crime? What patterns of police patrol, type of uniform, color of automobile will bring greatest effectiveness to police effort? What impact do differing police practice and appearance have on human behavior? Studies of such crime problems as bank robbery and police intervention in family disputes show that carefully developed techniques can prevent crime.

Rudimentary studies indicate that murders could be deterred by early counseling. An analysis of eleven murderers in Texas prisons showed common qualities present in each. The men were loners, highly deficient in their interpersonal relationships. This was due in large measure to such anxiety-producing factors through childhood as cruelty by parents, an absence of other children, broken homes, no fathers, and a resulting inability to face problems. In their early years they manifested strong tendencies to pretend problems did not exist, followed by sudden impulsive solutions. Preschool and grammar school guidance for children in high-crime areas and special counseling for youths who manifested poor social adjustment would have helped others beyond those given their chance—they would have spared the victims of the troubled youngsters.

A five-year study of 1,034 children between ten and eighteen years of age selected at random from poor homes between Houston and 125th Streets in Manhattan found that 12 per cent suffered from serious mental illness. Each child evaluated as seriously ill was totally unable to function in one or more of five important areas of behavior. A direct relationship between these disorders and the poverty of the slum environment and its life style was clearly seen. Cited as factors causing the mental illnesses were inadequate schooling, low income and constant tension over money, racial discrimination and family quarrels. No hereditary factors were discovered by the investigators headed by Dr. Thomas S. Langner of the New York University School of Medicine.

The sample was 60 per cent white, 30 per cent Spanish-speaking and 10 per cent Negro. Overall, 8 per cent of the white, 17 per cent of the black and 18 per cent of the Spanish-speaking children were diagnosed as seriously disturbed. Among children whose parents were on welfare the percentage was 28—three and one-half times the average. Summarizing the findings in April 1969, Dr. Langner said, "I think we should be alarmed by these findings. They are . . . the kind of kids that Oswald and Sirhan were."

Behavioral scientists can tell us how to condition violence from our personal capability. Psychiatry, psychology, anthropology and sociology hold the key. If we fail to make every effort now to curb our instinct to violence, the consequences in the years ahead will be disastrous. We can do this. It is more important than an ABM system to our personal safety.

The physical sciences promise much for the quality of criminal justice. We all get excited about the use of science in crime detection, but we have yet to become sufficiently excited to spend money. The identification of physical objects, the determination of where a fire started and what caused it, voice prints, computerized recording of prints for individual fingers and for palms, refined chemical analysis of weapons, blood, food and fiber, autopsy techniques that find the cause of mysterious death —these and other techniques could obviously take the mystery out of many crimes. A scientific research effort would also quickly expose the inefficiency and unreliability of many police techniques now used, such as continuous, intensive, untrained interrogation and identification by use of the line-up.

Computers—the only way to count or recall masses of facts swiftly in our society—are just being discovered by police, courts and corrections. Such steps as deployment of police in high-crime areas, tailoring programs of rehabilitation from the experience of all comparable cases, and pinpointing the causes of delay in courts require computers. There is no other way to organize and review the relevant facts. The police blotter, the intuition of the prison case worker, and the court docket sheet filled in by quill pen are no longer adequate. Computers must be enlisted in the cause of modern criminal justice.

Similarly, electronic communication is essential to crime prevention and control. A police officer with a club and gun patrolling on one side of a block may not know of an assault in an apartment on the other side of the same block. With a ten-ounce transistor radio he can be alerted immediately to any crime reported. An electronic board in the dispatcher's office can constantly show the location and movement of every officer on duty—or even off duty—in different colors to indicate the skills he has and the urgency of his present activity. Such techniques could multiply the impact of police presence. Today the deployment of police personnel is largely left to chance. When effective radio communication is needed for riot control, the Army has to supply it. Hundreds of walkie-talkie radios developed for Vietnam and other military needs are provided by the United States Army for police use in the streets of a great city in a riot emergency. They do not work very well in the city because they were developed for another jungle, but modern electrical engineering could adapt them to effective use.

Our saddest failure from many standpoints has been the lack of effort to provide nonlethal weapons for police. In terms of the effect of force, it is a long way from the hand or the club to the gun. The club risks injury—the gun risks death. There are thousands of Americans needlessly dead, and tens of thousands grieving for them and for our system, because the policeman had only himself and his gun to control a drunk, a psychotic, a looter, a person fleeing from a crime or apparent crime. The violence provoked by such incidents is immense. Police in Birmingham, Alabama, killed more than a dozen citizens in 1966; police in Washington, D.C., killed more than forty citizens during the last three years of the 1960's. The deaths measure only a fraction of the violence that flows directly from those incidents. The same story is retold in most major cities every year. Compared to all of this killing without the benefit of trial, there were only three legal executions in the United States from 1965 to 1970.

America spends billions on ways to kill—techniques of massive firepower, nuclear weaponry, biological warfare, ABM systems—but fails to spend the few millions it would take to develop safe and effective nonlethal weapons. Scientific skills could soon create a small weapon capable of firing a missile scores of yards with great accuracy. A chemical could be developed for such a missile capable of rendering a human being instantly unconscious but that would not be harmful to persons with bad hearts, diabetes or high alcoholic content in the blood stream. Professional police could be trained to use such weapons instead of guns, to use them only when absolutely necessary and then with great care.

Failure to develop effective nonlethal weapons contributes to the climate of violence, bitterness and hatred for the system. The black rage which causes a psychotic to shoot an officer may have begun a decade before, when as a child he saw the body of a black man lying in the street, a broken whisky bottle next to him and one side of his face blown off by a bullet from a policeman's revolver.

Police equipment is not built for police needs. It is only slightly modified from other stock. Cars designed for police— fast, safe, built to hold and carry dangerous people, to be conspicuous or inconspicuous, to warn or to surprise, as the need may be—would make a significant difference in police effectiveness. Helicopter patrols can safely and effectively control intercity and interstate escapes and even inhibit burglary and street crime in some areas, though used unwisely they can infuriate a whole neighborhood by their constant noisy presence. Sound recording and transcribing equipment could avoid weeks of delay in trials and on appeal while lawyers and judges wait for the court stenographer to decipher and transcribe his notes.

Science and technology must come to the aid of criminal justice. It can solve important problems. We are beginning, as with the small research capability of the National Institute for Crime and Technology created by the Omnibus Crime Control Act of 1968. But the beginning is slow—Congress appropriated only $3 million for the first year and $7.5 million the second. The Federal Judicial Center created in 1967 gives the courts their first chance to solve the very difficult problems of court administration in mass society by the use of research. As these efforts expand, and with the growing interest of companies in aerospace, chemical and systems-analysis industries, we can bring twentieth-century solutions to twentieth-century problems of man's great concern on earth—justice.

PART THREE

Liberty vs. Security:
The False Conflict

Our system of criminal justice fails to reduce crime. It is not working well. Police are not professional, courts are unable to process case loads, prisons make criminals of boys they could rehabilitate. We see the reforms that are desperately needed, yet we do not make them. But even if these public agencies were working at the most effective level possible, they could not substantially or permanently reduce crime while conditions exist that breed crime. Mere words of prohibition, with force and the threat of force their only sanction, cannot shape human conduct in mass society.

As turbulence, doubt and anxiety cause fear to increase, fear in turn seeks repressiveness as a source of safety. But experience tells us that the result of repressiveness is more turbulence and more crime. In frustration over the failure of law enforcement to control crime, new, quick and cheap methods by which police and courts and prisons might be made more effective are sought amid desperate hope and rising hatred. A public that be-

271

lieves the police alone are responsible for crime control, and therefore no other effort is needed, will vest any power in the police that seems to promise safety when fear of crime is great. But there is no such power.

Excessive reliance on the system of criminal justice is terribly dangerous. It separates the people from their government. It is the one clear chance for irreconcilable division in America. It puts institutions of government in which people must have confidence in direct confrontation with dynamics they cannot control. When the system is abusive, society itself is unfair and government demeans human dignity. Then there is a contest of cunning between the people and the state. The state can never win.

The dialogue over the proper limits of police action and barely relevant court rulings consumes most of the emotion and much of the energy that could be constructively used to strengthen the system of criminal justice. Instead of efforts to raise police standards, expand training, increase salaries, and improve judicial machinery, we debate in ignorance and anger whether police should be authorized to stop and frisk whenever they choose and whether the Miranda decision should be reversed. The resulting diversion of attention, emotionalization of concern and polarization of attitude damage the system of criminal justice. Those who stimulate prejudices in public opinion, who appeal to base instincts of fear, who protest their willingness—even desire—to sacrifice freedom on the altar of order add immeasurably to the burdens of achieving excellence in the performance of criminal justice agencies and commitment to eradication of the underlying causes of crime.

It is reasonable to assume that soldiers can provide safety. They have the immediate power to destroy all but the strongest sources of violence. But the assumption is wrong. Crime control is far too complex to be controlled by overwhelming power. Soldiers are completely untrained for it. Even the control of riots is beyond their ability unless they are retrained and garrisoned throughout cities. To do that would tragically undermine the capacity of local police to perform. Military organization and technique are the antithesis of the police role in a free society. Those police departments whose dominant quality is paramilitary will never be effective.

A narrow logic can even conclude that the use of deadly force —shooting looters, for instance—stops crime. After all, it does eliminate a criminal—if the right person is shot. Our total experience shows beyond question that the result of using such extreme repressiveness is always an increment to the dimension of violence and a new potential for more.

There are degrees of repression. Each demeans the dignity of the individual in its different way. Intimidation of speech or conduct by force or threat of force in essence says the state is supreme, the individual has no rights, he must do as he is told. We see this when police tell people to move along, when they stop and frisk without cause, arrest on suspicion, enter premises without a warrant or without knocking, deny permits to speak and assemble, break up meetings and raid places where unpopular people live or work, without legal justification.

Stealth and trickery as methods of repression mean that the state has no respect for the individual. It will deceive, lie, invade privacy, steal documents, do whatever it thinks necessary to catch people in crime. By wiretapping, the government says to its citizens: Do not trust us, for we do not trust you. We will hide, overhear, wait secretly for months for you to do wrong. If you do anything to displease us, we may choose to watch your every move.

Denial of bail and preventive detention are essentially premised on the belief that the individual must yield his liberty to the state if he is poor, ignorant, despised—and apparently dangerous. He can be tried later. Society will not presume him innocent. No respecters of human dignity, these measures imply that judges can tell who the bad people—the dangerous ones —are and can say that they should be denied freedom and punished as guilty until proven innocent.

The desire to compel confessions and to repeal the Fifth Amendment admits the impotence of the system of criminal justice to find truth and do justice. Instead, it seeks to crush the individual, to make him bend his knee to its sovereignty, to coerce from his own mouth words that will convict him, to question him—if he is poor, ignorant or afraid—until he cracks. Frustrated and frightened in its impulse, it ignores the unreliability of the emotional or psychotic response, seeking only conviction.

Finally, repression attacks life itself. We become so terrified we see safety in death imposed by courts and carried out in prisons. When all history says violence begets violence, when reverence for life is essential if life is to be dear, the state kills—encouraging some to do the same.

There is no conflict between liberty and safety. We will have both, or neither. You cannot purchase security at the price of freedom, because freedom is essential to human dignity and crime flows from acts that demean the individual. We can enlarge both liberty and safety if we turn from repressiveness, recognize the causes of crime and move constructively.

The major contribution the law can make is moral leadership. Only then can it hope to permanently influence the conduct of its citizens. The law cannot therefore impose immoral rules or act immorally. The government of a people who would be free of crime must always act fairly, with integrity and justice.

16

SOLDIERS, SAFETY AND FREEDOM

ONE phenomenon of the past few years—the use of troops, Army and National Guard—can create a direct and massive distortion of important balances in law enforcement. Its significance was largely lost in the immense emotional turmoil from which it arose. The matter deserves detailed consideration.

It is crises, of course, that test the strength of laws and constitutions. When all is well, their principles are widely extolled and staunchly defended. Their real vitality in government under law is determined in times of great stress.

The actual use of federal troops against civilian populations at Detroit in 1967 and Baltimore, Washington and Chicago in 1968 and the pre-positioning of troops for potential use in Chicago in August 1968 and Washington in January, October and November 1969 illustrate the pressures on adherence to a professed fundamental principle—the primacy of local law enforcement. It also demonstrates the dimension of the risks created by the turbulence of our times.

When the Union was formed, police powers were reserved to the states and the people. Federal enforcement was authorized only where necessary and proper to effectuate the purposes of acts of the Congress, and to protect the integrity of federal functions and property.

Police protection, by law and practice, has been vested in

local government. That it be retained at the local level is more important now than it was in 1787. Only local government can efficiently police our great cities. Only local government can be responsive to the infinite diversity of our peoples and their particular needs for police protection. Only local police can avoid the dangers of the police state.

The tensions of our time raise the risk of substantial and frequent use of federal troops against American citizens. When the chips are down and the fear of rioting is high, virtually every interest involved wants troops. The white suburbs and major business interests seek the apparent protection of troops out of personal fear and for the security of their property. The police themselves understandably hate riot duty. They often do not consider it as police work because its intensity involves crowds and manpower beyond ordinary police experience. The mayor of a town in the throes of a riot is besieged with demands to request troops. It takes a strong man to resist such pressure.

You do not *win* riots, however effectively they are handled. If a riot occurs, its psychological effect, whatever the physical damage, is devastating. Politically, it is much easier for the mayor to pass the buck to the governor or the President. The governors, once their inhibitions were broken by the request for the Army at Detroit, have been inclined to call quickly for troops. Their hesitancy, until Governor Romney asked for federal help at Detroit in 1967, stemmed in the main from a desire common to governors to seem strong enough to handle any trouble in their own states. With increasing fear, the demand for early overwhelming force grew. Reflection led to the realization that if a riot continues and troops are not called, leadership has not done everything possible to control a riot. If things go badly without troops, local and state leaders appear to have failed in their duty.

The National Guard offers a substitute for federal troops, but it does not satisfy many of the needs that give rise to requests for Army regulars. Generally, the National Guard is not nearly as well disciplined or as well trained. To rely on it involves risks to rioters from excessive use of gunfire and to the public from the failure to stop the rioting. The cost is burdensome on state governments. On occasion, governors have asked that the Guard be federalized to avoid state expense for supporting it. Governors have had to call special sessions of their legislatures to appropriate additional funds for the National Guard. In a very few places, principally Washington, D.C., which has a very small Guard unit, the National Guard will not have manpower of the magnitude that seems adequate to the dimension of feared disturbances. When parts of a state distant from a riot fear disturbances themselves, they resist transferring local Guard units to the scene of action, again causing pressure to call federal troops.

The Army, for all its protestations, loves war games. It came to riot control with alacrity. It has spent millions in establishing military command capabilities, riot potential intelligence, liaison and training with local law enforcement. Never doubt that the Pentagon will seek riot control duty if the opportunity arises. That it can do so in the posture of saving life and property makes its interest nearly irresistible. The assignment of a lieutenant general to full-time riot control command, and his presence among civilian law enforcement and Justice Department officials on a regular basis beginning in October and November 1969, shows how quickly and thoroughly the military can become involved.

Neither civilian nor military opposition to the commitment of federal troops for riot prevention will be encountered from any source in the Pentagon. When the issue arose of pre-positioning the Army in and near Chicago before the Democratic National Convention in August 1968, the Pentagon favored it without any dissent detectable from outside. There was no evidence of any need for federal troops to be located, on the ready, in the Chicago area. The principal reason given was the fear of the consequences if anything happened and the Army was not present. It cost nothing for the moment except dollars, but if the

Army was absent and riots were uncontrolled, leadership would look like Admiral Kimmel and General Short, insensitive to the risks at Pearl Harbor.

During the Baltimore riots of April 1968, when all intelligence indicated there was no need for federal troops and the officers on the scene for both the National Guard and the Army advance team found Army troops were not required, the Pentagon recommended the dispatch of two thousand men to the city. Four thousand three hundred soldiers went. Perhaps this kind of thinking is why so many American soldiers wound up in Vietnam.

Even the ghetto dwellers want the Army. Their reasons are many. Fear and hatred for the police are probably the dominant factors. The Army seems to bring safety, while the National Guard signals danger. Regular Army soldiers are like the GI's of the occupations following World War II. Soon they are giving candy to kids, and friendly crowds gather around them. Also, the Army is well integrated. Nearly every riot unit is more than 20 per cent Negro. The National Guard, in contrast, without the Army's long effort at integration, and often dominated by state politics, serves to remind blacks of repressiveness and discrimination. Nationally, the Guard was less than 2 per cent black in 1968. In many states the percentage was a minor fraction of 1.

Resistance to use of the Army is rare and, during an emergency, exceedingly difficult to support. When a President is asked for help by a governor, it is hard to decline. Every political pressure and every precautionary instinct support the use of troops.

Still, reliance on troops is undesirable from every standpoint unless they are necessary to save life. We are too quick to ignore principle when crises come. To be constitutional, commitment of troops against citizens presupposes insurrection beyond the control of state and local law enforcement. To rely on troops also means either that we will suffer extensive damage from riots before troops arrive, because of delays in the movement of the Army, or that we must garrison troops throughout our cities. It means that men, materiel and money desperately needed by local law enforcement—which is best suited from every standpoint to prevent and control riots—will be used for the Army. Devoting the same resources to local police could strengthen their performance in all the services they provide. Used for the Army, these outlays prove immensely wasteful. Men with little other beneficial function must be stationed around the country waiting to control what all law enforcement should be working to prevent—riots.

Except in Washington, D.C., after the murder of Dr. King, where specially trained troops were stationed nearby and National Guard capability was negligible, the Army was never deployed in direct street confrontation during the 1960's until a riot was substantially over.

The Army moves ponderously. It comes from distant points. On a four-hour standby, which imposes a severe limitation on any other activity, a brigade will not be airborne for six hours after the command to move. Add flight time, landing, establishing command posts and communication centers, organizing, loading in trucks and buses, moving miles to the city, then through strange streets—and many hours have elapsed.

The Army seeks overwhelming force. It carefully reconnoiters. At Oxford, Mississippi, on the evening of September 30, 1962, United States marshals, Border Patrol men, and prison wardens charged with enforcing a federal court order admitting James Meredith to the University of Mississippi Law School, waited in desperate circumstances for more than eight hours while a highly trained airborne unit specially deployed for this single purpose less than eighty miles away moved from Memphis to the Ole Miss campus. When it finally came, it came in torrents, but any foreseeable major outburst of violence would have occurred long before it arrived. Three days after Meredith was enrolled in his classes, 12,500 soldiers occupied Oxford, Mississippi, a rural county seat of 4,500. It was six months before the total dropped below 2,000.

It took troops at Fort Campbell, Kentucky, and Fort Bragg, North Carolina, on full alert, nearly eighteen hours to arrive in force on the streets of Detroit during the riots of July 1967. Most riots will have run their course in less than eighteen hours. When riots occur, the greatest damage is likely to come in the first few hours. For law enforcement to arrive six hours after a riot starts is to be late. Prevention has failed, the riot has occurred, suppression is past due, and commotion is waning without need of a counterforce.

Governor Raymond Shafer of Pennsylvania and Mayor Joseph Barr of Pittsburgh exercised rare restraint during the rioting following Dr. King's death. Informed on April 7, 1968, that troops could not reach Pittsburgh in force in less than twenty-eight hours, they carefully and personally assessed the situation and publicly stated troops were not necessary. The justification for calling troops in Pittsburgh exceeded that for Baltimore, which asked for troops through Governor Agnew.

The Army will never have a riot prevention impact, except psychologically, unless we dramatically transform our political system. It cannot deal directly and continuously with people in riot potential areas to prevent riots before they occur. To be effective, it would have to be garrisoned throughout areas of cities where riots may occur and retrained to move swiftly—and not with overwhelming force but with flexible control capability that expands and contracts sensitively to meet developing situations.

The waste and inefficiency involved in placing troops in cities and in special training would be great. Parts of cities would have an atmosphere of military occupation—perhaps interminably. Most of the time of the soldiers would be spent waiting for what we hope will never happen and should be working to prevent.

Police, using the same money necessary to provide an effective Army riot control presence, could be involved in the whole range of police activity. Crime prevention, crime control and community relations—all that police do would be enhanced. The prevention potential of such local expenditures would exceed many times over the riot control value. The police would be local people. They could be responsive to local government and local need. They would not create an atmosphere of military occupation.

To turn to the Army for riot and confrontation control would be a tragic mistake. It can happen. The vastness of the resources available to the Pentagon makes easy for it things impossible for others. It can set aside hundreds of millions of dollars and tens of thousands of men and never feel the difference.

In the spring of 1969 the Department of Defense rushed to completion a new control center primarily for use as a war room in the event of riots. Located in the Pentagon, the facility cost nearly $2 million, a figure exceeding any prior annual budget of the Federal Community Relations Service, which had been successful in preventing scores of riots. The Army can spend millions from an $80-billion defense budget while police struggle to secure $3 billion for their entire domestic service. The Army will send thousands of men to a city while the Justice Department strains to find a half dozen lawyers and community resource people.

Generals resent civilian presence and legal guidance. Their business is war. War knows few rules and forgets them when need arises. Attorneys from Justice concerned about civil liberties, excessive force and the rights of civilian populations and prisoners find it hard to influence military commanders on the scene. The situation has all the elements necessary for loss of civilian control of domestic law enforcement.

Local law enforcement is the first line of domestic defense. Where it is inadequate, combinations of local police from adjacent jurisdictions, the county sheriff's office and then the state patrol should be utilized. Only in extreme circumstances, where these other forces fail, should the state use its National Guard.

The founding fathers foresaw that times would come when local and state resources might be inadequate. They provided for the rare contingency in Article IV, Section 4, of the Constitution, which states: "The United States shall guarantee to every State in this Union a Republican form of government, and shall protect each of them against invasion; and on application of the Legislature, or of the Executive (when the Legislature cannot be convened) against domestic violence."

The provision is the bulwark of federalism because it applies at the most critical time in federal-state relationships—the day that state police resources prove inadequate, the day of insurrection, severe civil commotion or general lawlessness.

Following ratification of the Constitution, the Congress acted to implement this provision in 1792. The resulting statute in its present form is found in Title 10, Chapter 15, Section 331, of the United States Code. It reads: "Whenever there is an insurrection in any state against its government, the President may, upon the request of its legislature or its governor if the legislature cannot be convened, call into federal service such of the militia of the other states, in the number requested by that state, and use such of the armed forces, as he considers necessary to suppress the insurrection."

The Congressional debates preceding enactment of the statute reveal that the provision was intended to be used sparingly. Congressman John Francis Mercer of Virginia carefully distinguished civil and military police powers. He described the former as deliberative and the latter as not. He said, therefore, "in no free country can the latter be called forth . . . but under great restrictions." Congressman William Vans Murray of Maryland stressed that "a prompt and energetic execution of the law is considered of the first importance, while at the same time the military is never called but in the last extremity."

Historically, governors have been most sparing in their requests and Presidents even more so in authorizing use of the

military to control domestic violence. Essential differences between earlier times and ours must be distinguished. Before
World War II we did not maintain standing armies of substantial size. In 1939 the New York City Police Department had
more men than the United States Marine Corps. Change has
conditioned us to consider a large standing army to be as natural as the trees in the forest. The presence of well-financed,
highly trained, fully equipped soldiers invites their use.

Throughout American history before 1960, requests for federal troops had been made during fifteen domestic crises. A
number were denied and others granted only after careful study.
President Van Buren refused the request of Pennsylvania during the "Buckshot War" in 1838 because he deemed the state
militia adequate to the need. Tyler refused the request of the
Rhode Island governor in the Dorr Rebellion of 1842 because
the legislature was in session and had not applied for aid. Pierce
refused California in 1853 when the San Francisco Vigilante
Committee threatened to usurp state government, because the
state had not exhausted its powers. Theodore Roosevelt refused
Colorado's request for troops to suppress mining camp riots in
1903 because the state did not show it could not control the
riots and he further found its "request not made as contem-
plated by law." Requests in such instances usually followed
weeks or months of violence. It would have taken additional
weeks to provide Army assistance.

Under some circumstances the President need not have a request from a state to commit federal forces to maintain domestic
order. During the debates prior to enactment of Section 331,
Congress specifically rejected a provision that would have limited its use to occasions when state authorities sought federal
help. Restricting federal aid to occasions when state authority asked for help would have failed to meet the needs arising
when state authorities were hostile or indifferent to threatened
federal rights. In 1871, after ratification of the Fourteenth
Amendment and based on it, the Congress enacted a statute

codified as Title 10, Chapter 15, Section 333. It was a Reconstruction measure devised to provide federal protection for any group or class of people deprived of constitutional rights where the "constituted authorities of that state are unable, fail or refuse" to give protection. Directed generally at activity of, or condoned by, the state, it does not provide for any request from state authority. It was used extensively against activities of the Ku Klux Klan and in recent years was relied on in part in 1957 in Little Rock when Central High was desegregated, in 1962 in Mississippi and in 1963 in Alabama when the state universities were desegregated, and during the 1965 march from Selma to Montgomery.

Obviously, a strict limitation on the utilization of Section 333 is vital to federalism. It places the state and the nation hazardously close to conflict. This law has no application to present riot potential, where no one is more anxious for suppression than local authority. To rely on it when a governor, endeavoring to protect the rights of the citizens of his state, refuses to call for federal help would be extremely dangerous. It would be, in essence, a federal seizure of police power.

Until the riots in Detroit in 1967 just half of the Presidents who had served in this century had received any request for federal troops. Before 1967 only a single request for federal soldiers had been made in thirty-five years—during the race riots in Detroit in World War II while the Michigan National Guard was fighting overseas and unavailable. Governor Edmund G. Brown of California had not requested federal troops during the Watts riots of August 1965. Governor Richard Hughes did not seek help from the United States Army during the Newark riots of August 1967. Scores of other riots had been contained by local law enforcement and sometimes National Guard in dozens of cities from 1963 to 1968. By contrast, requests came from three places in 1968 alone—Baltimore, Chicago and Washington—and troops were committed.

The great importance of these constitutional principles and

presidential practices to the federal system and individual liberty is clear. Their importance to the public safety is also abundantly clear. Local police must be adequate to meet all but unforeseeable violence of the most extreme dimension. Then alert and well-trained state police, followed by the National Guard, should be committed to the full extent the circumstances warrant. Only as a last resort should the regular Army of the United States be called to confront citizen disorders.

We tend to forget the requirements of the law in times of crisis. These are the very times their observation is most important. Any President is going to provide federal troops where the lives and property of American citizens within the United States are unprotected. But they can and should be provided only when domestic violence of the most serious nature exists: when local and state law enforcement have fully committed available resources, the National Guard is activated and fully utilized, and still the serious threat exists and the violence remains uncontrolled. Federal force can be employed where soldiers are not garrisoned in cities with a minimum loss of time and added risk to life or property by cooperation and coordination of governments. Troops alerted early can prepare to move as a potential riot develops and, when necessary, move near the scene of a riot without being committed against civilians until the need is clear and constitutional safeguards are met.

Besides building local law enforcement, because it is the best chance we have to prevent the igniting and spread of riots, we need to train the National Guard, because it must move to suppress domestic violence before federal help is sought if our federal system is to prevail. But our primary reliance must be on local police. Who has the first, best chance to check a riot? Who can know the people, the area, the streets and buildings? Who is always present? To whom does the Constitution reserve the police power?

Our lives, our property and our liberty depend on excellence in local law enforcement.

17

THE WIRETAP:
DESTROYER OF INTEGRITY

IN bygone days the risks arising from eavesdropping were not great. Only by hiding could a person overhear. With the telephone the danger increased. Indispensable to life in mass society, electronics makes communication possible between individuals separated by blocks, or miles, or oceans. No longer can caution protect privacy. Even if you look behind the tree, in the closet or under the bed, you cannot be certain that your conversation is not overheard.

Developments in electronics beyond the telephone make it possible to totally destroy privacy. Privacy will exist tomorrow only if society insists on it. By placing a radio receiver-transmitter in a room, by directing a laser beam through a wall and focusing it on a resonant surface, by directing a parabolic scope toward two men in the middle of a field, every sound can be heard from afar. The speaker has no way of knowing who hears.

This invasion is only the beginning. Technology will soon bring the capability for audio-visual intrusion into every place. We can create a society where no one will know whether his every act is watched, his every word heard—or everyone will know they are. A generation later no one will see any wrong in it. The individual will be a different creature then.

Privacy has always been a precious commodity, but never so

rare as in our times. As populations grow, urbanization increases and science learns the secrets of the physical world, a clear commitment to privacy as an end in itself will be necessary if it is to survive in mass society. A conscious analysis of the meaning to privacy of every technological development will be essential. Science cannot make moral judgments. If morality is to be maintained, man must make those judgments.

Privacy is the basis of individuality. To be alone and be let alone, to be with chosen company, to say what you think, or don't think, but to say what you will, is to be yourself. Solitude is imperative, even in a high rise apartment. Personality develops from within. To reflect is to know yourself. Character is formed through years of self-examination. Without this opportunity, character will be formed largely by uncontrolled external social stimulations. Americans are excessively homogenized already.

Few conversations would be what they are if the speakers thought others were listening. Silly, secret, thoughtless and thoughtful statements would all be affected. The sheer numbers in our lives, the anonymity of urban living and the inability to influence things that are important are depersonalizing and dehumanizing factors of modern life. To penetrate the last refuge of the individual, the precious little privacy that remains, the basis of individual dignity, can have meaning to the quality of our lives that we cannot foresee. In terms of present values, that meaning cannot be good.

Invasions of privacy demean the individual. Can a society be better than the people composing it? When a government degrades its citizens, or permits them to degrade each other, however beneficent the specific purpose, it limits opportunities for individual fulfillment and national accomplishment. If America permits fear and its failure to make basic social reforms to excuse police use of secret electronic surveillance, the price will be dear indeed. The practice is incompatible with a free society.

Why do we think that the wiretap and the bug offer security?

What is the evidence that they are either effective or efficient? Surely those who favor their use have the burden of proving their value to law enforcement and that other means equally effective are not available before sacrificing privacy. This has not been done.

Manifestly, for most crime electronic surveillance has little utility. In murder, assault, mugging, shoplifting, robbery, burglary, larceny, no one seriously contends that tapping and bugging are useful, with rarest exceptions. In kidnaping, families nearly always consent to a police or an FBI tap. If they refuse, should their wishes be ignored?

The one area of criminal activity where proponents most fervently believe wiretapping to be essential is against organized crime. This is in part because law enforcement officials have played a losing game with organized crime for too long. Organized crime can be eliminated. Why should we merely dabble with it? There have been whole cultures free of its scourge, and today there are entire nations without it. There are states and major cities in America with no significant organized crime.

In several cities where organized crime is most severe, police and prosecution have in the past used wiretap without inhibition. It has not been effective. Organized crime still flourishes in these communities. In other cities where there has never been organized crime, police have never used wiretap. The massive programs required to end organized crime have no place for wiretap. It is too slow, too costly, too ineffective.

Organized crime cannot exist where criminal justice agencies are not at least neutralized and probably corrupted to some degree. The syndicates deal in goods and services people want. Gambling, dope, unsecured loans at high rates of interest and prostitution account for probably 90 per cent of the illegal income of organized crime. Their customers include hundreds of people in any city where they operate and thousands in some cities. Anyone able to flash a roll of bills who wants to gamble can find a game within a few hours if there is gambling in the city. The difficulty of finding a dope peddler or prostitute is little if any more difficult. The police know—they cannot escape knowing—of much of this illegal activity. The slightest investigation will reveal it.

Urban slums are the natural environment of organized crime. Here are tens of thousands of powerless people who can be victimized with impunity. Much of the activity of organized crime is visible and viewed from passing squad cars on ghetto streets. The numbers runners, addicts buying and selling, and prostitutes looking for a pickup are known throughout the communities in which they live.

The hypocrisy of society outlawing activity it knows exists and will continue—gambling, narcotics use, prostitution, usury —while refusing to make the effort necessary to reduce the demand for such goods and services, or to enforce its law, inevitably corrupts criminal justice. A few policemen, and occasionally a prosecutor, a judge or a jailer are paid not to cause trouble for organized crime they alone do not have the power to control.

How will wiretaps help law enforcement control organized crime against this background? Police know where numbers are sold, they know who's running the dice game, they know the prostitutes and bookies—they do not need a bug to tell them. They know the big shots, too. Most have criminal records. Their activities are knowable and known without wiretapping. If we really want to eliminate organized crime, we will not be distracted from the major effort necessary by cheap and degrading proposals to wiretap.

The more successful organized crime is, the more sophisticated its operations. Police use of electronic equipment against *capiregime* of La Cosa Nostra merely causes an escalation of technology. Jamming and warning devices, codes, secure lines, voice scramblers, false leads have all been used to counteract the law. A petty game, far from the arena of criminal action and wasting valuable time, electronic surveillance demeans law enforcement by involving it in an activity no one respects.

The FBI used electronic surveillance in the organized crime

area from at least the late 1950's until July 1965. Hundreds of man-years of agent time were wasted. As many as twenty bugs were used in a single city. So far as is known not one conviction resulted from any of the bugs. Scores of convictions were remanded for special hearings because persons charged with crime were overheard, but no evidence of any crime obtained by such surveillance, directly or indirectly, was ever introduced in a federal trial, so far as is known.

In 1967 and 1968, without the use of any electronic surveillance, FBI convictions of organized crime and racketeering figures were several times higher than during any year before 1965. The bugs weren't necessary. Other techniques such as the strike force proved far more effective.

Some transcriptions of tapes from bugs that recorded all sound in a room over a period of many months, even several years, fail to reveal any evidence of any crime, or any leads to crime—federal, state or local. Some reveal criminal activity. Some include talk of crimes that never occurred. Sometimes associations among surprising people are discovered. A few are saturated with unsavory details, but police knew or could have known of this by proper procedures.

There is a tendency to believe anything heard on a wiretap. We forget that the speaker may have intended to deceive the only person he thought he was talking to, may have been puffing, or may simply have been mistaken.

The great bulk of the conversations intercepted by tap or bug involve private conversations unrelated to crime. Most people overheard on nearly any surveillance are not criminals. Nearly everyone has family, friends, associates and acquaintances who are not partners in crime. They talk together and to others.

No technique of law enforcement casts a wider net than electronic surveillance. Blind, it catches everything in the sea of sound but cannot discriminate between fish and fowl. It is ineffective and inefficient because this world is too big to detect crime by gathering all the noise and silence of whole areas to sift for evidence.

District Attorney Frank Hogan of New York used wiretaps during the early and mid-1950's. His office disposed of tens of thousands of criminal cases annually. The number of convictions estimated to result from wiretapping in any year never exceeded several score. It took two to six officers to man each tap. There were more taps than convictions.

There must have been some suspicion of criminal conduct, if not actual evidence, before a tap was installed. If the same manpower had been used in other investigation, the number of convictions would have been higher. Certainly the professional pride of the police would be. An agent might get tired of monitoring a bug for five out of twenty-one eight-hour shifts per week, month after month. He has overheard children playing and dozens of television shows, for even criminals sometimes have children and television sets. He has heard nothing police have any right to hear for weeks: days of silence, water running, family quarrels, sneezing, housewives' gossip, lovers' meetings and snoring. How many eight-hour shifts sitting with a pair of headphones waiting for a suspected conversation will it take before a good man will decide digging ditches is more honest, healthy and constructive? He could have been learning an honorable trade—or investigating crime.

Since authorization of wiretaps and electronic surveillance in 1968, we have been repeatedly told by the FBI, by prosecutors and by the Attorney General himself that various indictments and arrests resulted from wiretaps. Nearly all have referred to gambling and narcotics activities. Some announcements have referred to hundreds, even thousands, of incriminating conversations. Obviously, had someone cared to, these activities could have been broken up and important seizures made without wiretaps. Police knew of the activity before the taps were placed. Some prosecutors seem more interested in justifying wiretaps than in controlling crime. They will even ignore the proprieties of pretrial publicity to tout their favorite technique.

Wiretaps waste great amounts of law enforcement time. Eighty-five per cent of all police expenditures are for salaries,

the time of officers and other personnel. To waste that time, too
scarce as it is, is inexcusable from a strict enforcement standpoint. It may take twenty men or more to install a bug. It is a
risky and difficult business. Police must carefully stake out the
area so that agents won't be caught in the act of installation, as
several have. This may involve following the suspect and others
who live or work where the bug is to be installed as well as
watching neighbors and friends who might visit the spot. Several
agents must guard doors and entrances to give warning if someone happens by. Several men must enter, sometimes breaking
in, to install the bug.

Surreptitiousness is contagious. If you invade privacy with a
bug, why not break and enter? Why not remove and photostat
documents? This too has happened. In an investigation of
Frank Peter Balistrieri, allegedly a minor underworld figure
from Milwaukee, Wisconsin, the FBI utilized three bugs over a
period of months. The Bureau contended, apparently accurately, that no evidence of the crime charged was obtained by
any of this surveillance. While entering the apartment of Balistrieri's secretary to install a bug, agents removed documents
from a file, photostated them and returned the originals without
advising the owner. This was a clear violation of law.

Law enforcement officers are human, too, and are subject to
all the weaknesses of man. Given an instrument of such power,
able to know so much about others without their awareness, can
we hope to structure safeguards against misuse? Since the practice itself is surreptitious, its concealment is easy. What of the
overzealous officer, the Javert? He is trained and equipped. He
knows he is right. What of known instances of police tapping
bookies to determine what their payoff should be for not shutting down the operation? Other illegal usages could easily arise.

Rather than fair investigative practices, how often might the
use be determined by some officers' likes or dislikes? The decision of whom to wiretap is necessarily selective. There is not
world enough or time with present methods to overhear more
than a few. The choice lends itself to persecution. Who is un-

popular? Whom would we like to get? Police can be interested in people's sex habits. Why have so many bedrooms been the site for electronic surveillance? Police may believe John Doe is a bad person. Or they can be racist. Are these the bases we want for investigation?

There have been repeated allegations that the FBI placed bugs in hotel rooms occupied by Dr. Martin Luther King, Jr., and subsequently played the tapes of conversations recorded in the room for various editors, Senators and opinion makers. The course of the civil rights movement may have been altered by a prejudice caused by such a practice. The prejudice may have reached men who might otherwise have given great support— including even the President of the United States. The public has a right to know whether this is true. If it is, those responsible should be held fully accountable. A free society cannot endure where such police tactics are permitted. Today they may be used only against political enemies or unpopular persons. Tomorrow you may be the victim. Whoever the subject, the practice is intolerable.

The line is thin between suspicion and probable cause to believe a crime has been committed. The civil rights leader, the lawyer, the newspaperman and others have been the subject of federal electronic surveillance. Why? Because we condone the practice and are unable to insure that only honest ends will be sought by such dishonorable means.

Many believe that if court orders are required before police may tap or bug, the risks will be eliminated. This is doubtful. The history of court approval in New York City reveals widespread rubber stamp approval without real judicial consideration. This has been a common experience with bail and search warrants. The opportunity of the judge to decide intelligently is limited. Only the police present the application. The judge knows little, if anything, of the individuals involved except what the police allege. Some judges in most major jurisdictions will probably give automatic approval.

If the Supreme Court establishes a standard of probable

cause, comparable to that required by the Constitution for search warrants, the lawful use of electronic surveillance will be drastically limited. Under this standard a phone could be tapped only when the police can demonstrate by evidence that there is reason to believe a specific crime has been or is about to be committed. There will rarely be such evidence and when it exists, a tap will rarely be needed. Such a test is the minimum protection the public should have.

Bugs and taps have rarely been used to gain evidence of specific crime. When this has occurred, it has almost always been happenchance. The real utility, though limited and inefficient, is the accumulation of information and misinformation about individuals, their habits, associates and business dealings, so a picture of all their activities can be drawn. From this police can hope to trace patterns of criminal conduct and eventually predict criminal activity and arrest whole groups involved. Joseph Valachi told the FBI as much as one agent could have learned if he spent fifty years listening to bugs.

Reliance on electronic surveillance, like other customary police techniques such as confessions and line-ups, inhibits the development of methods of investigation that are effective and efficient. Human nature finds habit so much more comfortable than research, development and change that we would rather do what we have done, however meaningless or harmful, than seek a better way. When ethical issues are involved, police inherently become emotional. Is the underworld ethical? they ask. Shouldn't we fight fire with fire? The chance for objective evaluation of an issue is thus diminished.

There is a profound and tragic moral in the fact that Congressional forces that favor wiretapping generally oppose professionalization of police, prisoner rehabilitation and research. They want to ignore any relationship between crime and slums, racism, poverty or mental health. To them, poverty is just an excuse; "bad people" commit crime. The elements of racism in the insistent political demand for law and order also become manifest when the same leaders oppose enforcement of civil rights. A tally card on the Congress shows a high correlation between the two positions.

Somehow, the hard-liners believe that all that is needed to stop crime is to catch crooks. But a person is not a crook until a crime has been committed, and our numbers are too vast ever to believe we can begin to protect the public by acting only after crimes are committed. With fewer than one out of fifty serious crimes resulting in a conviction, we clearly will not win such a contest.

Electronic surveillance has long been used in the field of national security. The meaning of such use is essentially different from use in domestic affairs.

It is a premise of political science that a government has authority to control unlawful activity within its borders. Among civilized people it must be assumed that this can be done fairly. As a corollary it must be understood that a government has no authority to control activity outside its borders. While we can endeavor to control criminal conduct at home, affording due process of law and without invading rights of individuals that are essential to the freedom of all, beyond our borders we are powerless to act.

Governments can know of significant activity within their territory without invasion of privacy. It is more difficult to know about foreign activity or plans. We live in a dangerous world. There are foreign powers with nuclear weapons. War is a constant peril in various parts of the globe. There can be more Vietnams. To discover whether missile sites are being built in Cuba, whether Communist China is designing new rockets, or massive troop movements are taking place in eastern Europe, nations engage in worldwide intelligence-gathering activity. The information gathered may be vital to national survival. The tradition, unfortunate as it is, has been for nearly all nations to maintain extensive intelligence operations. We spend billions for the purpose.

When electronic surveillance is used for national security purposes, it must be carefully limited and strictly controlled. National security matters have involved only international activities historically. This is their proper scope. They include only information relating to activities beyond our borders.

Efforts have been made to include major domestic crime within the national security definition on the theory that it threatens national safety. When so expanded any rationale justifying the practice is lost. Supervision under so vague a definition becomes difficult, and public confidence that usage is properly limited is destroyed. It was this play on the words "national security" that the FBI relied on to claim justification for electronic surveillance of organized crime. This caused its subsequent dispute with Robert F. Kennedy over whether such usage was authorized.

Similarly, Attorney General Mitchell claimed the right to use electronic surveillance under national security authority without court approval in pleadings filed in the Chicago Seven case in 1969, though no foreign interest was involved. Apparently his claim included the right to usage against such organizations as the SDS, the Black Panthers and La Cosa Nostra. It is a dangerous, insensitive and lawless claim.

Perhaps it is as immoral to use wiretaps in national security matters as in domestic cases, but it need not involve citizens living in their own land. The meaning to privacy is therefore substantially different. It is usually places of business, where private affairs are not so common, that are tapped. Most foreign missions and their agents assume they are tapped and act accordingly. Even so, we should seek to abolish the use of electronic surveillance in the national security field.

Tapping and bugging are as highly inefficient in the national security area as elsewhere. This is so even though international cable, telephonic and radio messages are essential to operations of foreign missions. Less than 1 per cent of all national security intercepts have any real value. But efficiency in the national defense area has never been an important criterion. We spend $80 billion for military defense and only $5 billion for all domestic crime control—federal, state and local. Perhaps this is why we have so much war—and so much crime.

It is deep-grained tradition that effectively constrains human conduct and particularly government actions. The naked word of the law has little force. It is powerless, unknown, forgotten, not important. If we do not establish the strongest traditions throughout law enforcement and attitudes among the public inhibiting invasions of privacy, privacy can be a lost concept in a few short years. Without such traditions, we will never control invasions of privacy by government, business competitors, spouses, enemies, blackmailers and extortionists or by merely curious or perverted people. Modern technology will become the master, not the servant, of mankind.

We cared enough for our privacy to prohibit unreasonable searches and seizures in the Bill of Rights. Physical search is a feeble instrument of oppression compared to a wiretap. Pervasive surveillance of the individual, his every word and deed, is possible through the wonders science will bestow on us in the next few years. The wonders are adequate now to create widespread belief among many people that their phones are tapped, or their rooms bugged. This hardly has a stabilizing influence on society. It does not create confidence in government or the purposes of our laws.

Fear causes us to condone government wiretapping. In calmer times we know better. Wiretapping is more than a mere dirty business—it tinkers with the foundations of personal integrity.

18

PRESUMED INNOCENT?

BAIL AND PREVENTIVE DETENTION

Ronnie brown was five years old when his mother brought him north to Brooklyn from rural South Carolina. Before he was arrested on July 25, 1969, for robbery at the age of seventeen, police had taken him into custody twice—once for assault, later for car theft. He had never been convicted of a crime. On August 14, 1969, at 5:20 A.M., he was discovered dead, hanging from a light fixture in his Rikers Island prison cell—a belt looped around his neck. He had been in jail nineteen days, though no grand jury had indicted him and no lawyer had advised him of his rights, when his aunt heard of his death on the radio. She told his mother, a nurse in a VA Hospital, twelve hours before the police found time to advise her.

Ronnie had written his mother, "Dear Mom, This is not the life I want. I am not really bad. . . . I want to get out and work and do something good." He didn't explain why he was "afraid to go to the bathroom." To persons familiar with American jails, it was not necessary. He did not want to be raped by homosexuals.

Ronnie Brown, dead at age seventeen, is still presumed innocent. Can the same presumption apply to a society that permits such inhumanity? The Commissioner of Corrections reported this death as the eleventh suicide in the New York City system during the first eight months of 1969. The problem, he said, was overcrowded jails and insufficient staffs. Hundreds perish this way each year in these United States. They never include the wealthy, the worldly-wise, or the famous among us.

The purpose of the Eighth Amendment provision that "Excessive bail shall not be required" was to prevent arbitrary imprisonment before trial. Its moving spirit was the presumption of innocence—a presumption arising from the importance of the individual in the hierarchy of American values. It meant that the dignity of the individual must not be demeaned by infringement on his liberty through imprisonment unless he is convicted of crime. The Eighth Amendment was included in the Bill of Rights to insure human dignity.

Intended to confer a right of constitutional magnitude, the prohibition against excessive bail came to impose a burden. Because the Bill of Rights spoke of bail—weighing freedom against money—liberty has been denied the presumptively innocent poor. For the want of a few hundred dollars millions of impoverished Americans have suffered in jail awaiting American justice. We can sense the misery, the utter loneliness, of the minstrel immortalized in our folk music who had only one old shirt and nobody to go his bail.

The single constitutional purpose of bail is to assure the presence in court of the person charged with crime on the date his case is set for trial. Unless the defendant is present the purposes of the law are frustrated. Trial cannot be held nor innocence or guilt determined. Therefore, even though we presume the individual innocent, we require a deposit of money so he will come back for his trial—or forfeit that money. In theory, the danger that he might commit a crime before his trial is never to be considered. This would conflict with the presumption of innocence.

Whatever its original concept, bail soon came to cause great and senseless injustice. Bartering liberty for money bail, the rich have been released while the poor accused of serious crime in most American jurisdictions have awaited trial in jail. It is only because they are poor that they remain in jail from arrest to trial. In the federal system the abuses grew from the Judiciary Act in 1789 until 1966 before the first corrective action was taken by the United States Congress. For 175 years we ignored a major imperfection in our system of justice.

The bail system generally jails persons accused of crime unless they post money or other security in an amount judged necessary to assure their appearance at trial. It demonstrates poignantly the incredible neglect our system can tolerate. Over the years we have deprived hundreds of thousands of people, never convicted of any crime, of their liberty because they were poor. The rich, the mobster, the well connected—they all made bail. Only the poor remained in jail, and as a result jobs were lost, families separated, and the best—sometimes only—chance to obtain evidence, find witnesses and prepare a defense was gone.

There were suicides—thousands of them. A fourteen-year-old Minnesota Indian boy accused of crime lasted forty-one days before he hanged himself in the Hennepin County jail in 1969. Sick people—diabetics needing insulin, for example—were ignored. Deeply despondent persons prone to self-destruction and left unsupervised in a brutal environment and the mentally retarded, frightened beyond self-control, who could not raise $500 bail, committed suicide.

Thousands jailed without bail were innocent. Hundreds of thousands were released after weeks or more in jail without trial. As to some, formal charges were never filed or were filed and later dismissed. Many prisoners served longer awaiting trial than the maximum sentence provided for the crime with which they were charged.

Thousands were corrupted awaiting trial in jail. Young boys, eleven or twelve years old, and teenagers were exposed to brutality, homosexual rape, drug addiction, insanity, senility and hardened human beings capable of any crime. The effect on those jailed for the first time and held for months before their trial was often to destroy their chance for rehabilitation. Many jails housed more prisoners than bunks, and some were so crowded it was difficult to find room to lie down on a cold, damp floor.

Bail was set in countless ways, but generally by formula and automatically—perhaps $100 for drunken and disorderly conduct, $1,000 for theft, $2,500 for burglary, and $10,000 for armed robbery. Often bondsmen, whose livelihood comes from the premiums determined by the amount of the bond, set bail themselves. Sometimes lawyers acting as both attorney and bondsman made bail. Defendants who could never quite pay the fee the lawyer sought would often raise the premium to make bail. There was no other way of getting out of jail. Bail premiums were a major source of income for such lawyers.

It is doubtful that bail made appearance at trial more probable except in the rarest case. Frequently no real security was risked by either the accused or his bondsman. In Texas lawyers collected 10 per cent of the dollar amount set as bail, or whatever lesser amount the client could pay, and signed the bonds themselves. The lawyer was supposed to have unencumbered land in the county of a value exceeding the amount of the bond, pledged to assure appearance of the accused at trial. Often he had none. In some counties decades passed without any forfeiture proceedings to collect on the bonds of defendants who failed to appear for trial. The system operated solely to extract money from persons charged with crime, not for their defense but to secure their liberty. Bail had become a tax on freedom for those accused of crime. Those who could not pay it stayed in jail.

In some areas, pressure was brought on bondsmen through the threat of forfeiture to produce defendants for trial. Private bondsmen without any public responsibility often crossed state lines seeking fugitives from trial. They shackled, kidnaped and transported thousands back to the state where the crime was charged. Untrained in the handling of prisoners and insensitive to human suffering, they had one motive—money.

A classic description of the bail bondsman's vast common law powers was given by the Supreme Court a century ago in the case of *Taylor v. Taintor,* 83 U.S. 366 (1872):

> When bail is given, the principal is regarded as delivered to the custody of his sureties. Their dominion is a continuance of the original imprisonment. Whenever they choose to do so, they may seize him and deliver him up in their discharge; and if that cannot be done at once, they may imprison him until it can be done. They may exercise their rights in person or by agent. They may pursue him into another State; may arrest him on the Sabbath; and, if necessary, may break and enter his house for that purpose. The seizure is not made by virtue of new process. None is needed. It is likened to the re-arrest by the sheriff of an escaping prisoner. . . . It is said: "The bail have their principal on a string, and may pull the string whenever they please, and render him in their discharge."

These pervasive powers over a bailed defendant have been based on the private contract between the parties to the bail bond—the accused and the bondsman—not because the bondsman stands in the stead of the state. Bondsmen have thus had techniques and opportunities—if not powers—exceeding those of the state.

The ancient justifications for such exercise of dominion by one person over another—return of runaway slaves and the paucity of law enforcement on the frontier—were never valid, but even more clearly have no place in today's system of criminal justice. Law enforcement has become, of necessity, a specialized profession and a public responsibility. The apprehension of alleged fugitives must be vested entirely in professional law enforcement officers. The return of prisoners to a demanding state should be conducted only by officials who are carefully trained and instructed to exercise whatever security measures may be necessary and to fully respect the rights of their charges. Criminal justice is public business. A free society can never place the liberty of individuals in private hands. Yet we do, and

Congress seriously considered regulating its practice in the late 1960's rather than prohibiting it altogether.

The bail system is worse than senseless—it discriminates for no reason against the poor. Bail diverts the criminal justice system from what matters—the individual—to what doesn't—his money. Rather than asking does he need treatment, has he violated parole, should he be supervised, might he leave the country, or is he dangerous, bail asks only—does he have $500?

Grandly the bail system plied its trade—money for freedom —without criticism until the early 1960's. As with many aspects of government activity, the practice then began to be questioned for the first time. The pioneering Manhattan Bail Project sponsored by the Vera Foundation moved most effectively. Other projects soon followed. For a few brief years in the mid-1960's bail reform was a major concern of the bench and bar.

The amount of liberty lost because of bail has been immense. The federal government detains fewer than 2 per cent of the prisoners held pending trial on any given day in the United States. In early 1963, several years before federal bail reform legislation was enacted, Attorney General Robert F. Kennedy instructed the United States Attorneys to exercise personal initiative in recommending the release of accused persons on their personal recognizance whenever they were satisfied that there was no substantial risk the defendant would fail to appear for trial. Prior to March 1963 only 6 per cent of all persons arrested and charged with a federal crime were released on their own recognizance without money bail. By March 1964 the percentage had nearly tripled, and by April 1, 1965, it stood at 39 per cent. Between March 1964 and April 1965 the percentage of all prisoners denied release on bail or on their personal assurance declined from 37 to 8.5 per cent.

During those years the average pretrial detention per prisoner was forty-one days. By a single administrative directive approximately 9,000 persons were saved forty-one days each during the course of a year—369,000 days of liberty, 1,000 man-years. The meaning of this when applied to state and local systems is staggering. Hundreds of thousands of people are detained in jails before trial every year.

The release of these thousands of people actually lowered the rate at which defendants failed to appear for trial. The rate of bail jumping in the federal system by those with enough money to make bail had been 3 per cent nationwide. Nearly 98 per cent of the individuals released on their personal promise to appear voluntarily came to court for their trials. The poor, theretofore held in jail before trial because they could not post a few hundred or a few thousand dollars, showed up for trial voluntarily with greater frequency than those who had been released on money bail.

In one federal court, the Eastern District of Michigan, 84 per cent of all prisoners accused of crime were released without bail in 1965. Only 1 out of the 711 thus released defaulted. With care this record could be equaled throughout the country.

Bail reform was a major step toward equal justice in America, but because it came at a time of increased anxiety over crime, it soon came under criticism. Many claimed bail reform caused crime. New ways of overcrowding jails were sought as protectors of the public safety.

At a time of towering need to reform and vitalize the entire system of criminal justice, the American people, who profess to love liberty, are entreated in the name of public safety to imprison people charged with crime and deemed to be dangerous, pending their trial. The plea flows from the fact that our system of criminal justice is not working. Courts are confronted with large and growing backlogs; the average delay in criminal cases from arrest to trial exceeds a year in many jurisdictions. Of course some persons charged with crime have committed additional crimes while at large pending trial. And repeated crimes by persons released pending trial make a mockery of the judicial system. But in nearly every instance those same persons were convicted of crimes and had served penitentiary sentences before their release on bail. It is the repeater who creates the problem. The person who commits a single crime is not likely to commit another crime in the months between arrest and trial. The problem of the repeater can be solved by effective techniques of sentencing and correction—not by pretrial imprisonment.

The public is reminded again and again of the cases where a person released pending trial is charged with another crime. Demagogues and those who seek easy solutions to crime while opposing the expense of essential action dramatize the stupidity of a system that cannot cope with such an obvious problem. We are urged to ignore the principles we profess—that every American is presumed innocent until proven guilty—and it is proposed that we jail the accused until his trial, because somehow we know he is a danger to society.

We call the proposal preventive detention. It would keep many persons accused of crime in jail pending trial. Preventive detention is neither necessary nor desirable to control crime. Inconsistent with our basic principles, it would deter correction of major defects in our system of criminal justice, violate important constitutional rights of citizens, and tend to cause crime. A glance at history and present practice tells us why.

Under a system of preventive detention, fear instead of money would determine whether an accused is to be released. In practice it would operate much like bail. In times of great concern over crime, bail has usually been set not at a norm or to assure appearance at trial but deliberately high to prevent release. During "crime waves," many judges release few people on bail. This is a part of the hypocrisy of the bail system. Under such circumstances bail has nothing to do with its stated purpose —to assure the presence of the defendant at trial—but is a judge's way of protecting the public from people he believes dangerous and himself from criticism.

If preventive detention is authorized, courts acting from community fear will release very few people when crime concerns the public. Poor and unpopular groups and individuals—the

Black Panthers, the Weathermen, ghetto dwellers—would be most affected. The test for a judge or magistrate in deciding whether to jail or release under a preventive detention statute— Will the defendant pose a danger to the community?—is necessarily subjective. His burden is greater than a jury's after trial, for juries at least have a rational assignment. They do not have to predict future human conduct. Juries determine past facts. There is yet little evidence that we can predict what people will do in the future. But the consequences of a decision to detain a person in jail until his trial may often be as dire as a verdict of guilt. A year in jail awaiting trial can be worse than a year on a prison farm after conviction.

Preventive detention could easily result in massive, destructive, needless jailing. The history of bail tells us what is possible. Have we overcome our capacity for neglect? It is tradition, not words, that protects rights. What good do the words of the Eighth Amendment do the poor Southern Negro or the urban slum dweller? Only the firmest commitment against unnecessary and wrongful detention will avoid filling jails with hundreds of thousands of people not proven guilty while we tell our young we presume all to be innocent. Strong traditions that inhibit officials from jailing persons before trial will force us to make the reforms essential to both justice and security. These include assurance of a speedy trial, jail and prison reform, and indeterminate sentencing procedures. Preventive detention will impede those reforms.

If we believe we can predict whether a person accused of crime will be dangerous upon release before trial, why not go one step further? Why should authorities wait until persons have been charged with crime before jailing them? If we can predict the next crime, we could have predicted the last one. Why not just round up those persons who look dangerous and put them in jail? We have done some of this, too. Preventive detention can lead us down such a road.

More to the point, if nearly all of the persons we would detain pending trial had been convicted of prior crimes, why were they released? Do not prison officials with professional assistance, in constant contact with an offender, have a better opportunity to estimate future conduct than a judge trained in the law who scarcely sees the accused? If they have committed another crime while on parole, they have violated the major condition on which all parole is premised—that the person released will not commit a crime.

Pretrial detention is not necessary to protect the public—even if it could—for a number of important reasons. The first and most critical has to do with the sentencing process itself. The greater part of all serious crime is committed by repeaters. It is these very repeaters who are least likely to be released pending trial. They constitute probably 95 per cent of the persons judges or magistrates in a properly functioning system would hesitate to release pending trial. The reason is that their future is predicted from their past. If the defendant is a four-time loser and suspected of many other crimes, he is expected, barring evidence of some change, to be capable of further crime.

But if he has been convicted before of any crime showing a capability to do serious harm, society had its best chance, indeed duty, to prevent him from committing further crime. If he has committed another crime, the system had failed. A correctional program tailored to his particular needs, based on a flexible sentence imposed to provide the opportunity for continuous effort, provides the best chance for rehabilitation. The only sentence that can do this is the indeterminate sentence.

The indeterminate sentence fixes an outer limit of potential imprisonment—five years or ten years, for example—but empowers correctional authorities to release the defendant whenever they believe he is capable of living in society without committing antisocial acts. Under such a sentence, professional supervisors can impose conditions of release designed to rehabilitate the releasee and prevent him from engaging in criminal acts. In a properly functioning system, most defendants might spend as much as 90 per cent of their sentences in community environments and half of their time without significant restraints on their liberty. Rehabilitating offenders through prison reform would greatly reduce instances where preventive detention might be used—and greatly reduce crime itself.

Any program will have failures. When a person serving an indeterminate sentence is accused of a subsequent crime, he can be taken into custody for violation of the conditions of his parole if there is evidence he has done so. If he has violated those conditions—perhaps by failing to return to a dormitory, by dropping out of school, by associating with the old gang or by being on the street at 2 A.M.—parole supervisors should know it before the police do. When they don't, the police can advise them. Society has a claim on his freedom for past wrongful conduct. The accused is entitled to due process in any parole revocation procedure, but the issue is whether he violated conditions of parole, not whether another crime was committed. There is no trial as such and no requirement of evidence beyond a reasonable doubt. If another crime has been committed, the earlier program has obviously failed and should be immediately redesigned in the light of new evidence. The offender, rather than being kept in jail until he is tried on new charges, should be placed in a correctional program based on professional estimates of need considering all the circumstances. Certainly, if he seems dangerous, he will not be released without supervision.

The use of indeterminate sentencing and community correctional control is slight and ineffective today. Nearly all felons spend the final years of their sentences at large. The time ranges from two-thirds in most federal cases to one-third in nearly all jurisdictions. While they are technically on parole, they are as a practical matter without supervision. The period of time on parole is longer and involves far greater opportunity for crime than the time between arrest and trial. Parole is the time of greatest risk of recidivism, because if further crimes are likely to be committed, they are most likely to occur soon after a prisoner is released from prison and placed on parole. Crime repetition becomes steadily less likely with the passage of time.

Proper sentencing and adequate community corrections control would make preventive detention virtually unnecessary. The importance of indeterminate sentencing, however, transcends many times over any security that might arise from jailing before trial. It provides the base for an essential protection for years because it can rehabilitate. Those months from arrest to trial during which preventive detention offers a dubious protection are but a small part of the time the public will be exposed to the risk of crime by the accused. He will be at large for years in between his times in prison. He will tend to be a little more dangerous each time he is let out.

An effective community supervision program will be designed to give high assurance that a convict does not have the opportunity to commit another crime until the probability that he may is very low. This is much greater protection than waiting until police have evidence that another crime has been committed, then jailing the suspect until his trial. Preventive detention can do no more.

Under existing law there are three important classes of crime where the issue of preventive detention is not presented. Combined, they eliminate any remaining vestige of rationality in preventive detention and offer an opportunity for an effective resolution of the pretrial detention dilemma.

In capital cases throughout our history we have reserved the power to detain an accused pending trial. The Eighth Amendment was written and ratified against a background permitting detention of persons charged with capital crimes. Money bail, it was thought, might not assure the appearance of a defendant charged with crime where life itself was at stake. Life was the only thing this theory valued above money.

In practical terms this rule means that persons accused of the most serious offenses—murder, rape, armed robbery, assault with intent to kill and other major crimes of violence—for which the death penalty can be invoked need not be, and are rarely, if ever, released pending trial in most states. Wrong in principle, the practice has at least the gloss of history and because it is limited to very serious crimes is preferable to an untested technique of preventive detention. It provides a better basis for public protection than preventive detention, pending accomplishment of essential reforms. But it should be abandoned.

Second, preventive detention authority is not needed to detain juveniles. The law will develop in time to grant juveniles more of the protections afforded adults under the Constitution. Today, however, juveniles can be and are arbitrarily detained pending trial on criminal charges. Indeed, they are often detained without the formality of charges, as when the state stands in the place of the parent where there are allegations of neglect or delinquency. Curfews, compulsory schooling and juvenile detention homes often restrict the freedom of the young without trial or due process. While these practices are themselves wrong, they afford a protection today that gives time for needed reform of the judicial system without resorting to a new expanded pretrial custody.

Finally, preventive detention does not address itself to the problem of the mentally deranged. There are madmen who can pose a danger to the community. But they are not made sane by holding them in jail pending trial. Indeed, if incompetent, they may not face trial. Their need is for medical judgment and treatment and the issue is not whether to release or detain them pending trial, but one of health or sickness. The lines between mental commitment and trial for a crime are not precise, and clearly the present judicial techniques of determining mental capacity are fraught with risk and full of abuse, but preventive detention has no relevance to the problems of crime by the mentally ill. They are detained today through procedures of commitment designed to determine their sanity, without regard to whether they might commit a crime.

The remaining potential for crime by persons released between arrest and trial is slight but the public has additional protection without jailing persons presumed innocent. A well-financed and adequately staffed community supervision agency can provide services that reduce the chance of crime by employing techniques for pretrial release used effectively in parole and probation cases. Services will include health care, school, vocational training, job placement, counseling and family assistance. Conditions under which an accused is released and which he must obey to remain at liberty can reduce the risks of crime. Some conditions are designed to assure presence at trial and do not infringe on the assumption of innocence. Other conditions may be acceptable to an accused and therefore raise no legal issues. If necessary, special surveillance can be ordered by a court.

Conditions of release have included room inspection, requirements that the accused be at home at night, daily observation of conduct, checking presence at employment, school and home, restrictions on associations, and regular reporting in by phone or at an office designated by the court.

Civil commitments for alcoholics and addicts that give some supervisory power over an individual but avoid the stigma of criminal charges may be substituted entirely for criminal prosecution, or applied in modified forms for pretrial purposes. These same techniques of supervision, essential to successful probation and parole, are also meaningful in some pretrial situations. They are clearly the greatest restrictions society can justly place on an individual where, even on a finding of guilt, probation or a short jail sentence is the most severe sentence probable.

Until the last few years no supervision of persons released on bail was possible. There was no one to provide it. The choice was jail or unrestricted freedom. With bail reform, staffs capable of supervising accused persons released pending trial have been established. Strong bail agencies, professionally staffed with adequate manpower, with reduce crime, while pretrial jailing will often cause crime. Agencies to supervise persons between arrest and trial should become an important part of our system, closely coordinated with police, prosecution, courts and corrections.

Then, there is the absolute necessity for an early trial. The

Bill of Rights was concerned primarily with the rights of the accused when it sought to assure what is usually denied—a speedy trial.

Clearly now, the public safety as well depends on speedy trial. A chief deterrent of the entire activity of the system of criminal justice is lost when months or years elapse between crime and conviction. The only time the average person will see any connection between his criminal act and the consequences of conviction is when conviction follows the criminal act quickly.

A speedy trial is a far greater deterrent than a lengthy sentence. Longer criminal sentences are often imposed when public concern over crime is high. This is a reaction of courts to the public's, and perhaps the courts' own, concern. But it is an emotional reaction. Long sentences have not deterred crime. The question is not how long the sentence, but what happens to the individual while he serves it. Is he rehabilitated or hardened?

If many months pass between the criminal act and a conviction, the connection between the two is remote and seems happenchance. Punishment, as the punished view it, does not follow swiftly and inexorably from crime. The greatest deterrent for the person capable of committing crime is the belief, when he decides whether to act, that if he does he will be quickly apprehended and convicted as a direct result of his conduct.

Preventive detention would tend to prolong the time between arrest and trial. In addition to relieving the pressure for speedy trial, preventive detention would require additional hearings that courts are ill equipped to handle. Should the accused be released? Is he dangerous? What facts has the prosecution assembled that show he is dangerous? What evidence has the defense to show he is not? What of appeals from decisions denying release? Is this the way courts should spend their time?

An early trial reduces the risk that an accused will commit another crime pending trial. If trials are held within sixty days instead of sixteen months, the opportunity for additional crimes is reduced.

With conviction, the presumption of innocence is lost. Then the burden is on the individual to prove that his trial was unfair, or that he is not guilty. Accordingly, there is no right to release from custody while a case is on appeal just as there is no right of appeal. Once the accused is convicted, the question of release pending an appeal is at the discretion of the court. Danger to the community may be a factor in the court's decision, though the overriding question is the probability of reversal. In practice, courts generally provide for the release of persons convicted pending appeal. Only rarely are the rich and powerful such as leaders of La Cosa Nostra denied bail pending appeal. This illustrates the discrimination inherent in pretrial detention.

Lethargy pervades human conduct and institutional reform. Pressures are necessary to produce essential action. Preventive detention would relieve just those pressures that will force reforms far more important to public safety than the insignificant and doubtful security it can offer. We can accomplish needed reform safely without reliance on preventive detention.

If we place people in jail before their trials, a major incentive to reform sentencing, provide speedy trials and improve jails and prisons is lost, because we think we are safe. For the moment, the public may be, but life is longer than a moment. Persons confined cannot hurt anyone except themselves or other prisoners. To many on the outside these do not matter, but prisoners will be at large again someday. If upon release they are even more likely to commit crimes, we have not provided for our safety.

Prison reform can rehabilitate most prisoners who presently are condemned to lives of crime. In time, correctional reform would eliminate most of the risks of crime between arrest and trial. Preventive detention is another cheap and immoral excuse for failing to meet the needs of modern society. It will create crime.

How many kids lost their last chance for an education while waiting in jail for a trial? If 90 per cent of our crimes are committed by dropouts, we might ask whether greater safety does not lie in putting these youngsters back in school instead of in jail. These are the ones who live lives of crime, spurred to it perhaps because an ill-functioning system of justice kept them from school.

How many thousands of families have been broken by pre-trial detention? Things were bad enough before the arrest, but that was the final straw. Because a husband spent months in jail before his trial, the last chance for his family to stay together was lost and perhaps two generations or more of criminals were made. If two-thirds of the prisoner population of the United States comes from broken homes, we should inquire whether we really want to break up more homes, particularly in areas of high crime potential, by reliance on preventive detention, which cannot protect the public anyway.

If we reform prisons, protect the public from crime by repeaters through indeterminate sentencing, provide speedy trials and adequately staff bail supervision agencies, how great is the risk of crime by persons awaiting trial? If we fail to make these reforms, can preventive detention—which denies human dignity, keeps youngsters out of school, breaks up families and exposes persons to jail brutality—reduce crime? If during the time required to make essential reforms in judicial administration and prison and jail reform the public is protected from crimes committed between arrest and trial by repeaters, by persons charged with capital crimes, by juveniles and by the criminally insane, is there any need for preventive detention?

The presumption of innocence should not be lightly discarded. It has elemental force. Its spirit is embodied in the Eighth Amendment. It establishes the relationship between the individual and the state, implying that every person is worth something, may have dignity and be deserving of trust. In questions between citizen and state, the presumption is—and must remain—that the individual will prevail until society proves him a criminal beyond a reasonable doubt. He cannot be jailed on suspicion, nor held pending investigation and trial, merely because he is poor, or even if he is despised. The Nixon Administration has referred to the presumption of innocence as a "mere rule of procedural evidence." Liberty and human dignity will never be secure among a people who place so little value on so fundamental a principle.

In these turbulent times, when the individual is easily lost, when he can do so little to affect things vital to his very being, actions that depreciate his dignity are extremely harmful. The young, the educated, the disadvantaged in mass society sense the heavy pall on their chance to be somebody, to do something, to fulfill themselves. They sense our hypocrisy, professing one thing, practicing another. They sense how slowly our institutions change to meet clear needs—our reluctance to make vital reforms. Preventive detention would be a tragic step backward at a time when we must move swiftly on.

19

CONFESSIONS, THE FIFTH
AMENDMENT AND HUMAN DIGNITY

THE history of confessions is full of torture, treachery and lies.
From biblical times to the present we read of morally weak,
emotionally disturbed, often innocent people cruelly used, made
to convict themselves by words forced from their own mouths.
We also read of those, guilty or innocent, who refused to bend
their knees—and know all too well of their fate.

Three books of the New Testament relate the story of Jesus'
trial. Charged with capital crime, the accused was asked by
prosecutor Pontius Pilate, "Art thou the King of the Jews?" But
the only answer Jesus would give was "Thou sayest it." He refused to be humbled by the state. If Caesar would convict, he
must do so himself. As is so often the case when confessions are
sought, the purpose of the state was not to discover facts, but to
satisfy public emotions in a political trial. The penalty was
crucifixion.

Efforts of King Henry the Eighth to force Sir Thomas More
to state facts and views he chose not to reveal also failed. Because he would not succumb, he was taken to the Tower of
London and beheaded. Insistence on both the confession and
the oath arises from man's inability to know the heart and mind
of others, his lack of faith in them and his desire to control their
destiny. He seeks to master their spirit by force, but it cannot be
done.

Most of us thrill at the courage and dignity of those who sacrifice all for their principles. Yet many who thrill most at such strength lament our refusal to force or trick confessions from persons they deem evil. Can this be consistent? Can we assume the government will know the good from the bad and will pursue only wrongdoers? Perhaps Jesus and Thomas More were despised and feared by Caesar and Henry. Perhaps human nature has not changed.

Millions of powerless people have been crushed by the state's insistence that they testify against themselves and those they may know. The Wickersham Commission, reporting of the 1920's in the United States, found that police regularly used force and fear to coerce confessions. By isolating and beating men until they confessed, police further segregated themselves from the communities they served and the facts of crime. The "third degree" was commonly practiced and the phrase was a part of everyone's vocabulary. Many feared the police. As a result, law enforcement officials could not learn of crime from the people who suffered it most, and they were unable to identify offenders through the application of science to fact discovery.

In St. Louis, where police practices were typical of those around the country, persons arrested on insufficient evidence were often "sent around the Horn." It was a long trip in rough water. The reference to Cape Horn actually meant that the prisoner would be held incommunicado, transferred every few days from one precinct station to another, and questioned intensively for as long as a month in the hope he would break down and confess.

In modern law enforcement the effort to obtain confessions usually arises from an honest desire to solve crime. But this questionable means to a desired end necessarily implies that other evidence, equal or better, is not available and that confessions are reliable. Experience disproves both implications as general propositions.

Beyond the desire to solve crime is the not unknown motive of assuring the public of police effectiveness, whether the person charged is guilty or not. This is particularly true of notorious and horrible crimes and explains in part both the frequency of confessions in such cases and the low conviction rates for murder and other major crimes which go to trial. Confessions also contain the same psychological satisfactions that derive from punishment. We see the confessor suffer. Many would rather hear an admission from the mouth of an accused than see clear and incontrovertible evidence from independent, objective sources. Such an impulse does not arise from a desire for truth. It demeans human dignity.

Emotion enables us to obscure the purpose of vital constitutional safeguards. The American public has been conditioned for many years now to see the Fifth Amendment as a weapon for criminals and a barrier to justice. It says, "No person . . . shall be compelled in any criminal case to be a witness against himself." Its very words bring to mind long lists of unpopular people, hearing rooms with bright lights, and the phrase "I refuse to answer the question on the grounds that I might tend to incriminate myself" ignominiously repeated a hundred times or more.

We have so debased the use of the Amendment in the public's mind that many automatically ascribe guilt to those who assert it. This undermines the vitality of essential constitutional safeguards and erodes the quality of justice. Assaults on the Fifth Amendment, and particularly on cases construing it, are a favorite tactic of the demagogue. Those interested in truth and human dignity must rise to its defense.

The techniques of eliciting confessions inevitably lead to unfairness and abuse of other rights. The person accused is helpless in the power of the state, and that power unrestrained corrupts justice. Danny Escobedo, held in Cook County, Illinois, jail for questioning, was denied access to his lawyer even though he could see him through the doorway when police interrogators entered and left the room. What possible value can the right to counsel contain if it is a right that can be so denied?

The most controversial Supreme Court case in the field of criminal justice during the 1960's—*Miranda v. Arizona*—dealt with confessions. Ernest Miranda is famous far beyond his importance. So is his case. That an issue of such limited significance and a rule of such elemental fairness could set off a major controversy shows how little we know about crime and how little we care.

Miranda, a young Mexican-American, was arrested and charged with rape. After his arrest he was questioned by police and confessed to the crime. The police never advised him that he did not have to answer their questions and that if he did his answers could be used against him. Nor did they tell him that he could have a lawyer and call a friend if he wanted. At his trial his confession was admitted as evidence and he was found guilty by a jury.

On appeal, the Supreme Court said a person accused of crime must be clearly advised that he does not have to answer questions asked by police when he is in their custody and if he does, his answers can be used against him. Further, the Court said, he must be told that he is entitled to call a friend and to have a lawyer, and that if he cannot afford a phone call or a lawyer, these will be provided. Because the police questioned Miranda without advising him of his rights when he had no legal representation and a confession he gave was used against him at his trial, his conviction was reversed.

The crime with which he was charged was horrible, but if principles of criminal justice have value, they must be applied in horrible cases, too. This is where principles are tested and are needed most—because emotions are so strong and issues so critical.

If justice is our concern, how can *Miranda* be wrong? Educated people—aware of their rights—know they do not have to answer questions. They know that if they do, their answers can be used against them. They know they are entitled to counsel. Experienced criminals, gang members and Mafiosi also know these things. Common sense will tell a rational and reasonably intelligent person that if he chooses not to talk, no one is likely to force him—even if he does not know his rights. The rich have lawyers; so do the mobsters, whose first act on arrest is to call their lawyer. The police know they will call lawyers and do not often try to interrogate powerful or wealthy people, because their rights will be vindicated.

There are few times when a lawyer may be more important to an accused than when he is first interrogated. Then, if ever, a person is likely to be emotional, confused and bewildered. Then only the police are present. At the trial a judge presides and has the duty under law to protect rights.

All *Miranda* means is that we must not take advantage of the poor, the ignorant and the distracted—that government will be fair and has self-confidence. Are the rights of the poor and uneducated so unimportant that they are not to be accorded what others cannot be denied? Can it be that law enforcement is unable to control crime if it must advise the poor and the ignorant of rights the rich, the educated and the professional criminal automatically enjoy? How much respect for law can then be expected from the poor and the ignorant? We may assume they will never know they have been denied rights by government itself, yet they cannot help but sense how few breaks they get in life and fewer still at the bar of justice. As a result law enforcement becomes a contest of cunning, principles become irrelevant and faith in the system is lost—far beyond those poor few directly engaged in the confrontation.

Seizing on *Miranda,* a handful of men, among them Senators John McClellan and Strom Thurmond, and later Richard Nixon, made it seem as if the Supreme Court were emptying the prisons of criminals—that law enforcement would never again be effective. The hands of the police were tied, they told us. The Court was causing crime—it was primarily responsible for the wave of crime that was drowning the nation. They attacked the most vulnerable institution of government and sought to undermine the confidence of the people in our courts.

Constitutional amendments were introduced to reverse *Miranda*. And some of those calling for law and order—and strict construction of the Constitution—would ignore that Constitution and the supreme law of the land for 175 years by amending the Constitution by a mere statute. Most of these same men have opposed every measure to professionalize law enforcement, add manpower, raise police salaries, modernize courts, control guns, tear down prisons which manufacture crime, rehabilitate offenders—spend money on the criminal justice process. Most of them also deeply opposed civil rights legislation and the Supreme Court for its civil rights decisions. This was no mere coincidence. They represent vested power that has no compassion, that has brutalized blacks for generations and that will have its way by sheer force if necessary.

Even if we are prepared to abandon common morality, we deceive ourselves if we believe greater safety will come from the denial of rights guaranteed in *Miranda*. That case has not tied the hands of the police. Ernest Miranda and each of the defendants in the four other cases reversed with his have been convicted after a new trial for the same offense, or have pleaded guilty rather than face another trial. Justice was done and the confessions that had been unlawfully and unfairly obtained earlier were not used and were not needed—all defendants stand convicted without them.

Even if the police had habitually come to rely on questioning persons under arrest without advising them of their rights, how important can the practice have been to effective law enforcement? In 1931 the Wickersham Commission reported widespread police use of third degree methods, including solitary confinement, beatings and other means of securing involuntary confessions. Was law enforcement better then? Were people safer? The courts must never hesitate to tie the hands of police if the police are misusing their hands. That is what the Bill of Rights is for. It protects the citizenry from tyrannical government. If courts fail to enforce the rights it guarantees, then we have no rights and no freedom.

The occasions on which confessions can play a role in crime solution are rare. Interrogation of suspects is not an effective method of investigation. The police in countries such as Sweden, where a far greater proportion of serious crimes are solved, abandoned the use of confessions a quarter of a century ago or more. Since 1948—eighteen years before the Supreme Court decided *Miranda*—the FBI has given a warning that meets all the *Miranda* standards except one. The FBI could not offer an attorney to a person unable to afford one, because the Bureau had no means to do so. Its decision to give the warnings was not dictated by the Attorney General or a court but by the Bureau itself in the interest of effective investigation. As a result, the FBI has developed stronger cases on better evidence. It rarely makes an arrest without substantial evidence and often only after a grand jury has indicted. Today, more than two decades after the FBI began giving *Miranda*-type warnings, guilty pleas are entered in 86 per cent of its cases, and 96 per cent of its investigations that are prosecuted end with a judgment of guilt. Obviously *Miranda* has not impaired its performance. The FBI gets the facts. It is difficult to argue with facts.

Another result of the FBI's fairness with persons in its custody is public confidence. The Bureau does not suffer the disastrous impairment in its community relations that unavoidably follows from prolonged questioning of persons under arrest. If there are thousands who have experienced the unfair and heavy hand of police interrogation, law enforcement will not be effective.

Local police must deal with types of crime that are often more difficult to solve than the generally sophisticated offenses over which the FBI has jurisdiction. Thousands of thefts, burglaries, muggings and robberies can overwhelm an undermanned and poorly trained police department. Unable to make thorough scientific investigations, police whose relations with the community are so impaired that eyewitnesses and sometimes even victims will not cooperate often resort to relentless questioning of suspects or people whom they believe to be capable of crime because they do not know another way. The more professional the police department, the less it relies on interrogation. It is the small forces that ask questions—the rural police and the ghetto precincts, where investigative skills and resources are slender and where police know little else. As a fact finder, interrogation is a pathetic substitute for investigation.

Sadly, *Miranda* has had insignificant effect on police conduct. In the main, it is ignored—the accused is not accorded his rights —or the warning is given in so perfunctory or hostile a manner that it has no value, and rights are not exercised.

A thorough study of police interrogation in New Haven, Connecticut, in 1967 by five editors of the *Yale Law Journal* concluded: "Our data and our impressions in New Haven converge to a single conclusion: Not much has changed after *Miranda*. Despite the dark predictions by the critics of the decision the impact on law enforcement has been small." Explaining that unless criminals are caught red-handed or witnesses are available, police are usually unable to secure adequate evidence to support even an arrest, the editors find interrogation unnecessary, since where evidence is sufficient to authorize arrest, conviction is usually assured. But they also observed that questioning did occur and "the *Miranda* rules, when followed, seem to affect interrogations but slightly. The police continue to question suspects, and succeed despite the new constraints." The reason was the "inherently coercive atmosphere of the police station."

Other surveys have indicated that police have obtained as many confessions after giving *Miranda* warnings as they did before warnings were given. In some areas few accused persons have asked for lawyers. There is even some evidence that as many—or more—statements are given by people after consulting lawyers as are given by those who do not consult lawyers. This is understandable if, as many experienced prosecutors and judges believe, confessions are usually obtained in cases where the police already have overwhelming evidence of guilt. The accused, knowing he is caught, confesses. In such cases, of course, confessions are not needed and may jeopardize prosecution.

It is dangerous to permit police to ignore the law, or to comply begrudgingly with its letter while destroying its spirit. If the system is to have integrity, the law, whether wise or foolish, must be followed. If police, through ignorance or by putting themselves above the law, do not comply with *Miranda,* ours is not a government of laws. Unless police are trained to implement rules and to execute sensitively the laws in accordance with executive direction, legislative statute and court orders, the system will be chaos. This lawlessness and our attendant hypocrisy will alienate the young, the educated, the poor and the blacks.

We must go beyond the letter of *Miranda* to implement its spirit. The police must not unfairly question suspects who are not fully apprised of their rights. Inhibited in his exercise of essential rights and inadequately represented, an accused will not believe in American justice. We have suffered long enough from the incommunicado detention and the interrogation that abuse the rights of an accused, breed fear and sometimes cost the quick discovery of vital evidence.

There may have been some harm to police performance following the *Miranda* decision. If so, it was psychological. A resentment, inflamed by demagogues, arose against what seemed to police to be an unwarranted interference with their conduct. From their vantage point, they could not understand why a court should object if a man admits a crime. It is difficult for police without training and caught in all the emotion of crime to see how inefficient, unreliable and potentially abusive the technique is. The old habit is comfortable and they are practiced in it. No one likes to change his ways, particularly when there is a charge that the old way was wrong, and when the new ways are unknown, require skill and are imposed by courts that have never walked a beat or faced a criminal in the street.

In fact, *Miranda* can help police. It will force professionalization if it is implemented. No longer permitted to sit around in station houses asking endless questions, police will be compelled to use scientific methods of crime solution. We will all be safer. So will our freedom.

Any potential value of confessions obtained from an unwitting suspect is more than offset by the harm arising from abusive interrogation. Most crime is never reported to police. Until government can come to know of crime, its solution is impossible. The impairment of police-community relations caused by the third degree has greatly decreased police effectiveness in crime solution.

Police are not authorized to arrest persons unless they have probable cause to believe the suspects have committed a crime. As a practical matter the evidence giving rise to such cause is usually more than adequate to prosecute, or will lead to additional evidence if police are trained in scientific investigation. Interrogation is no substitute for intensive pursuit of objective evidence. Many prosecutions have failed because confessions have been relied on without adequate police effort to seek independent evidence of the crime. Then the confessions have been withdrawn, disbelieved, or have caused unnecessary and harmful disputes to follow as to whether force was used to extract the admission.

The failure to solve serious crimes often results from reliance on efforts to obtain confessions. This also explains the failure to convict in many murder cases, where 38 per cent of all prosecutions result in acquittals or dismissals. Former Dean Edward Barrett of the University of California Law School at Berkeley has estimated that 25 per cent of the persons arrested for felonies are released without charge. Frequently the reason for the arrest was questioning. Many cities have questioned scores, even hundreds, of people about a single crime. When that fails, other efforts to solve the crime are abandoned. Had effort been made to investigate fully instead of merely to question, many crimes might have been solved. The impact of so many arrests on such serious grounds without resulting charges is severe. Often a technique of intimidation, hostile questioning embitters thousands annually. The time wasted and opportunities lost are immense.

The *Miranda* decision has not been expanded to protect juveniles in the custody of authorities. While it should be, and surely will be ultimately, it cannot be alleged as a cause of increased juvenile crime during the 1960's. It therefore was irrelevant to the increase in crime, which was nearly all in the juvenile age group. Juveniles can be questioned now while in custody without first being given essential warnings—and they are.

The efficacy of interrogation comes into serious question when the condition of those who are questioned is considered. With rare exception the emotional content of the moment is extreme. Something traumatic has just happened. Even when the interrogation is remote from the crime at issue, there are few whose pulse does not beat faster when they are questioned in the custody of the police.

More difficult still is the problem of mental health. How reliable will the statements of the mentally or emotionally disturbed be? How fanciful and deceptive might a confession be—and with what motives? There is a compulsion in many so afflicted to confess and in some to mislead, but more frequently there is such a disorganized and erratic personality that comprehension is lacking. The difficulties of interrogation of the mentally retarded are well known to those who are experienced with them. They often do not understand and can be led by suggestive questions to say or do things they do not understand.

This makes the chances of mistake—of false or erroneous confession—very real. Legal history is full of examples. The truth will out if we seek it, and sometimes even if we do not—but the mouth of the perpetrator of conduct society abhors is not the place to find it.

We should not forget the experience of one very able and

conscientious young assistant district attorney. Two young girls were brutally murdered and dismembered. The accused, having made a full confession, pleaded guilty to the crime. In a speech the young prosecutor later publicly excoriated the Supreme Court for its decision in *Escobedo v. Illinois,* which would have prevented the use of the confession had his case gone to trial, because the accused was denied counsel.

There was no way, he said, that a conviction could have been obtained without that confession. It was all the evidence the state had linking the convict to this horrible crime. Was society to go unprotected because the courts were concerned about the niceties of police interrogation, he inquired.

Less than a year later the man who had pleaded guilty and was sentenced to life imprisonment was set free. He did not murder those girls. Evidence disclosed that it was physically impossible for him to have been present. Another man, arrested on another charge, was shown to be the murderer. There was no other evidence found by police linking the man sentenced to life in prison with the crime—because there was none.

It sometimes seems we feel it more important to appear to solve a major crime, to convict someone, than to find the real wrongdoer. Never believe it. The public may be placated for the while, but out there somewhere the real killer is at large and he—and through him others—sees a system that is unjust, a technique that fails. Crime is stimulated. If I may be convicted of a crime I did not commit, should I hesitate to commit crime? Then I at least reap what may seem a benefit for the jeopardy I assume. Maybe someone else will pay for me.

An emotionally well balanced and intelligent man knows he need not confess to a crime whether the *Miranda* rule exists or not. No one can make him talk. The hardened criminal, however dull, will never talk to police. This is instinctive with him. The rich man, the powerful man and the mobster will be surrounded by lawyers. The police are left with the sick, the poor and the powerless to interrogate.

The *Miranda* decision does not say police cannot question people. It has no bearing on people who are not in custody. Police can screen persons by questioning near the scene of a crime to find out what they know so long as once they suspect a person they advise him of his rights. A person capable of deciding whether to make a statement and fully and fairly apprised of his rights may be questioned with or without a lawyer if he chooses. For those who want to confess or plead guilty, *Miranda* imposes no barrier—except to assure that such people know what they are doing. Is this too much?

People who do not know their rights have little advantage over people who have no rights. If rights are to have value, they must be known and protected. Many live in fear and with a hostility that will continue to characterize the relationship between segments of the public and the police until rights are secure. If we are to accord rights to all our citizens, should we be embarrassed to say so? This is what *Miranda* does.

Police interrogation has also led to the abuse of other rights. Prompt arraignment—the early appearance of an accused before a magistrate to determine whether an arrest is legal—has been an area of major abuse. Police have held persons incommunicado for long periods of time solely to question them. This was the issue before the Supreme Court in *Mallory v. United States*. Questioned for many hours and never presented to a magistrate, the accused finally confessed. The Supreme Court reversed the case because the defendant had been denied the right of prompt arraignment assured by the federal rules of criminal procedure. There is no more frightening power in a police state than the seizure of citizens and holding them apart from all help until the authorities choose to act. At the hearings on the nomination of Justice Abe Fortas to be Chief Justice, Senator Thurmond shouted, "Mallory, Mallory, let that name ring in your ears." The Mallory case had been decided seventeen years before Justice Fortas was nominated to the Supreme Court. Its relevance to the Fortas appointment was remote at best, but its rule is essential to freedom.

There are rules of law by which the prosecutor can grant immunity from prosecution to an individual and force testimony. Since the person cannot be prosecuted, his testimony cannot be used against him in a criminal trial. He cannot therefore invoke the Fifth Amendment as a reason not to testify. More than thirty federal statutes and the laws of many states empower prosecutors to grant such immunity. Its use by prosecutors is frequent, though not always successful in eliciting the testimony sought. Sam Giancana, alleged boss of La Cosa Nostra in Chicago, was brought before a federal grand jury, granted immunity and interrogated about his activities in the mid-1960's. He refused to testify. As a result, he was held in jail for contempt of court for nearly eighteen months but never testified. This is an abuse of judicial power. He was not charged with any crime except refusal to speak, a right of a free man that the state cannot waive.

Abuses of the immunity power are many. We might first ask whether the state is so powerless that it cannot find facts except by agreeing not to prosecute one person in return for testimony incriminating others. Can equal justice be achieved this way? What if immunity is granted and serious crimes—perhaps murder—are thereby excused? Should the state have such power?

We are in the midst of an assault on the Fifth Amendment. Frightened people would repeal it. They want government to have power over individuals to crush them, to humiliate and humble them. The individual is a lonely, feeble, anonymous creature in technologically advanced mass society. He is being slowly dehumanized. Human dignity is the central issue of our time. The Fifth Amendment is essential to human dignity. It says that even in contests with the state, we shall respect the individual. We will not force or trick him. The government will be fair. Liberty and safety are both lost before the Grand Inquisitor—so is human dignity.

20

THE DEATH PENALTY AND
REVERENCE FOR LIFE

MORE than seventy nations and thirteen American states have acted to reduce human violence by abolishing the death penalty. Among advanced nations the United States remains the chief advocate of death as a punishment for crime. We are characterized in the eyes of millions as much by our executions as by the general violence of our environment. Indeed, the two phenomena blur into one. The inhumanity of Vietnam and the death there inflicted further persuade the citizens of many nations that Americans are a violent, a dangerous, people.

Most of our states and the federal government itself reserve the right to kill and actually impose the death penalty, though it has been rarely exercised in recent years. Compared to 199 executions in the United States in 1935, there were but one in 1966 and two in 1967. There were none in 1968 and 1969. Only one person has been executed in the past decade under the twenty-nine federal statutes authorizing death, and no life has been taken by federal justice since 1963. Still, as the 1960's closed, more than 500 men waited under sentence of death while the Supreme Court reviewed cases which challenged the constitutionality of capital punishment.

History shows that the death penalty has been unjustly imposed—innocents have been killed by the state, effective rehabilitation has been impaired, judicial administration has suffered—and crime has not been deterred. Our emotions may cry for vengeance in the wake of a horrible crime, but we know that killing the criminal cannot undo the crime, will not prevent similar crimes by others, does not benefit the victim, destroys human life, and brutalizes society. If we are to still violence, we must cherish life. Executions cheapen life.

The major argument for capital punishment today is the belief that fear of death will keep people from committing serious crimes. But most studies of the death penalty have concluded with Professor Thorsten Sellin that "it has failed as a deterrent." A comprehensive United Nations report found that abolition of the death penalty has no effect on murder rates. With or without capital punishment, murder rates are much the same.

Why should we expect a deterrent value? Do we really believe most capital crimes are rational acts? Are they not more often committed on impulse—in a moment of passion—without thought of gain or loss? Only extreme fear of punishment—so emotionally severe that basic instincts are cowed—can deter unpremeditated crime. It is, after all, meditation before the act that may cause a person aware of the risks and consequences of being caught to refrain from prohibited conduct.

Premeditated crime, in the view of scholarship on the subject, is committed by people who believe they will not be caught. They do not really weigh the penalty. If this is so, the best deterrent for premeditated crime is to give potential offenders cause to believe they will be caught and proven guilty. Swift apprehension, effective prosecution and quick conviction will do this. When these are achieved, people can see that in fact they are paying society's price. Professionally trained police, the application of science and technology to criminal justice, successful prosecution and speedy trials can thus prevent violence—while capital punishment only makes crime a more deadly game.

The hardened criminal, devoid of human compassion, will not be deterred by the fear of death or severe punishment. He lives among the springs of American violence, where sudden death is no stranger. Society must protect itself by rehabilitating him or isolating him. To seek some public satisfaction from his execution will only brutalize others.

George Bernard Shaw believed, "Murder and capital punishment are not opposites that cancel one another, but similars that breed their kind." His view has scientific basis. The death penalty is observed by many psychologists to be an incentive for some mentally unstable persons to commit capital crimes. Recognizing the high correlation between murder and emotional disturbance, as well as a psychotic compulsion to gain notoriety, to shock sensitive people and to injure oneself, they see the death penalty as a cause of serious crime. Unquestionably, it has this effect on some. Just as arson, assassination, murder and rape inspire others who hear of them to consider and sometimes commit similar crimes, the news of executions affects mentally disturbed people, who have been known to emulate the offenses of the condemned.

It is tragic that President Nixon reacts to public fear of bombings by seeking a new federal death penalty. To make such purely local crime a federal offense is bad enough. Are the police of our great cities unable to protect their citizens? But adding the death penalty only further emotionalizes. Can we believe death will be a deterrent to bombings? Are they the work of people who will change their conduct from fear of such a penalty? President Nixon's action only dramatizes our widespread fear and makes the revolutionary purpose of the bombers more effective. Deeply disturbed young people and those who are violently revolutionary can only be stimulated to further effort by such overreaction. In truth, never have so many been so frightened by so few. To the world, as a solution for bombing we prescribe the expected American answer—violent death.

The death penalty causes violence in many ways. The effect of executions on other inmates in a prison where the condemned wait to die is devastating. The "big houses," major penitentiaries where the executions usually occur, frequently confine several thousand men. They are the most dangerous offenders convicted of crime, many deeply disturbed emotionally. Inmates there are constantly aware of the men on death row. Seeing them wait month after month, they wonder what kind of people we are. What kind of game this is we play—as if society were a giant cat and the condemned man a mouse to be toyed with before being killed. Even when prisoners who have lived in the presence of the condemned are released—and nearly all are —we know most will be convicted of crime again, because we fail to give them a chance. For how many of those later released has the final image before pulling the trigger of a pistol pointed at a police officer been the eyes of the men on death row and the thought, not me?

The impact of the death penalty on other prisoners has several dimensions. In *Soul on Ice,* Eldridge Cleaver described the many handicaps of clergymen working in prison, concluding, "Besides, men of the cloth who work in prison have an ineradicable stigma attached to them in the eyes of convicts because they escort condemned men into the gas chamber."

Wardens and guards are deeply affected by death row. The ugly details—the last meal, clothing that will not retain poisonous gas, the frequent failures on first attempt, the fear that a last-minute commutation may come too late, working with warm flesh that knows it is about to die—are not pleasant experiences. The roll of wardens who have spoken out strongly against capital punishment is long. It includes Clinton Duffy of San Quentin, James Johnston of Alcatraz, Lewis Lawes of Sing Sing and John Ryan of Milan. They know the inhumanity of the death penalty and the effect of executions on the other men in their custody.

Capital punishment harms everything it touches. The impact of the death penalty on the administration of justice has been terribly damaging. Lawyers have long noted that hard cases make bad law. There are few cases harder than those which take a life. Justice Felix Frankfurter strongly opposed capital punishment for this reason. "When life is at hazard in a trial," he said, "it sensationalizes the whole thing almost unwittingly." He regarded the effect on juries, the bar, the public and the judiciary as "very bad." President Johnson's Crime Commission found that the emotion surrounding a capital case "destroys the fact-finding process." Realization of the consequences of error permeates the entire proceeding. A jury may acquit because of its fear of the death penalty when the evidence clearly establishes guilt of a serious crime. Justice Robert H. Jackson believed that appellate courts in capital cases "are tempted to strain the evidence and even, in close cases, the law, in order to give a doubtfully condemned man another chance."

Fear of mistake produces excruciating delays in executions. In the late 1960's there were more than four hundred persons on death row at all times. Most spent years in the shadow of death. Their ages ranged from fifteen to seventy. The unbearably long wait adds immeasurably to the inhumanity of capital punishment and, combined with the infrequency of actual execution, eliminates the one deterrent effect the penalty might otherwise be thought to have. The punishment is not only slow; it usually never comes.

In a 1961 study the American Bar Foundation found that long delays such as those in the Caryl Chessman case weaken public confidence in the law. This is an understatement born of self-interest. Such cases have disgusted millions. In a more outspoken vein, the President's Crime Commission noted: "The spectacle of men living on death row for years while their lawyers pursue appellate and collateral remedies, tarnishes our image of humane and expeditious justice."

We torture ourselves through delay, indecision and doubt because we do not really believe in taking human life. No one in the process feels comfortable with himself, or about his government. The resulting hesitation further heightens the harm of the penalty. This is part of the price of hypocrisy.

History is full of men who have opposed capital punishment. Because the death penalty is irrevocable, Lafayette vowed to oppose it until "the infallibility of human judgment" was demonstrated to him. Fear of error has caused many to oppose capital punishment. It should. Innocent persons have been executed. In addition, some incapable of knowing what they did—the mentally retarded and disturbed—have been sacrificed to our lust for punishment and vengeance. Judicial determination of mental competence, a prerequisite to a finding that a person is legally responsible for a criminal act, remains far from a precise science. The legal standards are neither clear nor sound, and the decisions are made in emotional contexts. But fear of a mistake, that the person was innocent or knew not what he did, ignores the greater reason for abolition. We must be humane.

Death has been visited in a discriminatory fashion. A small group of offenders selected by chance have been destroyed. Most who committed similar crimes were never caught. Nearly all of the persons caught and convicted of the same crimes for which a few were killed have been imprisoned—not executed. There are thousands of prisoners serving life sentences or less whose crimes were more inhumane than those of the men on death row.

The poor and the black have been the chief victims of the death penalty. Clarence Darrow observed that "from the beginning, a procession of the poor, the weak, the unfit, have gone through our jails and prisons to their deaths. They have been the victims." It is the poor, the sick, the ignorant, the powerless and the hated who are executed.

Racial discrimination is manifest from the bare statistics of capital punishment. Since we began keeping records in 1930, there have been 2,066 Negroes and only 1,751 white persons put to death. Negroes have been only one-eighth of our population. Hundreds of thousands of rapes have occurred in America since 1930, yet only 455 men have been executed for rape— and 405 of them were Negroes. There can be no rationalization or justification of such clear discrimination. It is outrageous public murder, illuminating our darkest racism.

Why must we kill? We are finally beginning to realize that

crime is preventable and rehabilitation possible. The medical sciences, psychiatry, psychology, sociology, education, training and employment can prevent crime. Modern penology offers effective methods of protecting society. Pre-delinquency guidance and assistance, treatment centers, halfway houses and work release programs are evidence of the movement toward community programs that offer so much. They are the future of corrections. It is a sad commentary on how much we care that this wealthy nation spends 95 per cent of all funds for corrections on pure custody and only 5 per cent on hope—health services, education, employment and rehabilitation techniques—while still killing those who offend it the most.

If an offender cannot adapt to community programs, he can be retained in prison. If he is dangerous, he can be prevented from doing injury. Through employment in industries within the prison he can be productive. If he is unable or unwilling to work, he can still be treated kindly and allowed to live. Society can be fully protected. We no longer need to kill from fear.

Murderers, the persons for whom the death penalty is most frequently invoked, generally make well-behaved prisoners. They are rarely a threat to the safety of others. A study during the 1940's of 121 assaults with intent to kill in the prisons of twenty-seven states showed that only 10 were committed by prisoners serving life sentences for murder. There is nothing in prison experience to indicate that the death penalty would protect prison personnel from assaults by life-termers, whatever their earlier crime.

The death penalty is inconsistent with the purposes of modern penology. It deters rehabilitation. It is a disastrous substitute for the effort and money needed to develop correctional knowledge and skills.

Surely the abolition of the death penalty is a major milestone in the long road up from barbarism. There were times when self-preservation may have necessitated its imposition. Later, when food, clothing and shelter were scarce and often insufficient, inordinate sacrifices by the innocent would have been required to isolate dangerous persons from the public. Our civilization has no such excuse.

There is no justification for the death penalty. It demeans life. Its inhumanity raises basic questions about our institutions and our purpose as a people. Why must we kill? What do we fear? What do we accomplish besides our own embitterment? We must revere life and in so doing create in the hearts of our people a love for mankind that will finally still violence. A humane and generous concern for every individual, for his safety, his health and his fulfillment, will do more to soothe the savage heart than the fear of state-inflicted death, which chiefly serves to remind us how close we remain to the jungle. So long as government takes the life of its citizens, the mandate "Thou shalt not kill" will never have the force of the absolute. Our greatest need is reverence for life—mere life, all life—life as an end in itself.

EPILOGUE

A PASSION FOR JUSTICE

The days and years ahead will be turbulent. Nothing else is possible. We cannot cringe at the prospect, rather we must welcome it—for it is to be. Turbulence is life force, the manifestation of change. It offers happiness and fulfillment if we have the courage to master it. Shaw called Beethoven "the most turbulent spirit that ever found expression in pure sound." He was, and without his turbulence he would not be remembered two hundred years after his birth. The power of the Ninth Symphony is the turbulent joy of humanity.

We can fear change. Or we can withdraw into the apathy of affluence and indifference. Neither reaction is alien to the human spirit. Both turn us to narrow self-interest and incapacitate our will to find solutions and meet needs. Together they pose the greatest threat to our future. As turbulence increases, fear will turn to force—brute force—as its technique for preventing change it does not want, and apathy will not object. But force cannot stop the irresistible movement of change. The result, if fear prevails, can only be violence.

Change will accelerate with increasing population and pro-

liferating technology. We will experience more change in the way people live their lives in the remaining three decades of the twentieth century than in all history to date. The trauma of change with its uncertainties and newness, the anonymity of mass populations and the dehumanization of technology will cause dislocations in people's habits and well-being, with accompanying frustrations and anxieties far beyond anything we have ever known.

As we approach absolute interdependence, the welfare of each nation will depend on the welfare of all. Stability and the good life will not be known by any if they are not shared by all. Park Avenue can no longer be placid while Harlem seethes nor Beverly Hills dignified while Berkeley is tumultuous. Crowded in urban dwellings, moved by mass transit systems and supersonic aircraft, instantly informed of major events and made aware of all living styles by electronics and other communications, every person will depend for his essential needs on the uninterrupted performance of millions of others. Food, water, clothing and shelter were simple wants. Now we must have not only the means to obtain those, but systems of production, distribution and delivery to supply them—and much more. Our fragile cities, barely functioning, must effectively provide transportation, education, power, labor, telephone service, mass communications, garbage collection, sewage disposal, health services, police and fire protection, parks, recreation opportunity, and environments free of pollution, noise, anxiety and violence.

Interdependence makes the consequences of violent revolution unbearably inhumane. These are not the simple days of Concord. Castro cannot harvest Cuba's sugar cane without help. What revolutionary leadership could seize and operate the essential services of an American megalopolis? What happens to man when no water flows from the faucet, the supermarket shelves are empty, buses, trains and planes stop, gasoline is gone, electricity fails and with it, television, radio, telephones, elevators, stoves and heating systems; when truck drivers, teachers, firemen and police do not show up for work? Romanticists notwithstanding, violent revolution is no longer tolerable. We must reform without disruption.

Change will create new conditions of poverty unlike—and more severe than—the gentle poverty of simple wants. Antisocial conduct will find new forms reflecting the greater strains on the individual arising from poverties of health, opportunity, power, decent living conditions, humaneness, dignity, peace and love. The new poverty will feed crime among the young, the anxious, the unstable and the powerless. The impact of that crime will be felt by all. There is no place to escape. New Phophets of Doom will cry with Ezekiel, "The land is full of bloody crimes and the city is full of violence."

The different meanings of racism in technologically advanced societies and a world divided into continents of emerging blacks and browns and yellows will require an early resolution of injustices and inequalities. Integration will be essential in America to avoid violent conflict and to show the world, which will have billions more blacks, browns and yellows in three decades, that the races can live together with dignity, respect and love.

If the challenge of change seems staggering, our capacity to meet it is overwhelming. There was never a people that so clearly had the means to solve their problems as Americans today. Movers, builders, doers—we have proven the ability of man to dramatically change his destiny. Now we must show that he can control that destiny. A nation that doubled its productive capacity in four years during World War II can supply the needs of its people and the techniques and assistance by which other nations can supply theirs. It is only a question of will. How much do we care? How much foresight, initiative and energy will we devote to the quality of life and the human condition in the exciting years ahead?

If institutions are to serve people meaningfully, provide for their needs and afford them a chance to participate in decisions vitally affecting their future, they will have to learn to change with conditions. The science of institutional change must become a major endeavor. Old institutions will have to adapt constantly to be relevant to developing situations, and new institutions with new techniques must be devised to meet new problems. Ways must be found to release the energies of our people. Today we fail to find constructive outlets for half of our energies. A million people now on welfare in New York City alone could add greatly to the wealth of the nation, provide needed goods and services and fulfill themselves if we work to find the way.

That we permit conditions of ill health to prevail among millions is perhaps the most devastating contemporary commentary on our character. We could end this in a few short years. Malnutrition, brain damage, retardation, mental illness, high death rates, infant mortality, addiction, alcoholism—these are principal causes of crime. But crime is a small part of the pain they inflict on society. Health is a key measure of the human condition. There is little chance for quality in life with poor health. Doctors, nurses, medicines, vaccines, clinics, hospitals, research, counseling and physical fitness facilities, clean air and water, some quiet and reasonably orderly environments are essential to reduce violence. We can supply them abundantly if we care. We can build 20 million housing units in five years if we want to and tear down the ugliness of the slums where crime is cultivated.

With vision, courage and compassion, America can unleash

forces that will bring us through the turbulence ahead. We can devote our greatest talents to our most important business—education. We can give everyone the opportunity to absorb all the education he can. Education in its largest sense—understanding and individual fulfillment—is a major end of civilization. Through it we can salvage thousands of lost lives and avoid future losses. Education must be more than something we suffer through because it is the thing to do. It must be a first priority, a growing, reaching, searching quest for each of us through which we seek to know the truth, to understand, to prepare to make our contribution.

An all-fronts effort to meet the challenges of change will be required of our institutions. Churches, government, business, industry, trade, labor, schools, health services, charities—all must disenthrall themselves, think anew and act anew. Law must be in the vanguard as an effective instrument for social change. It will have to create new rights adequate to the needs of the individual in mass society. The old laws, such as caveat emptor and negligence as the basis for liability, are not sufficient. New rights constantly refined to assure human dignity will require effective means of enforcement. The law must devise effective techniques for fulfilling its word, and where the law is unable to do so, it must help regiment the power within society necessary to that fulfillment. We cannot continue to deny essential rights and expect our system of government to survive.

In the main, regulation and control of technology must be through law. Man will have to make moral judgments by democratic processes, encase them in the rule of law and enforce them equally throughout his society. The delicate balances of interpersonal relationships in crowded urban life must be sensitively defined and carefully enforced by law. Law must soon be brought to the solution of all international disputes. Our capacity for violence is too great to tolerate its further use in international problem solving.

Science must also be brought to bear on human attitudes. Old instincts must be altered. Our reflex to violence can be conditioned out of the American character. We should work to make violence socially unacceptable and personally unthinkable. Today we glorify the power of violence while ignoring the pity of it. Violence is ugly and in its criminal forms is the ultimate human degradation. We must see it as such.

We must also contain our acquisitive instinct. Selfishness must be relegated to the past, when scarcity created preciousness and made man covetous. We can produce more than enough for all. We must understand that if we fail to do so and to distribute our product equitably, all will suffer. There will be no social stability if major segments of society are excluded from the mainstream and millions go on living in poverty. There is no longer room enough for us to ignore one another. Service to others now best serves oneself. Social injustice will be shared by all in the form of anxiety, frustration and crime.

A conscious, constant and effective effort will be necessary to maintain freedom. The pressures of population and technology on the chance of the individual to be himself will overwhelm us if society does not strive to create liberty. There is no contest between liberty and safety. We have the means of enlarging both. Unless we do, we will lose both, because neither freedom nor security can long endure without the other.

Divisions arise over injustice. Underlying such divisions as those between the powerful and the powerless, young and old, rich and poor, educated and ignorant and black and white are different perceptions of and experiences with the quality of justice in America. St. John told us, "And if a house be divided against itself then that house cannot stand." He was right. Injustice in its many forms is the basic cause of disorder. It takes rather substantial injustice to arouse man from lethargy. From one side of America's house divided we hear the demand for order: There must be order! It is the voice of those who resist change. From the other side of our house comes the plea for justice: Give us justice! This is the voice of those who seek change. But the long history of mankind says you will have neither order nor justice unless you have both.

We are divided with repressive inference when we must join with constructive purpose. The fear and anger of the too comfortable and the unconcerned is catered to at the cost of greater alienation of the miserable and the involved. Behind the phrase "law and order" many conceal their opposition to civil rights enforcement and to dissent—to the supreme law of the land. Blinded by prejudice, they will not see that through decades of civil wrongs we have bred crime, caused it, and will continue to do so until wrongs are righted. People cry for order, but blush at the mention of justice. One of the blessings of technologically advanced mass society is that it makes injustice intolerable. We must not be ashamed to speak of humaneness, to be gentle, to seek rehabilitation—these are essential to the spirit of man. Without them he will be hard, cruel and violent.

Will the immensity of our problems—population, world peace, nuclear arms, rising racial strife, student unrest, the decaying hearts of our great cities, crime, pollution, the sheer numbers in our environment—so strain our understanding that we confuse essential liberties with the cause of our grief? Will we come to fear the strength of diversity, the virtue of difference? Will we see some nonexistent contest between liberty and security, between the rights of the individual and the safety of society? Will we seek a little more safety by giving a little less liberty? Can fear, affluence or lethargy overpower our will to enlarge both liberty and security? Can complexity and anxiety cause us to doubt that fulfillment is the flower of freedom, borne of no other tree, that freedom is the child of courage? Shall we fail to remember that nothing can so weaken security as the loss of liberty?

Tolerance, patience, humaneness and a gentle untiring hand will be essential to avoid division. Too, we must create ways for the exchange of views among all of our people. Agencies of criminal justice must be fair and effective if they are to hold us together in the turbulence of the years ahead until we have removed the underlying causes of crime in America. Our laws must provide moral leadership and cannot therefore be themselves immoral. Our purpose as a people must have a clear and generous meaning of equality for all. We must strive to fulfill the obligations of a great nation, to achieve needed reforms, to offer fulfillment, human dignity and reverence for life.

Guided by reason, America will soar on wings of humane concern. Passion is the vital spring to human action. Fertilized by ideas, passion alone has the power to activate millions. America's passion must be justice.

ABOUT THE AUTHOR

Ramsey Clark, born in Texas in 1927, was educated at the University of Texas and the University of Chicago. He served as Assistant Attorney General in the Kennedy Administration and as Attorney General in the Johnson Administration.

Mr. Clark currently practices law in New York City and Washington, D.C.